B·A·S·I·C
MONTESSORI

B·A·S·I·C

MONTESSORI

Learning Activities for Under-Fives

DAVID·GETTMAN

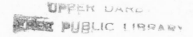
St. Martin's Press
New York

First published in the United States of America in 1987

ISBN 0-312-01215-2

ISBN 0-312-01864-9 (pbk)

Library of Congress Cataloging-in-Publication Number: 87-61086

372.21
G

CONTENTS

FOREWORD

Desmond Swan, Professor of Education, University College Dublin

A whole generation has passed since Maria Montessori died in 1952, while it is more than twice that time since her rising star shot like a meteor across the educational firmament. Lionised by political leaders in three continents during a long life-time, she was by the same token declared anathema by Mussolini and Hitler. But already at the zenith of her public acclaim in the United States of America, Montessori's theories and method of education rather suddenly fell out of favour among some leading professors of education there, as well as elsewhere in the English-speaking world. This in turn was followed by a slowing down in the growth of Montessori schools in these countries, notwithstanding her great and growing popularity in Continental Europe, India, South America and Australia, where she exercised an influence far outside the Montessori schools as such.

Yet a few years after her death, Sputnik went into orbit, and a certain amount of American complacency about their schools was shattered. Among the beneficial outcomes of the resulting reappraisal was a resurgence in the popularity of Montessori schools in the United States, a development that continues to the present day.

Nevertheless, among many teachers today whose teaching has been enriched by her legacy of thought, she is accorded scarcely more than the status of a footnote in their history of education, or is vaguely known as the inventor of a method of teaching and founder of a somewhat marginal system of schools. But to leave it at that would do less than justice to her creative genius as an educator and overlook her pivotal role in the evolution of modern educational theory and practice. This is why the present volume is greatly welcome, presenting as it does a new and comprehensive synthesis of her encyclopaedic and painstaking approach to early childhood education.

A visionary by nature, Maria Montessori looked to educational reform as the vehicle *par excellence* for the regeneration of mankind. She stood at the point of convergence of mass schooling in Western countries with the emerging discipline of modern empirical psychology. The freshness of her pedagogical perspective was informed by her scientific training in medicine and anthropology. Besides, she was thoroughly practical in her approach to solving problems of education and instruction. Her unique blend therefore of vision and practicality, of disciplined thought in psychology, medicine and anthropology, as well as her total commitment to improving the lot of the individual child — all combined to produce both the pedagogical method and the system of schooling which stand as the most visible memorials of her greatness today.

Montessori marked a revolution in psychological and pedagogical thought that would eventually distinguish the twentieth century from the nineteenth. The latter emphasised the functions of receptivity and conservation in attempting to explain the life of the mind. This had been conceptualised essentially in terms of passive or static elements, reducing intellectual activity to combinations of inert psychic atoms which were identified, on a physical analogy, as sensations and images bound together by means of passive connections (habits and associations). This 'connectionism' laid the basis for the behaviourist school of thought which would continue to dominate Western psychology for many decades to come but would make a meagre enough contribution to education, a field where it claimed to have much to contribute. The behaviourist psychologists gave full weight to the role of environmental forces in cognitive development, but this was a position with which Montessori would only partially agree at most and would differ in significant ways. Environment can shape development, she held, but it can never create.

Another strand in the complex web of contemporary child psychology, especially in the United States, was the belief in a fixed intelligence, genetically predetermined. With this also Montessori was at variance, despite the strongly biological orientation of her theories. Intellect was, to her, the outcome of a unique set of interactions between heredity and environment, not in a fixed way but in a developmental model, growth adapting to its unique environment with the latter providing (or failing to provide) appropriate nourishment at any given stage.

Cognitive functioning, according to Montessori, is an active principle, spontaneous action on the environment being the touchstone of its development. In this she was indeed in tune with other emerging psychological theories of the twentieth century, e.g. the Würzburg and Gestalt schools in Germany. Her stress on internally based motivation rather than external control of behaviour, as well as on mental growth resulting from spontaneous activity, were, according to Piaget, the key to the successful revolution in pedagogy in this century; in these too she of course anticipates much of Piagetian psychology — 'Action is prior to thought — thought is internalised action', he held.

This inseparability of mind and body, of thought and action, is central to Montessori. It will explain much of the stress she laid on graded activities in the classroom, which of course occupy many pages of the present volume. Learning occurs physically, mentally and sensorially. In education we ignore the motor and sensory development of the pupil only at the peril of his mental development. Movement is intrinsic to life itself, while its contribution to mental growth is as crucial as that of oxygen to the brain. Hand and brain have evolved in such a degree of interdependence that the proportional representation of the hand (especially the thumb and forefinger) in the cerebral cortex fairly exceeds that of any other comparable part of the bodily surface. In an important sense then, in the context of individual development, the human mind is 'hand made'. Correspondingly the mind has no outlet but through the body, while the body has no orderly purpose unless its actions are controlled by the mind.

Again, sensation commences in some dim way before birth but only begins to become differentiated in infancy so that the different sensory modalities come to function in their proper ways thereafter. The sensory impressions received in infancy and childhood become the warp and woof of mental structures, while these modalities gradually become key sources in the traffic of information from outside the organism to its executive seat in the brain.

Maria Montessori's genius has explicated, perhaps more clearly than anyone else, the necessary inter-relations in question here. 'The organisation of man has three parts: brain, senses and muscles. Movement is the final result to which the working of all these delicate mechanisms leads up. In fact it is only by movement that the personality can express itself', she wrote in *The Absorbent Mind*.

Montessori showed that human development necessarily follows an orderly sequence as the genetic pattern unfolds in maturation, thus leading on to new levels of synthesis in mastering increasingly exact and complex tasks. She defines maturation as development carried out by the individual interacting with his environment. In particular, orientation, exploration and manipulation co-ordinated with sensory activity itself lay the foundations upon which the child constructs himself, mind and body, as an increasingly efficient, free and autonomous being.

Some commentators have found difficulty in reconciling Montessori's emphasis on the freedom of the child with the highly elaborate structure of the graded materials which the Montessori teacher uses in the classroom. But it is not freedom in any absolute sense that she seeks to cultivate. Rather it is a freedom from undue intrusion by others (especially the teacher); and the liberty for the pupil to make his own choice within the structured possibilities offered. She holds that it is only by choosing to submit to the discipline of learning from this responsive environment, that personal autonomy is achieved.

In this, Montessori anticipates in a remarkable way the emergence of modern humanistic psychology of the person. This psychology, like hers, views the person as an integrated whole, stresses the individual as well as the universal aspects of human nature, and above all the importance of personal autonomy as a goal of education. The notion of the individual as self-creating, self-actualising and self-enhancing is central to both. Indeed her notion of freedom itself coincides remarkably with the following definition given by Carl Rogers: 'Freedom, rightly understood, is a fulfilment by the person of the ordered sequence of his life' (*Freedom to Learn*).

These concepts of the developing person constitute some of the essential foundations on which Montessori's pedagogy was built. The role of the teacher, now known as a directress, would be that of servant rather than master — a reversal of the prevailing role model of her day. Scientific detachment, informed observation and sympathetic mediation of the prepared environment would characterise the directress' work. Like the art that conceals art, say in directing a play, she should know when to intervene and when to stand in the wings while the central character, the developing child, creates the drama of his own unfolding personality. But for all the minute prescription she gives, Montessori would never see teaching as the slavish working out of someone else's recipe. Indeed the directress as a versatile and caring facilitator of human development is now becoming an appropriate model for the emerging age of the new information technologies in education, when the older pupil is already acquiring skills and accessing databases far beyond the ken of the most knowledgeable teacher. In this context it is not fanciful to suggest that all of us, pupils, parents, teachers and teacher trainers alike, will have everything to learn from a deeper study of the Montessori concept of education.

1 MONTESSORI AND HER THEORIES

INTRODUCTION

Maria Montessori, who lived from 1870 to 1952, was a brilliant and original educator, scientist, healer, humanitarian and philosopher.

In Montessori's time, a woman in Italy was not given the same educational opportunities as a man. But even as a child, Maria won special opportunities because of her intellect. She attended an all-boys' technical school, and there expressed an ambition to pursue a career in engineering. When she was not given professional encouragement in this, she developed an interest in biology, and settled on becoming a doctor instead. At university, Maria, the only girl, was shunned by her colleagues, and she spent many months pent up in a room to study by herself – until, near the end of her first year, when she was called to deliver a paper to the class, the other students found themselves cheering and applauding her brilliance and insight. After becoming the first woman to graduate in medicine from the University of Rome, Montessori practised surgical medicine for the next ten years. During this period, when she could have gloated over her unusual place of honour among women, she instead helped other women through their own higher education, and campaigned heartily for equal rights for all women.

Soon after graduating, stimulated by her further studies in psychology, and having begun to teach in the psychiatric clinic at the university, Montessori became involved in visiting the patients in the nearby mental institution. Believing instinctively that mental deficiency was more of an educational than a medical problem, she arranged to remove the younger children from the institution and work with them separately. Every day for two years, Montessori did her best to help these disturbed and handicapped children learn and develop, basing her teaching methods on the principles of two prominent French physicians whose research she had read and admired: Jean Itard – teacher of the famous 'Savage of Aveyron' – and Edouard Sequin. Remarkably, a number of the children progressed so quickly that Montessori signed them up for ordinary school examinations, which they passed without difficulty. But she was not impressed by her accomplishment. Instead, she wondered what was wrong with the schools who gave such examinations if two short years of her improvised methods could bring seriously disturbed and handicapped children to the same standard of education as that expected of ordinary children.

Montessori then turned her thoughts to the education of the ordinary child. She returned to the University of Rome for further academic work in educational philosophy, psychology and anthropology – which she undertook with such distinction that in 1904 she was appointed Professor of Anthropology. At the same time, she continued to study childhood nervous conditions, and to publish her findings in medical journals.

In 1907, an opportunity came for her to begin to work with ordinary children. In a reconstructed tenement in San Lorenzo, an impoverished quarter of Rome, a children's day nursery was set up by the housing authorities, and it needed a director – someone to be in charge of about fifty wretchedly poor three-to-six year olds, mainly to keep them from playing on the stairs and dirtying the newly painted walls. Little did the tenement's authorities suspect that this humble nursery, which Montessori called her 'Casa dei Bambini', or Children's House, would become a place of great discovery for the shy, tearful children who came there, and for Montessori herself.

Montessori began by attempting to use in the Children's House some of the same teaching techniques she had used at the mental institution. She found that the children enjoyed the exercises, but that they preferred to do them independently, without her help. As Montessori introduced more and different materials for the children to work with, some materials were accepted enthusiastically, while others were left untouched. She did not force anything on the children, but offered and presented each new activity like a gift, to be taken up at will by any interested child.

Some time into this process, Montessori began to notice something very strange and wonderful about some of the children. Those who freely participated in the activities began to reveal a facet of childhood which Montessori had never seen before. Some of the more experienced children began to evidence a kind of inner calmness, and they were able to concentrate contentedly for very long periods of time. Not only did they quickly absorb complex skills and sophisticated knowledge, they also developed a self-discipline which relieved any need for external authority. In their dealings with adults and other children, they began to show great thoughtfulness, compassion and understanding. It was as if their work at the Children's House lifted some great weight off their minds, freeing them to focus on their own inner thoughts and purposes. Montessori herself scarcely believed what she was seeing, but the pattern persisted. She continued to introduce new self-teaching materials that built upon the principles of the earlier ones, carefully observed the children's use of them, and if the children were not spontaneously and repeatedly drawn to the activities, those materials were taken away and not offered again. Montessori's method developed and grew purely on the basis of what the children showed her about themselves.

It was not until much later, after two decades of working with young children and sensitively observing them, that Montessori began to tie her observations together in the form of theories. This chapter aims to summarise Montessori's basic ideas about development and learning, and about why children in Montessori classes all over the world exhibit that remarkable sense of self-assurance and contentment in their work. Throughout Montessori's own writings, she repeatedly reminds us that she did not just sit back in an armchair and dream up these theories. Montessori wanted us to remember that it was the children themselves who, by their free and natural inclinations, revealed to her the true nature of their growth and development.

THE YOUNG CHILD'S SPECIAL MIND

The most basic principle in Montessori's theory of education is that the learning capacity of a young child is fundamentally different from that of an adult. To realise this ourselves, we need only think of one learning task attempted by both adults and young children – learning to speak a new language.

We know from adult experience that learning to speak a new language is an enormously complex and difficult task, requiring prolonged concentration, a well-developed memory, and a strong sense of grammatical logic. How is it possible that a very young child is able to master his or her first language, having only a very temporary attention span, a weak ability to recognise people and objects, and no apparent sense of logic at all? When an adult undertakes the task, the vocabulary and grammar of the new language are systematically related to those of the adult's native language; the native language serves as the vehicle that gives meaning to the new words and phrases. But the young child starts with no language whatsoever. In what world of meaning does the child interpret its new language? Also, the adult who learns a foreign language rarely speaks it well enough to pass as a native; most travellers or immigrants have accents and tendencies to misuse local syntax which betray their own native languages. How does the young child learning its first language invariably speak it so perfectly, utilising the exact portions of the mouth, tongue and throat necessary to reproduce the language's sounds, and acquiring a precise national accent, a regional dialect, all the local idioms, and even neighbourhood or family idiosyncrasies? No one but a one-to-three year old can accomplish this remarkable feat.

Clearly, the young child has a unique and extremely powerful capacity for learning such skills as language, a capacity which is mysteriously lost, or perhaps buried, somewhere on the way to adulthood. The difference between the adult and the young child is not merely in the quantity that can be learned; unlike the adult, the child appears able simply to absorb, through activity, but without effort, certain complete and precise abilities and skills, with a completeness and preciseness that an adult cannot even conceive of. Montessori called this unique early learning capacity the young child's 'absorbent mind'.

The absorbent mind makes possible the transformation of a helpless, gurgling infant into a young personality with all the basic physical and mental abilities needed for daily human existence: feeding, cleaning and dressing oneself; sitting, climbing, grasping and a wide range of fine motor skills; as well as language, recognition, memory, will, grace, courtesy, cultural customs, and a self-identity. This feat of self-creation is accomplished by the child's simply living in and 'absorbing' the surrounding cultural environment.

Montessori used the term 'absorb', not in the sense of 'take in' as a dry sponge absorbs water, but rather in the sense of 'combining into itself'. One imprecise but useful analogy is a crystal growing in a saturated solution. Like a growing crystal, the child's absorbent mind dwells in a rich environment, and as it absorbs impressions of its surroundings, new behaviours and thoughts become incorporated additions that alter the mind's pattern or direction, and increase its surface area for further growth. In contrast with the child's absorbent mind, the adult mind maintains its basic form and capacity, and acquires knowledge not by absorption but by intentionally testing hypotheses and logically synthesising conclusions. This is why a child, unlike an adult, enjoys and seeks the repetition of the same stimuli many times over. Each impression slightly alters the child's perspective, so that even the same stimulus appears slightly different each time. The adult, who laboriously draws inductions from experience, and draws deductions from inductions, but whose perception remains essentially unchanged, finds the repetition of previously assessed stimuli to be boring and tedious.

In Montessori's experience, the young child's absorbent mind usually lasts about six years, a period which she observed to be divided into two three-year phases. Its mode of action subtly changes between the first phase and the second phase.

The first phase of the absorbent mind's activity, from birth to three years, is the most formative in childhood. During this phase, the child absorbs almost all available impressions in full detail, and each impression is instantly incarnated into and superimposed on all previous ones. The absorbent mind acquires nearly any impression, simple or complex, with equal ease and accuracy. It primarily responds to human stimuli, especially the human voice, but within the full range of human activity it is impartial and non-selective, using every sense to perceive the child's entire emotional as well as behavioural and cultural environment. For example, a baby in the living room of its home will absorb the complete and detailed actions and attitudes of mother reading, father tinkering, and brother and sister playing a game, even if all these activities are going on at once. Because the absorbent mind in this first phase does not have to be awakened by any exercise of the child's will, Montessori called its operation 'unconscious'. However, despite its effortless operation, the early absorbent mind is active and not passive, involving the child in imitation, movement and manipulative play, to capture, vary and augment the available field for experience.

Utilising the surrounding cultural environment as substance to absorb, the early absorbent mind helps create, in about three years, the child's basic human abilities. These creations do not appear gradually, but seem to be formed by an inner development that is only occasionally manifested in quantum leaps of ability. This creative transformation becomes readily apparent when you compare the behaviour of a newborn infant with that of a speaking three year old.

In the second phase of the young child's development, from ages three to six, the absorbent mind continues to function, but it now appears more specifically focused on certain impressions gained through intentional interaction with the material as well as human environment. These new experiences solidify, further develop and, most importantly, integrate the abilities earlier created. While the first phase of the absorbent mind consisted mostly of a quiet inner development that occasionally surfaced in surprising gains, the second phase appears busy and the maturation of skills is open and continuous. Also, whereas previous activity in the environment had been largely unconscious and spontaneous, the three-to-six year old interacts with the environment consciously and intentionally, strongly preferring certain experiences to others. These special impressions pursued and captured by the three-to-six year old, like the largely accidental experiences of the nought-to-three year old, continue to be acquired by the absorbent mind without effort or strain, no matter how complex they appear to us.

AN ORDERED GROWTH

Having been born with an 'absorbent mind', a young child simply 'absorbs' most of the various goings on in its immediate human environment. But to say that 'the child has an absorbent mind' isn't really enough to explain how a baby uses what it absorbs to create all the various human characteristics possessed by a child of six. Obviously, the child does not just reproduce, like a video and sound recorder, everything that the absorbent mind perceives. Even if we take into account the cumulative metamorphosis of the absorbent mind, a young child's human nature still consists of something more than just a highly superimposed image of the surrounding human environment. We need to ask how the absorbent mind goes about turning its accumulated impressions of a culture into an intelligence which will later participate in and contribute to the culture being absorbed.

Montessori's answer was that the child's absorbent mind indeed receives impressions, but it also processes, categorises and otherwise interprets them, filtering bits of impressions through, and fitting them into, an inherited intellectual structure. She also deduced that this structure is not static, but gradually changes and unfolds as the child grows. The structure and its pattern of unfolding appear to be basically the same for all children everywhere. What makes each child's intellectual development different are the varying experiences that the absorbent mind has been exposed to at each stage of the structure's unfolding.

So although the absorbent mind's first phase is unconscious, it is not undirected. At any one time, the child's unfolding intellectual structure makes special use of certain aspects of the impressions it absorbs. It is the effect of absorbed experience on the underlying structure that actually creates the child's intellectual abilities. By the second phase of the absorbent mind, starting around age three, the structure's developmental work has progressed sufficiently to give the child enough mental faculties to express interest consciously in the particular experiences that will henceforth most benefit the evolving structure. So, from ages three to six, the child feels and shows preferences for the types of stimuli needed to refine and integrate the basic abilities created from ages nought to three.

This may be illustrated by use of a simple analogy. Consider how one would go about building a house. It isn't enough just to gather together the various materials which go into a house. All you'd have then is a pile of bricks, wood, metal and glass. It also wouldn't do simply to re-create disjointed impressions of a finished house – to build the stone facade there, the interior of the bedroom over here, the patio up there. One really needs three things to build a house: first, a detailed structural blueprint of the finished house; second, a building schedule, to tell us that the foundation must be laid first, then the frame, then the plumbing, then the outer walls, then the electrical work, and so on; and third, sufficient labour and materials to build the house with. But as the house is actually being built, there comes a time when the builders no longer need to refer constantly to the blueprints and the schedule. The house itself begins to take on a definite shape, and what needs to be done next presents itself very clearly to the builders.

When Nature constructs a young human being from a helpless infant, its blueprint is that underlying, inherited intellectual structure, its building schedule is the pre-determined unfolding of this structure over time, and the labour and materials are the many experiences and impressions received by the absorbent mind. When the work is well under way, Nature makes self-evident what needs doing next by awakening and exercising the child's will.

In her many years of observing children, Montessori was able to work out a very general outline of the 'building schedule', that is, what kinds of faculties are being developed at various points in the first six years of life. She was able to deduce this rough order of development by noting which sorts of activities and experiences seemed to benefit, and for the older ones, seemed to appeal to, the children most. The general order of the hidden construction work going on within the young children was thus suggested by special, transient sensitivities to certain categories of stimuli. Montessori called these broad, but distinct and temporary sensitivities, the 'sensitive periods'.

In all, Montessori noted six of these sensitive periods.

The first one, a sensitive period for the development of 'sensory perception', begins at birth and continues all the way through age five. During this sensitive period, the child needs to exercise all the sense faculties as fully as possible. A great deal of frustration in many young children is caused by parents' constant admonitions not to touch anything, and by plasticised, deodorised and highly sheltered surroundings.

The second sensitive period, which is for 'language', doesn't begin until age three months, but it too lasts to about age five or five-and-a-half. The many stages of this sensitive period, which Montessori traced in some detail, include for example an early sensitivity to the sound of the human voice and the sight of the human mouth speaking. It may seem obvious that a baby will begin to imitate the speaking sounds it hears. But a baby hears many sounds, including for instance musical melodies, dogs barking, and kitchen noises. The fact that these sounds are not imitated or incorporated into the child's communicative behaviour supports the theory that the baby has a special sensitivity to, and can unconsciously select from all the varied sounds in the environment, just human conversation.

A sensitive period for 'order' usually starts around the child's first birthday, peaks at about age two, and subsides when the child is three. This sensitivity is rarely recognised by parents and is probably the cause of much of that inconsolable crying and fretfulness long associated with the 'terrible two's'. At this time in the child's development, the construction of the intellect appears to be going through a vital organisational phase. Impressions and experiences are being placed in ordered patterns that will form the basis for the child's emerging world view, which is in turn beginning to make possible the ordered expression, in language, of ideas about the world. If order in daily experience is constant, this allows the child to build an understanding of life on the foundations of the patterns perceived. External order will facilitate the child's development of an internal sense of order.

This means that the child aged one and two will greatly benefit, and be happiest, when the world all around appears constant in its patterns and arrangements. External order would include such constancies as: keeping most material objects, like furniture, toys, and clothing, in the same location from day to day; following the same daily routines, such as where and when meals are taken, how and when family chores are done, and when family members depart and arrive; and using the same procedures in doing things with the child, such as how the child is picked up and held, how meals are fed, and how baths are given. When a child of two seems unduly upset for no apparent reason, it is often because some small thing has been inadvertently changed – something which may be totally unimportant to the adult, but which is a vital cornerstone of consistency in the child's understanding of how life is conducted. When some disorder is necessary in the young child's surroundings, we should be sympathetic and supportive, and should stress the things that haven't changed.

A brief but important sensitive period, which occurs right around age two, is the sensitive period for 'small detail'. Now it is rather easy to see how sensitivities to sensory perception, language and order can help the unfolding inner structure, in combination with the absorbent mind, to create a human intellect. But the creative value of a transient sensitivity to 'small detail' is not immediately apparent.

First of all, what did Montessori mean by 'small detail'? During this sensitive period, the toddler will, for example, be strolling slowly along with you on a hillside path that permits a breathtaking view of the town below. But instead of standing with feet wide apart gazing out upon the edifying panorama, as you had intended, the child will be on all fours following with great interest the zig-zag crawl of a little black ant. Or later, with the two-year-old on your lap, you are leafing through a big colourful picture book with scenes of the zoo, and you are naming the animals featured on each page. But instead of taking note of the bright orange, roaring tiger, the child will be asking you about the "lolly", and you will notice that in the bottom left corner of the picture, there is a small drawing of a little girl, standing away from the tiger's cage, holding a tiny orange ice lolly in one hand. Why should the child be preoccupied with these insignificant details?

Consider Sherlock Holmes, the fictional detective. Holmes was always being clever for two reasons: first, he gave equal weight to all evidence, no matter how insignificant it seemed; and second, he had a special ability to concentrate very deeply on one specific problem at a time. Sherlock's friend Watson was invariably drawn to only the most obvious of clues, and always tried to solve the whole mystery, with its many unanswered questions, at one fell swoop. The Sherlock Holmes stories point up two vital components of human intelligence: we must be capable of widening our powers of observation to include all phenomena, since the meaning of a situation is not always to be found in the most obvious phenomena; and second, we must be able to concentrate our intellectual powers on specific problems. It is also essential to early development that a child be able to broaden the field of observation available to the absorbent mind, and to tighten the concentration of the inner intellectual structure in processing what is absorbed. This is the purpose of the sensitive period for 'small detail': to awaken the mind's control over the child's attention. The sensitivity to small detail draws the child to the tiniest objects, the separated fragments, the faintest noises, the hidden corners – all the phenomena previously overshadowed by the brightest, biggest objects, the fastest moving or the loudest. Also, when the child is drawn to a small thing, the sensitivity holds the child's attention there for an extended period, fostering the ability to focus on that one small stimulus to the exclusion of all else.

Just as that sensitive period is completing its work, at around age two-and-a-half, the child enters the sensitive period for 'co-ordination of movement', and this lasts until about age four. Co-ordination of movement essentially means bringing the body under the control of the will: being able to use one's fingers, hands, legs, feet, mouth and so on, precisely the way one wishes to. This does not mean that a child of this age can more easily acquire complex physical skills – in other words, this is not necessarily the ideal age for becoming a violin virtuoso or a prima ballerina. Having a sensitive period for co-ordination of movement only means that there is an involuntary inclination to perform and repeat movements purely for the sake of gaining greater and more precise control. For example, a child aged about three loves washing hands, not for the sake of getting them clean, but simply to be able to work on the manipulative skills involved: turning taps, holding slippery soap, rubbing to make lather, rinsing, and finger-drying. By contrast, children aged four or older will normally only wash their hands to get them clean (if you can get them to do it at all). The importance of this sensitive period is that it helps the child become physically capable of pursuing activities that – in the absorbent mind's second phase – are consciously selected to provide the greatest benefit to the unfolding intellectual structure.

The last sensitive period in the life of the absorbent mind is a sensitivity to 'social relations', which starts around two-and-a-half, and persists through age five. This helps to orient the child towards intellectual development after age six, which occurs mostly in a social setting, and consists largely of the acquisition of social and cultural knowledge. In this sensitive period, the young child pays special attention to the effect of one's behaviour on the feelings and actions of others, and how one's behaviour is in turn affected by the judgements and tendencies of a group of children. Whereas the under-three year olds tend to play alone or just 'alongside' one another, the work of this sensitive period enables recognisable affections and friendships to develop, allows play to be somewhat co-operative, and makes mischief begin to appear conspiratorial. The two-and-a-half to five year old is also quite interested in, and readily absorbs, the basic rules of social relations, such as manners, mealtime customs, graceful movement, and showing consideration for others.

LEARNING BY CONNECTING

The 'absorbent mind' is Montessori's answer to the mystery of how a baby is dramatically transformed into a thinking being. And 'sensitive periods' are the essence of Montessori's theory about how basic human skills are systematically developed. But one should now ask: given a basic intellect and certain general abilities, what equips the child to then acquire specific information and know-how? We've discussed how the absorbent mind feeds an unfolding, inherited structure, and how the sensitive periods help provide the right materials for the building of particular skills. But when and how are these general skills integrated, expanded and filled out with the knowledge and understanding that makes them useful in the real world?

You will recall that by age two-and-a-half or three, the special sensitivities to certain impressions needed by the absorbent mind's inherited inner structure, in each phase of its unfolding, start to be expressed consciously. They begin to appear in the child as purposeful activity and explicit expressions of curiosity and interest. For example, the child wants to be shown how to place blocks in a row, to see what we're doing in the kitchen, to hear what noises come out of the telephone receiver, and to discover where the water in the bath goes when it disappears down the drain. This age marks the onset of what we usually think of as 'learning'.

'Learning' is one of those words we use without really knowing what we mean by it. When a person lacks an ability one moment and then displays the ability the next moment, we say that the person has 'learned' it, and by the word 'learn' we imply that some sort of operation has taken place that installs the new ability in the person. But what sort of operation accomplishes this and how does it work? We know that repetition often leads to learning, but we wouldn't want to say that learning consists entirely of repetition. Even when we are the ones learning, we are hard pressed to describe what actually goes on in our heads at that moment of realisation, if there is one, or over that long period of practice. All we know is, suddenly we are able to do or think what we could not do before.

In Montessori's view, the act of learning does not involve the acquisition of anything new. Simply being awake to the world, the absorbent mind is constantly acquiring the substance of whatever will be learned by the young child. The 'learning' itself is the act of joining or connecting these previous acquisitions in such a way that they are bound together by use or meaning, and so that they have a place in a larger system of uses or meanings. Whatever is thereby learned then becomes, like each earlier acquisition, a piece of knowledge that can be further bound to other pieces, in some later act of learning.

Educators have long observed that learning, this binding together of what was earlier absorbed, occurs in three basic stages. In terms of Montessori's theories, these stages can be described as follows.

The first stage is absorbing, via the absorbent mind, a full impression of all the various separate components that will later be joined. This can occur naturally, over many months, or it can be intentionally provided in a few minutes. Because of the child's propensity for movement, this is always a participatory event on the child's part, rather than a passive reception. Also, in order for full absorption to take place, an effort of concentration is required; it will not work if the child is at all distracted. In this first stage, whatever is being absorbed, because it is being processed through that inherited inner structure, is already starting to become loosely associated in the back of the child's mind. Consequently, the child senses a motivation to strengthen and complete these associations. In brief, this first stage is the absorption of certain component phenomena, which if complete, creates a motivation for learning.

The second stage of learning consists of repeatedly acting out connections between the absorbed phenomena, which for the young child again usually involves physical activity. This firmly bridges the absorbed phenomena that were only loosely associated in the first stage. Through repetition, the child explores and establishes all the different ways that the component phenomena fit together, so that in the end they are irrevocably joined. In order to make the connections, such as between a verbal sound and a letter of the alphabet, the child must clearly perceive what is being connected and what is being left unconnected. Similarly, the primary aspect of any intentional activity, such as hammering a nail, is accurate control over what is being acted upon, distinguished in the actor's mind from what is not to be acted upon. In essence, then, this second stage of learning solidly binds, through repeated and carefully controlled activity, certain previously absorbed phenomena, and thereby draws clear distinctions around them, making of them a unified concept.

The third stage of learning is the conscious application of the now bound and circumscribed concept to tasks and situations that will give it a meaningful place in the child's world. This could mean, for example, using the new sound-letter combination to write a word in a story the child is composing, or using the hammer and nail to help build a 'Wendy House' in the child's garden. When a concept, such as an abstract mathematical relation, has no obvious practical application, the child may create an application by inventing a game that makes use of the new concept. Sometimes, putting the concept into language is enough to give it a meaningful place in the child's mind. Alternatively, the child may give application to the new concept by trying to teach it to someone else. However it is done, the object of this last stage is to make the concept meaningful for the child, by giving it a purpose in the child's daily life, and a relationship to other concepts the child has learned.

So learning is essentially connecting – a set of related perceptions motivating connective activity that is in turn given application. Going back to Montessori's larger view of the child's development, we can now explain how the child, in the second phase of the absorbent mind, is able to integrate and expand the skills and abilities created in the first phase – and so starts to acquire real knowledge and skills.

As we've noted, the three year old's activities begin to be more purposeful, because the child's development has progressed to a point which awakens the will. Purposeful activity starts to integrate the child's abilities by bringing them into a personally managed relation with the world. Also at this age, the child is first made capable, partly by the sensitive period for small detail, of giving concentrated attention to any activity intentionally selected. At the same time, the sensitive period for co-ordination of movement is developing the physical skills needed to pursue those activities.

So at this point, three stage learning can begin to operate: the child's new powers of concentration support the first stage; repetition and striving for control, which are characteristic of the sensitive period for co-ordination, help drive the second stage; and purposeful activity, guided by the will, becomes the basis for the third stage. Together, these enable the child to perform 'learning by connecting' – the three stage process which fills out early basic skills with knowledge and understanding.

THE CHILD'S WORK PLACE

Because of the importance, especially in the second phase of the child's absorbent mind, of having particular stimuli and experiences available at critical periods of the intellectual structure's unfolding, early development may be greatly assisted if the three-to-six year old is in an environment that makes these stimuli and experiences likely.

In accordance with the principles we've been discussing, such an environment would ideally offer purposeful experiences that permit the exercise and integration of the abilities newly created in the child's first few years. These experiences would make clear, tangible and accessible to the child's absorbent mind the basic patterns of the culture's customs, practices, beliefs and perceptions. The experiences would be generated largely through physical activities, each of which would be presented to the child in accordance with the principle of three stage learning. And the experiences would be made accessible only when they were required at each point in the child's inner construction, but thereafter they would be freely available for the child to seek out at will.

Purposeful physical activities, reflecting the culture, presented by three stage learning at critical periods, and later available for use by the child at will – this is precisely the sort of environment that Montessori, in response to the expressed desires of the children, developed at her Children's House in San Lorenzo.

The Montessori environment is a place that fully satisfies the requirements of the absorbent mind, the sensitive periods, and the three stage learning process. Montessori called this place the 'prepared environment', since it is specially prepared to meet all the child's developmental needs. The 'prepared environment' is the ideal work place for the young child's vocational pursuit of self-construction, to create from a baby an independent, thinking human being.

Most parents consider the home to be the ideal environment for their young child. Montessori agreed that in the first stage of the absorbent mind, when basic human abilities, feelings and attitudes are being unconsciously created by close and constant exposure to people, the secure and direct effect of parental love and attention is most conducive to early growth. But in the second stage of the absorbent mind, which requires true freedom, purposeful activity, and cultural involvement in order to function, the child can greatly benefit from additional exposure to an environment specially prepared to meet these needs.

The main distinguishing features of Montessori's 'prepared environment', in contrast with an ordinary nursery school, are the many specially selected learning and cultural activities, each of which is introduced precisely when the child is ready, and is thereafter freely available for the child to conduct independently. Most of the remainder of this book details the basic activities and how to present them. But there are other aspects of the Montessori environment which should be discussed first, since their absence could lessen the activities' effectiveness. Although it is easiest to appreciate the importance of the activities themselves, the whole Montessori environment is designed to complement the activities and the children's participation in them. Remember that all aspects of the 'prepared environment' were originally included by Montessori because they were repeatedly favoured by the children she worked with, and not because they seemed desirable by adult standards.

A Montessori environment can be created in a home, a school building, a church hall, or a community centre, or even in an empty shop, the ground floor of an office block, or any place that child-minding would be permitted. Nothing fancy is required; the very first Montessori environment was a room in a working-class tenement building. The site need not be luxurious, but like any area for children it must be clean, warm, secure, pleasant in appearance, brightly lit, and isolated from dangers like building work or busy roads. You do not need a lot of space: one separated half of a playroom would do fine for one or two children at home; for a group of children, one large room or two smaller rooms, with ready access to a WC and a fenced outdoor play area, would be best. If you're thinking about opening a Montessori school for children other than your own, you probably also need to ask local authorities about planning, licensing, fire safety, and building regulations – including rules about the amount of space required per child.

The room or rooms should be furnished very simply, with child-size furnishings. You'll need a child-size table and chair for each child, and some child-size open shelving. By 'child-size' I mean comfortable for the child to be working at: for the chair, the child's feet should rest flat on floor; for the table, a seated child should be able to rest elbows on the surface; for shelves, the child should be able to see the contents of a bowl on the top shelf. The tables, chairs and shelves should have water-resistant surfaces for easy cleaning, and should of course be free of splinters and sharp corners or edges. The only other essential furnishings are 'table mats', each made of a two-foot-square piece of felt, and also, even if the space is carpeted, 'floor mats' of stiff, thick felt, each about three feet by four feet, rolled and stored upright in a low bin. Optional furnishings might include: a child-size easel for painting; two large plastic buckets, one as a water source (with a ladle) and the other to put used water in; a well-lit reading corner with a small bookcase and a soft child-size chair or fluffy pillow; interesting pictures to hang on the wall at the child's eye level; and for each table, a vase to put flowers in. For yourself, you might want a lockable cabinet for supplies, and a low but comfortable stool to sit on when you are working with a child at a table. With the exception of these two last items, everything in the Montessori environment is designed for use by children.

The most notable elements of the 'prepared environment' are the specially-constructed materials used by the child to conduct the Montessori activities. In principle, you should try to get professionally-made Montessori materials for as many of the activities as possible. However, there are only a few manufacturers in the world who produce them commercially. The largest and best of these companies, 'Nienhuis Montessori', is based in Holland, and has a mail-order catalogue obtainable from the following address: Nienhuis Montessori International B.V., PO Box 16, 7020 AA, Zelhem (Gld.), Holland. The professionally-made materials are best because they will last longer, and their lasting beauty and perfection make them more enticing for children to use. Also, a number of the materials would be difficult for anyone but a master craftsperson to make – if you want to provide these materials, you will probably have to buy them.

However, professionally-made Montessori materials can be expensive, and you may need to make do with some home-made materials. A handy adult will be able to make many of them from readily available household items, supplemented by modest purchases from a sewing supplies shop and a hardware or DIY shop. For those Montessori materials which are easiest to make, a few 'DIY hints' are included with the activities descriptions in this book. (Incidentally, the glossy, full-colour Nienhuis Montessori catalogue would be a very useful visual aid to anyone trying to make their own materials.) Finally, there are some Montessori materials which cannot be bought at all, and for these I provide detailed suggestions on how to make them.

Many adults are surprised and delighted when they see Montessori materials for the first time. The objects are simple, basic shapes in pure, wholesome materials – small wooden cabinets and containers with neat, enamel-painted elemental forms inside, squares of wool and cotton fabric, plain ceramic jugs and basins, and other similarly uncomplicated artefacts. To some adults, the materials may seem a bit too elemental, or even old fashioned. But Montessori discovered that young children actually prefer this simplicity, and seek it out in their environment.

There is a recent trend in nursery and primary schools to conduct lessons for young children with computers, calculators and other implements of high technology. The rationale is that these are the tools of modern times, and that every child should become comfortable with their use and operation. Montessori would have agreed that because these machines are an important part of modern society – like cars, say – their presence should be a natural occurrence in the child's general environment, and their identity and purpose should be known to young children. But Montessori would no more have suggested that four year olds use a computer than that they drive on a motorway.

The successful and creative use of high technology, such as computers, requires a complete understanding of what the automated operation would consist of, if it were performed by hand. Young children do not have this understanding. Rather than leap into advanced techniques, the Montessori method always starts with the concrete and gradually builds up to the abstract – for example, grouping and counting beads to understand in a literal, material sense what is meant by adding quantities, before proceeding to work with numbers in themselves as abstractions. Montessori's hands-on activities give a solid grounding for later abstractions, which are thereby more fully understood, and are not carried out as mere rote operations.

All Montessori materials which the children may wish to use and to which the children have been properly introduced, should be kept out and available on the child-size open shelves. Also each piece of material should have an assigned place and position on these shelves. Although it is not necessary, you may wish to group the materials on the shelves by subject matter (e.g. Mathematics, Language, Sensorial). It is essential, however, that the children be able to see and retrieve, without any adult assistance, all the materials and supplies needed to conduct any activity which has been presented to them. Unless these materials are being used by someone else, the children must always find them in precisely the same place and position on the shelves every time they look for them. This will help the children become independent, and will help them understand what is expected when putting the materials away.

The 'prepared environment' is ideally open every day throughout the child's waking hours, as the child is then able to work and learn whenever the urge strikes. This is quite possible in the home, by simply leaving open, all day long, the room with the Montessori materials, and occasionally devoting a half-hour or so to introducing new activities or observing the child's work. But with groups of children not living under the same roof, some compromise is usually necessary.

All-day nursery facilities, which may run from early morning to early evening, often find that they and the children only have sufficient energy to devote part of their long day to Montessori work. Some all-day nursery schools concentrate on Montessori presentations from 9.00 to 12.00 in the morning, interrupted only by snack time, and then the materials are left out for free access throughout the afternoon. I've also seen day nurseries that focus on Montessori work for two separate one-hour-and-a-half sessions: one session in the morning, say from about 10.00 to 11.30, and the other in the afternoon, from about 2.00 to 3.30. I would not suggest restricting Montessori work much more than this, since different children reach their peak concentration time at different hours of the day. Short Montessori sessions tend to end just as a child is getting involved, and may cause some children to flit superficially from one activity to another in order to pass the time until the end of the session is announced. Nursery schools or play groups which are open only in the morning or in the afternoon for a few hours, sometimes only a few days a week, are obviously able to maintain the Montessori environment for only a limited time period, but they can more easily offer it without interruption.

The time arrangement you settle upon will obviously depend upon what is practical and possible in your situation. The main points to remember here are: the Montessori environment is intended only as an aid to the child's self-development; it is no use forcing the activities on any child at a particular time; no harm whatsoever is done if a child does not wish to participate at a particular time, or indeed at all; and whatever exposure a child has to the Montessori environment, no matter how small or temporary, cannot hurt, but will only help.

HOW THE ADULT CAN HELP

The bright room, the furniture, and the Montessori materials together constitute only half of the 'prepared environment'. The other half is you, the adult.

The adult in the Montessori environment can serve the child in three ways: as the main 'caretaker' and guardian of the work space, its furnishings, and the materials; as a 'facilitator' of the child's interaction with the materials; and as an 'observer' of the child's work and development. You can be all three of these things at once, but never the child's teacher in the traditional sense, since in the Montessori environment the child learns through active discovery, rather than through passive reception. Montessori called the adult who assumes the above three roles the environment's 'director'.

The director's 'caretaker' role is a more important one than it sounds. Because the child accomplishes self-development by independent work with the materials in the environment, these objects and the way they are arranged must be sufficiently pleasing and attractive to draw the child to them, so to speak. Although as an adult you will tend to think of your own tastes and needs, always try to consider how the environment could be more pleasant and more convenient for the child.

To start, the materials must always be complete, with no parts or pieces missing, and with any supplies such as paper or pencils ready to use and available in plentiful amounts. All materials and associated supplies should be nicely arranged on the shelves, perfectly aligned in their designated places, and easy to take off the shelves without disturbing other things. The materials should be in perfect repair, that is, any scratch or scrape should soon after be touched up with matching paint and any broken or chipped parts replaced as quickly as possible. The materials, the shelves and the work tables should also be immaculately clean, which means dusting them every day, and removing grime and fingerprints with a moist cloth about once a week.

These tasks should not only be performed as a matter of routine, but also in light of the child's responsiveness to the materials. For example, if a certain material has been ignored, perhaps it is because it is too difficult to get at, in which case you could announce its move to a more accessible spot, or perhaps it is ignored because it is damaged, in which case it should be repaired or replaced. Incidentally, if you are carrying out these caretaker duties in the presence of any child, you must do your work in precisely the same manner that you would want the child to do Montessori work. For instance, even if you are in a hurry, do not carry more than one object at a time, do not move about hastily or carelessly, and do not handle your working materials roughly, because you will find the child absorbing these bad habits and reproducing them.

The 'facilitator' role is what will take up most of the director's time and attention. In this role, the director actually presents the Montessori activities to the child. The activities are presented one at a time, usually to only one child at a time. In conducting these presentations, the director has three distinct responsibilities.

First, each activity should be presented at precisely the right moment in a particular child's development, so that it will challenge the child's intellectual and physical abilities, and tie together certain of the child's previous experiences, thereby stimulating the child to observe the presentation closely and later to attempt the activity independently. To help create a challenge, the director doing the presentation must conduct the activity as perfectly as humanly possible, with a strong sense of confidence and an appearance of facility and grace. Rather than put the child off, this vision of perfection will be absorbed by the absorbent mind, and will lead the child to repeat the activity many times in pursuit of that perfection. The director must perceive when the initial challenge has been met in the child's daily attempts, and then introduce the additional exercises that build on the activity and its principles.

Second, after an activity has been presented to a child whose curiosity was sufficiently stimulated by it, the director must have the restraint to allow the child voluntarily to select and independently attempt the activity, and to attempt it many times without interference, comments or assistance. In other words, you must resist your sentimental impulse to help, and the child must be permitted to explore the new material freely and to struggle towards reproducing your presentation. However, if for some reason the child did not fully grasp the whole presentation, or seems hung up by the lack of an important step or technique, then sometime in the near future the director should repeat the presentation.

When repeating a presentation, the director chooses a time that the child will not relate to any failed attempt, and simply says, 'I would like to show you this material again', without reference to the child's previous attempts or to the earlier presentation. In the repeated presentation, the director makes especially obvious the points in the activity which the child previously missed.

There is a fine line between difficulties that the child, through practice, will gradually be able to overcome, and difficulties which indicate that something in the presentation was missed; it is up to the director to recognise the difference. If a child has missed something important in the presentation, and this is not soon after corrected by repeating the presentation, the child is very likely to begin misusing the materials – that is, giving up the activity's original goal, which seemed impossible to achieve, and inventing a different, more achievable way to use the materials. For example, in the PINK TOWER activity, ten cubes of different sizes are built into a tower of cubes of consistently decreasing sizes. Without having absorbed the point in the presentation where you locate the next smaller cube to put on the tower, the child will be unable to build it properly. If the director does not note this difficulty and its reason, and does not repeat the presentation, the child will eventually abandon the idea of a diminishing tower, and may decide to arrange the cubes in the shape of a house or castle, or to pretend they are train cars, since these would be more achievable goals.

Third, when a child, after much practice, is finally conducting an activity and its related exercises with proficiency, the director must help the child realise that something has been learned in the process. This is done by placing the principles disclosed by the activity, and the skills and knowledge gained by the child in doing it, in a wider context of meaning and application. Often the next Montessori activity in the sequence accomplishes this purpose, by building on the concepts of previous activities. But the director should also provide other opportunities for applying new skills, by making up and playing little games, or by asking the child's help in some small job that needs doing around the environment. For example, a child experienced in building the Pink Tower might be invited to stack a scattered set of books from largest to smallest. The Sensorial Activities are especially easy to adapt as game-playing, when the child is ready.

The director's responsibilities in presenting Montessori activities are clearly related to the theoretical concepts we were discussing earlier. The director's presentation depends for its success upon the workings of the absorbent mind. The child's responsiveness is dependent upon the readiness of the unfolding intellectual structure, broadly manifested in the sensitive periods, for the particular challenge the presentation poses. Lastly, the three responsibilities of the director as a facilitator – creating a challenge, allowing the child to practise, and placing what was learned in a wider context – are based on the three stages of learning – absorption, connection and application.

The purpose of the director's third role, that of an 'observer', is mainly to assist the director's work as a facilitator. As we've noted, to be sure that a presentation will pose a challenge to the child, the director must know precisely when to offer it. This sense of timing is based on the director's long-term observation of the child's development, which has shown that the child is far enough along in the appropriate sensitive periods and that the child has had sufficient experience with preparatory activities. Also, when giving a presentation, the director must closely observe the child's level of interest, and provide sufficient opportunities for involvement to maintain the child's attention. When the child is attempting an activity independently, the director must observe from a distance where difficulties arise in these attempts, to determine whether another presentation is needed, and if it is needed, what special points to emphasise. These observations will also suggest when a child has mastered an activity, and therefore needs the further challenge of the next exercise, the next activity in the scheme, or practical application through simple games and tasks.

More generally, the director must constantly observe all the activities selected by the child each day, to see where the child's natural interests lie. These overall observations of the child's work are vital because the several schemes of activities described in this book are not intended to be followed like a syllabus; decisions on what new presentations to offer should follow the child's natural inclinations. For instance, if the child is selecting a lot of physical activities, the director should offer activities that involve much movement; if the child seems particularly interested in reading and printed material, the director should offer activities that use charts or tags or books. Also, special interests shown by a child in particular subjects, like boats or rocks or clothes, should be incorporated into the activities whenever possible – for example, by providing 'rocks' to count in the MEMORY PLAY activity in Mathematics. In brief, if the director is successfully to direct the environment on the child's behalf, then the child must be allowed to direct the director.

If it is helpful, all these daily observations may be recorded in a diary. If a director is working with a number of children, a summary may be drawn up for each child at the end of each day, indicating what presentations were given, what presentations were repeated, what presentations should be given again with what points to emphasise, what work the child did, and what special tendencies the child displayed. At the end of each week, the director should review these records to understand each child's needs and inclinations better.

The three roles of a Montessori director – taking care of an environment specially for a child, facilitating a child's independent activities, and patiently observing progress – are difficult and somewhat unnatural roles for most of us to play. For example, if the facilitator role were left to our instincts, we would probably want to fumble a presentation to make it fun and humorous, so as not to intimidate the child. We would later want to give constant suggestions to aid the child's attempts at the activities, and to do part of the work for the child if it seemed too hard or slow. And we would be endlessly overlooking imperfect work, never repeating a presentation, attributing a child's mistakes to laziness or naughtiness, and in the face of difficulty, always pushing the child on to the next activity in the scheme rather than dwelling on the difficulties. But the Montessori activities, as remarkable an educational aid as they can be, would do the child little good if conducted in this manner. Because the adult behaviour which is most beneficial to a child's development is so unnatural to us, we all need to prepare ourselves to be Montessori directors, emotionally and in our attitudes, if all of those carefully prepared activities are to derive any benefit for children.

Our over-riding attitude should be that we do not wish to teach the child, or in any other way dominate the child, but only to help provide the child's natural development with the best environment in which to unfold freely. Second, we should realise that although the use of the Montessori materials will generate cultural and intellectual matter for the child's mind to absorb, it is up to us to provide the absorbent mind with emotional, moral and spiritual substance. In this respect, we should strive to be compassionate in our emotions, tolerant in our ethics, and humble in spirit. Third, when we present the child with our emotional, moral and spiritual substance, we need to know our weaknesses, to be alert to our preconceptions and prejudices, to reassess our motives constantly, and to acknowledge and learn from our mistakes. In a word, we must be honest. Children will absorb what we do, and then compare it to what we say. We should never put on an act with children, for not only are they sure to see through it, but we may risk permanently losing their trust. Finally, we should believe in the innate potential for goodness in every child, so that even when we don't see an angel before us, we know there is one in there somewhere, and that by providing the right freedoms and opportunities, we can help the goodness to surface.

Montessori believed that we adults, as part of the child's world, will necessarily either be a hindrance or a help to the child's development. As Montessori directors, our goal is to understand the child sufficiently that we will only ever be a help.

THE ACTIVITIES

The Five Subjects

Over her many years of directing Children's Houses, Montessori developed a great number of fun and interesting activities for young children to engage in. These activities provide the child with stimuli and experiences that, in terms of our theory discussions, nourish the absorbent mind, fulfil the needs of the sensitive periods and the child's unfolding inner intellectual structure, and follow the process of three stage learning. To help the director know the order in which to present the activities, so that the availability of new experiences will correspond to the changing needs of the unfolding inner structure, Montessori organised her activities into five disciplines or subjects, and within each subject worked out a general sequence for presenting the activities. From the child's point of view, the distinctions between these subjects are blurred and unimportant, and indeed most of the activities create experiences that give benefits in more than one subject area. It is therefore not useful for the director to stress to the child the purely rhetorical distinctions between the subject areas. The five subjects are themselves not sequenced; they are conducted more or less in parallel. But as shown in the lists below, certain activities in one subject area are best conducted before, at about the same time as, or after certain activities in the other subject areas.

One subject area consists of the Practical Activities, which develop basic personal and social skills used in daily living, like dressing oneself, cleaning things, and being polite. Another subject area is represented by the Sensorial Activities, which serve to enhance and enlarge the child's sense perceptions of the world. Another two subject areas are the Language Activities, which start the child reading and writing, and the Mathematics Activities, which introduce counting and arithmetic. The last subject area, called Culture Activities, exposes the child to such fields of inquiry as physical science, history, geography, anthropology and biology.

An Overview of the Sequence

The main reason for presenting the Montessori activities to the child is to provide appropriate experiences that satisfy the child's changing developmental needs. Each activity, in itself, provides some such experience to aid some particular stage of development. Taken together, the activities also build on one another to create an inter-related web of experience that helps integrate the individual abilities developed along the way.

In this web of Montessori experience, everything the child does is preparation for something the child will do later. This principle of 'indirect preparation' is incorporated into the design of each and every Montessori activity, and is reflected in the sequence for presenting the activities. Indirect preparation occurs in the Montessori environment in three ways: first, by the separate introduction, in two or three activities, of the component parts of a later activity; second, by the training of the child in specific, often physical, skills that build in stages toward a more complex skill; and third, by the creation of broad abilities or sensitivities that will generally be important in later work.

An example of the first form of indirect preparation is how the analysis of word sounds in the I SPY activity, and the association of sounds with letter shapes in the SANDPAPER LETTERS activity, are combined in the later MOVABLE ALPHABET activity to become the expression of words by arranging letters. An example of the second form of indirect preparation is how the small wooden knobs on the CYLINDER BLOCKS prepare the child's fingers for small grasping, which is further refined through the SORTING GRAINS activity, is given motor control through the METAL INSETS activity, is given lightness of touch in the SANDPAPER LETTERS activity, and is finally applied to handwriting in the WRITING INDIVIDUAL LETTERS activity. An example of the third form of indirect preparation is how the Practical Activities generally help develop the child's sense of order, through the organisation of the materials used in one's work. This is a skill that becomes crucial to successfully conducting many of the Mathematics Activities and the later Sensorial Activities.

Every Montessori activity, then, has a special place in the sequence, because it satisfies some transitory need that will arise at a particular point in the child's development, and because it provides at least one form of indirect preparation for an activity that will come later.

The following lists indicate the general sequence in which the Montessori activities may initially be offered to the child. For simplicity, I have divided the overall Montessori nursery programme into seven time 'Periods', under each of which is listed activities in the five subject areas. A child just starting out in the Montessori environment should be presented with activities in Period One, and thereafter the child may progress, at an individual pace, numerically through the other Periods. (The names of activities which are fully described in this book are printed in CAPITALS. Although there are seven Periods, this book mainly covers activities through Period Four, and some in Period Five; hence the title, *Basic Montessori*.) Usually, a child working within a particular Period in one subject area will also be working in the same Period in other subject areas. Note that these lists only indicate when an activity is first presented; the activity and its derivative exercises will continue to be conducted by the child in later Periods.

While the Periods tell you the proper sequence of the activities, you should, as has been mentioned before, only follow a particular series of activities when the child has shown an interest in pursuing such directions. This is an important qualification to the use of these lists: your over-riding responsibility is to follow the child's inclinations. Within the scope of the child's inclinations, these lists will help you know what doors to open next. To expand on this metaphor, you should not lead the child down these corridors, but rather follow closely behind the child, so that whichever direction the child turns, you can reach out and open a door.

Period One

(Early Practical Activities, introductory Sensorial, Culture, and Language Activities, no Mathematics.)

Practical: POURING BEANS BETWEEN TWO JUGS; opening and closing containers; BUTTONING; buckling; other simple Dressing Frames; carrying and laying floor mats and table mats; SAYING 'THANK YOU'; other early grace and courtesy work; carrying a tray; lifting, carrying and putting down a chair; sitting down on and getting up from a chair at a table; climbing and descending stairs; WALKING ON THE LINE; folding; hanging clothes on a hook; brushing hair; dusting.

Sensorial: CYLINDER BLOCKS; PINK TOWER; box 1 of the COLOUR TABLETS; presentation tray of the GEOMETRIC CABINET; SENSITISING THE FINGERS; TOUCH BOARDS; presentation (1) of GEOMETRIC SOLIDS; STEREOGNOSTIC BAGS presentation.

Language: CLASSIFIED PICTURES exercises (1) and (2); SPEECH; stages (1), (2) and (3) of I SPY; BOOK CORNER AND LIBRARY.

Mathematics: none.

Culture: LAND AND WATER presentation.

Period Two (Building fundamental skills in all subject areas except Mathematics, concentrating on sight and touch in Sensorial work.)

Practical: pouring water from a jug; medium difficulty Dressing Frames; simple braiding of rope or yarn; laying a table for a meal; polishing brass, glass surfaces, shoes or furniture; washing hands; washing cloths; scrubbing a table top; SWEEPING SAWDUST; brushing clothes; folding clothes; hanging clothes on a hanger; HANDLING A BOOK; asking for and receiving scissors; greeting people; kindness to visitors; BEING SILENT.

Sensorial: advanced CYLINDER BLOCKS exercises; BROWN STAIR; RED RODS; boxes 2 and 3 of COLOUR TABLETS; GEOMETRIC CABINET exercises (1) through (4); BINOMIAL CUBE; BLINDFOLD; TACTILE TABLETS; later GEOMETRIC SOLIDS presentations; STEREOGNOSTIC BAGS exercises; SORTING GRAINS; SOUND BOXES; preliminary presentations of BELLS; Three Stage Lessons on the names of Sensorial qualities.

Language: CLASSIFIED PICTURES exercises (3) and (4); stage (4) of I SPY; exercise (1) with the single-letter SANDPAPER LETTERS; METAL INSETS; frequent SPEECH 'Questioning'.

Mathematics: none.

Culture: LAND AND WATER exercises; first MAPS; PLACES classified pictures; preliminary work for CLASSIFICATION BY LEAF.

(Developing more advanced Practical skills, concentrating on other senses in Sensorial work, completing preparatory work in Language, fully entering Culture work, starting Mathematics.) **Period Three**

Practical: pouring water from a jug, also through a funnel; bows, laces and other difficult Dressing Frames; advanced braiding, then plaiting hair; tying a tie; simple cooking chores; ironing; making beds.

Sensorial: GEOMETRIC CABINET exercises (5) through (8); CONSTRUCTIVE TRIANGLES; SQUARE OF PYTHAGORAS; TRINOMIAL CUBE; FABRICS; THERMIC BOTTLES; BARIC TABLETS; presentations of BELLS.

Language: exercise (1) with the double-letter SANDPAPER LETTERS; stages (5) and (6) of I SPY, frequently; exercise (2) with all SANDPAPER LETTERS.

Mathematics: NUMBER RODS exercise (1).

Culture: all MAPS; PLACES picture folders; PAST AND PRESENT; STORIES ABOUT THE PAST; AIR; WATER; MAGNETISM; CLASSIFYING ANIMALS; CLASSIFICATION BY LEAF; PARTS OF ANIMALS; PARTS OF PLANTS.

(Advanced Sensorial Activities, early Language reading and writing, Mathematics Group 1 and starting Group 2.) **Period Four**

Practical: responsibility for certain daily Care of the Environment duties; helping and advising younger ones in a group.

Sensorial: GEOMETRIC CABINET exercises (9) and (10); THERMIC TABLETS; MYSTERY BAG; VISUAL WORK WITH BLINDFOLD; BELLS exercises (1), (2), and (3); TASTING CUPS; SMELLING BOXES.

Language: MOVABLE ALPHABET; WRITING INDIVIDUAL LETTERS; WRITING FAMILIES OF LETTERS; POSITIONING LETTERS ON LINES; SANDPAPER CAPITALS; Box 1 of OBJECT BOXES; ACTION CARDS; Box 2 of OBJECT BOXES; READING FOLDERS exercise (1).

Mathematics: NUMBER RODS exercise (2); SANDPAPER NUMBERS; NUMBER TABLETS (with the Number Rods); SPINDLES; NUMBERS AND COUNTERS; MEMORY PLAY; LIMITED BEAD MATERIAL; NUMBER CARDS; FUNCTION OF THE DECIMAL SYSTEM; FRACTIONS.

Culture: GRAVITY; SOUND; OPTICS; PLACES artefacts.

(Further development in Language reading and writing, essence of counting, adding, subtracting and multiplying in Mathematics.) **Period Five**

Practical: assisting with group activities; attending to visitors; comforting other children.

Sensorial: Knobless Cylinders; BELLS exercises (4), (5), and (6).

Language: Matching and Writing Capitals; The Alphabetic Sequence; Writing Copies; PUZZLE WORDS; READING FOLDERS exercise (2); Classified Reading; Environment Cards; Articles; Adjectives; Conjunctions; Prepositions; Verbs.

Mathematics: FORMATION OF COMPLEX NUMBERS; INTRODUCTION TO TEENS; INTRODUCTION TO TENS; Unlimited Bead Material (ADDITION, Subtraction and Multiplication); Counting; Stamps (Addition, Subtraction and Multiplication); Dots; Fractions exercises.

Culture: PLANT LIFE CYCLES; TIME LINE.

Period Six (Advanced Language work, basic division and arithmetic memory work in Mathematics.)

Practical: serving snacks and meals; subtle etiquette.

Sensorial: advanced Bells work.

Language: Margins; Punctuation Cards; READING FOLDERS exercises (3) and (4); Adjective Matching; Detective Adjective Game; Adverbs; Command Cards; Adverb Matching; Verb Games; Plurals; Feminine and Masculine; Root Word Charts.

Mathematics: Unlimited Bead Material (Division); Stamps (Division); Addition and Subtraction Snake Games; Addition and Subtraction Strip Boards; Multiplication Tables; Multiplication Bead Board; Addition, Subtraction and Multiplication Charts; advanced work with Fractions.

Culture: reading 'Classified Cards' in Geography, Nature Studies and History; fact books from the library.

Period Seven (Application activities in Language, abstraction in Mathematics.)

Practical: helping the director prepare the environment; presenting Practical Activities to younger children.

Sensorial: presenting early Sensorial Activities to younger children.

Language: Written Questioning; Free Writing; READING FOLDERS exercise (5); Reading Analysis.

Mathematics: Unit Division Board; Division Charts; Short Bead Frame; Hierarchies; Long Bead Frame; Simple Division.

Culture: definition stages of 'Classified Cards' in Geography, Nature Studies and History; field nature observation work.

Presenting an Activity

When a child has been enthusiastically pursuing a subject area and has gained experience that would appear to provide the requisite preparation for a particular new activity, then the director needs to respond at the earliest convenient time with a 'presentation' of the new activity. Unobtrusively place out the activity's materials in the spots you have set aside for them on the shelves, privately tell the child, with evident excitement, 'I have something new to show you ...', and proceed to present the new activity.

For each Montessori activity in this book, you will find: a statement of the activity's *Aim* or purpose in the Montessori programme, which explains how the child can benefit from it; a list and description of the *Material* needed for the presentation and the ensuing exercises; in some cases, 'DIY *hints*' or suggestions on *How to Make the Material*; a discussion of any *Preliminary Activities* or *Preliminary Presentations* or any special *Preparation* to be done by the director; a full step-by-step guide to giving the actual *Presentation* or *Presentations*; and complete descriptions of ensuing *Exercises* and how to present them. 'Exercises' are the work that the child does independently, after the presentation. The first exercise is usually simply the child independently trying to reproduce what you did so perfectly in the presentation. You later briefly present each of the other exercises, one at a time, when and if the child has mastered what's been presented so far. Although it is not always part of the description, every presentation and exercise concludes with the child putting all the materials back in their places in the Montessori environment, perfectly ready for another child to use.

As you will see, the step-by-step course of a presentation usually follows the process of three stage 'learning by connecting', described earlier. First, you simply show the material – naming it, showing where it is kept, identifying the scope of experience it provides, and inviting the child to handle it and otherwise become familiar with it. Second, you demonstrate the 'connection' or concept embodied in the material, and distinguish the material's purpose from that of other materials, by showing precisely how to use it and how best to observe and experience the 'connection'. Third, you give application and context to the concept, by immediately inviting the child to attempt what you have shown, and to try it again later, independently. Occasionally, the presentation is simply a Three Stage Lesson, which is a special method, based on the process of three stage learning, for helping the child memorise terms or other abstract associations.

Similarly, the overall structure of an activity parallels the process of three stage learning: the presentation is simply providing the activity to the absorbent mind; early exercises enable the child to act out the connections and concepts embodied in the activity; and later exercises – such as the memory exercises in the Sensorial Activities – allow application of the concept in a meaningful context.

When you are first teaching yourself an activity, you may follow the step-wise instructions given in this book, in the same way you would follow a recipe. But never give a presentation to a child while reading the directions for the first time. All the materials and supplies you will need for the presentation must be complete and in their designated places in the environment before you begin, and you will obviously have to work out in advance what you'll need and where to keep it. Also, before giving any presentation, you must fully understand its process and purpose, and have a great deal of experience in conducting the activity yourself. This means that you must practise it, and practise it often enough to keep yourself well trained, so that whenever you need to present a material you will be ready to give a flawless demonstration of how it's used.

Each presentation you give must be absolutely perfect, for three reasons. First, the child will benefit most by repeating and repeating an activity, and only the image of perfection created by your presentation will draw the child on to repeat the activity in pursuit of that perfection. Second, the child's absorbent mind will pick up every single little error you make, no matter how subtle it is or how quickly you correct yourself, and these errors may later frustrate or prevent the success of the child's independent attempts at the activity. Third, you must be able to conduct the activity with complete ease and familiarity, so that rather than concentrating on getting it right, you can concentrate on keeping the child's interest and attention.

You may often think that a presentation sounds so simple – 'after all, a three-year old can do it' – that practice on your part seems unnecessary. Although many of the activities are indeed based on comparatively simple procedures, without a lot of practice you will find it nearly impossible to conduct an activity without hesitation or mistake, while exuding absolute confidence, and while simultaneously trying to keep the child more interested in what you're doing than in what's going on across the room.

Keeping a young child's attention, while not diverging unnecessarily from the main flow of the presentation, is a subtle art that is best learned by experience. If you're working with a group of children, you will find that different children respond best to different techniques. For some children, an atmosphere of fun will keep their attention, while others are more fascinated by a sense of wonder and magic. During your presentation, you can occasionally invite the child to do some small physical task, like handing you something or putting something back in its box.

Also, you can make the child's observation of what you're doing involve some activity; for example, invite the child to re-count the beads you've just counted, or to feel the cloth you've just felt. If nothing seems to be working, and the child is simply not absorbing the presentation, then gracefully conclude it in the middle, and wait until another day to try it again from the beginning. Never, in desperation, conduct the activity jointly with the child – you doing some, and the child doing some – since unlike an adult, it is difficult for a young child to grasp the essence of an activity by alternately taking directions and observing. More generally, a presentation to a young child should never consist, in whole or in part, of verbal instructions. Remember that the young child's mind does not analyse nearly as well as it absorbs. Therefore, the essence of a good presentation is that you don't explain the activity to the child – you show it.

Whether a presentation is successful depends partly on the director's skills in conducting it, and partly on the child's readiness to respond to it. If a child, when later working independently, has continuous difficulty with an activity or appears to be manipulating the materials aimlessly, then either another presentation is needed, or the child is not yet ready for the challenges which the activity presents. If the child makes no errors at all when first attempting the activity, it is likely that the child is already too advanced and may lose interest in the activity before benefiting from it. When the child has grasped the purpose of the activity from the presentation, but there are occasional errors in judgement and technique, then the child is at just the appropriate stage of development. The challenge to perfect the activity will induce repetition and concentration, resulting in that remarkable self-directed, self-motivated learning that Montessori first witnessed in her Children's House.

The Child Freely at Work
Imagine that the child has recently been given a number of very high quality presentations, the cleaned and polished materials are neatly stored in their designated places in the carefully ordered Montessori environment, you are sitting expectantly in the corner waiting to observe some of that remarkable Montessori self-teaching, and what is the child doing? Playing with the cat.

Sounds frustrating? Well, it shouldn't. We must be very careful not to get in the frame of mind that there is anything whatsoever wrong with the child's playing with the cat, nor indeed with any typically childlike behaviour. The point cannot be emphasised too strongly that the Montessori environment is only there to help the child. Forcing it on the child, making evident our expectations of the wonders that Montessori's method can work, or in any way coercing the child to give up behaviour that comes naturally, will only cause harm and distress. If the Montessori environment is to help and not harm, it must be offered like a loving gift, without expectations or conditions, as a place for the child to be absolutely free – free to observe presentations or not observe them, to work or not work, to join in activities or just mess about, to be active or to rest.

Montessori observed that if she prepared the environment and presented it to the child properly, and allowed the child sufficient freedom to respond to those presentations at an individual pace, then a kind of space for natural growing is opened in the child's life.

The young child starting off in the Montessori environment is usually quite incapable of working on anything for very long, and typically flits from one activity to another, acting either in a frenzied manner or withdrawn. Then gradually the director's presentations begin to arouse the child's interest, focusing attention on a small number of activities. This aroused interest is delicate, and when it is exhibited it should be nurtured and protected from distractions. One day, when the child is attempting one of the simpler activities, the attempt will go on a lot longer than usual for no obvious reason, and then abruptly end, with the child looking around, as though just awakened from a daydream. Later in the same day, this experience of prolonged work may be repeated, perhaps several times, separated by distinct periods of restlessness. In the next stage, these extended work periods occur more often, and the times of restlessness between the work periods become shorter and less frequent. Also, a daily pattern evolves, wherein the child engages in a number of activities, not delving into any of them too deeply, before coming to the 'main activity' of the day, on which the child focuses quite intensely for a considerable period of time. Now, rather than end in a state of restlessness, each activity ends in a state of repose, during which the child contemplates and digests the work just experienced. This newfound ability to 'concentrate', as Montessori formally termed it, and the ensuing periods of tranquil contemplation, apparently fulfil a deep inner need, and this fulfilment begins to be expressed as a subtle increase in gentleness, kindness and thoughtfulness towards others. In the last phase, concentration continues, and spreads to other activities of the day, so that there are many focused activities rather than just one 'main activity'. Perseverance becomes a habit, and calmness and serenity a permanent aspect of the child's personality.

This is, of course, the ideal, but we can look for signs of it as we work with the child each day. Again, we cannot force the child to awaken into 'concentration'. It is in large part an awakening of the child's conscious will, which can only flourish in an atmosphere where it is fully free and respected.

Directing a Group of Children

The original Children's House had a considerable number of

children, at various ages and stages of development, all working simultaneously, and this is the way all Montessori classes have been organised since.

One would suppose that putting together children of different abilities, who are all working at different stages, would create jealousies and competition among them. However, the truth is precisely the opposite. It is the grouping of children who are all at roughly the same stage of development that invites comparisons and breeds jealousies. In a mixed-age group, each child, at any one moment, is working on something different and unique, and comparisons in 'performance' are not possible.

When we are uncertain of something, we often have as our first impulse the desire to seek help, or simply a vote of confidence, from another person who we believe to be more experienced. It is also a child's natural impulse to consult the more experienced. In a group of children of mixed ages, this older, more experienced person need not be the director – it can be another child.

Having a mixed-age group, and directing a child, who needs minor help, to another child more experienced, has a number of distinct advantages. First, for materials like the SOUND BOXES, which provide no inherent feedback that an error has been made, the director can ask an uncertain child to consult another more experienced child. This approach suggests to the first child that there are no absolute or final answers to certain questions, but only people working together to improve their perception and understanding. A second advantage is that a child who lacks self-esteem can be greatly encouraged by having someone else come to him or her for help. All children are good at something, and if the director keeps in mind several things that each child is good at, then whenever children want a check on one of those activities, they may be sent to the 'resident expert' for help. Another advantage of this approach is that having to show or explain something to someone else forces a child to organise it mentally, and so deepens the child's own understanding of it. Also, new children in the group can be given certain simple presentations by older children, especially of the Practical Activities and early Sensorial Activities, which helps welcome the new ones into the group, and incidentally, frees up a little time for the director.

A mixed-age group working together provides indirect preparation for younger children, who watch and begin to absorb the activities they will be doing later, and it helps the older children realise their progress when they see the younger ones attempting things that they themselves mastered some time ago. The general social atmosphere of the group benefits from children helping one another, as it becomes a fact of life that some people are more experienced in some things, but that everyone needs a little help from others.

The Montessori environment is thus a lively, social place, in which the children are free to work together if they like, and in which they often observe and discuss one another's work. Montessori children are encouraged to look to one another for answers and ideas as much as they look to adults.

Although the original Children's House had a large group of children, there is no reason that most of Montessori's principles and activities cannot be put to use in a private home, with just one or a few children. You will find that some of the activities discussed in this book are described as though they will be conducted with a small group of children. But with a little imagination, and where necessary, by assuming the roles of the other children yourself, you can readily adapt all the activities to a single child working alone.

GROWTH TOWARDS INDEPENDENCE

In devising her method, Maria Montessori had but one aim: to assist the child's natural development. Because the endpoint of a child's development is, one hopes, a self-sufficient, well-adjusted adult, any assistance we offer to 'development' must by definition foster independence and self-sufficiency. Our reason for practising the Montessori method is thus to aid the child's growth towards independence.

The Montessori method fosters independence in two ways: first, in the short term, it provides freedom and independence in learning; second, in the long run, it helps the child acquire tools for living, that is, the skills and abilities which give a person greater choices in life, and which make one free from dependence on others.

Let's first consider freedom in learning. We have all heard about educational methods that are based on 'freedom', in that they permit any activity or non-activity that strikes the child's fancy, provided it doesn't hurt or disturb anyone. Freedom in the Montessori environment is different from this. The Montessori method is not a licence for the child to act out momentary whims; instead, it introduces and upholds the child's right to make thoughtful choices. Although 'acting out whims' feels like freedom at first, a person eventually finds it quite limiting. Following our every whim, we would incur consequences we didn't want, we would make no progress towards fulfilling our deeper desires and, unable to make serious decisions, we would repeatedly find that our long-range choices had been made for us. True freedom, in Montessori's view, is control over one's own destiny, and that means controlling our whims, working towards long-range goals, and making conscious choices about our actions and their consequences. In other words, every act of truly 'free' choice is preceded by an act of judgement. This is a kind of freedom that must be learned, and to which we must lead a child, little by little.

When the child is new in the Montessori environment, we

verbally offer very simple choices between clearly contrasting experiences, for example, a choice between a quiet activity like working with a 'Dressing Frame', and an energetic activity like dusting all the table tops in the room. To help the child grasp the idea that thoughtful choosing requires self-evaluation, it is important that these early choices be between genuinely different activities, presenting a contrast that a young child can readily appreciate. Later, after we have presented many activities to the child, we give a greater number of choices, say four or five, any of which would pose the right level of challenge to inspire practice and stimulate growth. As has been stressed before, we must pay attention to and follow the interests demonstrated by the child in making these choices, and then create new opportunities in directions suggested by the child's natural inclinations. Gradually, the child's choices need not be pointed out as often by the director, since they become self-evident in the wide range of interesting materials that we have presented to the child and which are waiting attractively on their shelves.

Corollaries to the child's freedom in choosing activities are the freedoms to conduct those activities when, where, as long as, as often as, and at whatever pace the child likes. For example, the child in a home Montessori environment can set to work with an activity at dusk or daybreak, can set it up under the piano bench or in the bedroom, can work on it for ten minutes or for eight hours straight, can set it up just once or twelve days in a row, and can work intensively at great speed or intermittently between roaming around and daydreaming. In a group environment, in addition to the above sorts of freedom, the child can also share an activity with another child, provided they have both been properly presented with the material. These freedoms aren't so much a matter of liberty, as they are a matter of respecting the child's dignity as an individual. Respecting children teaches children to respect themselves; it builds their trust in their own judgement, and so supports their basic freedom to make thoughtful choices.

The second type of independence fostered by the Montessori environment is the cultivation of certain skills and knowledge, like reading, writing, maths, geography, social courtesy, physical grace and household skills, all of which help a person live competently. This sort of competence in daily living frees us from dependence upon others, it often frees us from manipulation by others, and by enabling us to deal efficiently with mundane matters, it frees our minds for more profound and rewarding pursuits. The world in general, and human society in particular, have forces and pressures which are larger and more powerful than any one of us. If we do not understand these forces, they will forever drag us along in their wake. But if we can acquire insight into these forces, and learn to adapt to them, we can use their momentum to propel us in our own creative directions.

Montessori characterised the child's gradual growth towards

independence as a continual emergence, or liberation, into ever-larger spaces to adapt to. Birth is the first liberation, freeing the baby from containment by the womb, but leaving the baby vulnerable to the changeable environment outside. A second emergence, which comes in the first month or two, is a deliberate facing of the world and its sensory impressions, which the baby's absorbent mind begins to incarnate. A third liberation is weaning, making the baby independent of its mother's body, but also making it responsible for the complex set of actions necessary to feeding one's self and expressing needs. With the onset of speech, the baby emerges into social life, and is liberated from the isolation of the solitary thinker, but must also begin to cope with social expectations and judgements. At about one year of age, the child begins to learn to walk, emerging into a greater field for exploration, but also becoming responsible for knowing when and where not to explore. With each emergence into a greater space come new freedoms and new responsibilities.

In the Montessori environment, it may be useful for us to think of the child's progress in just this way. It implies that we, as directors, can help equip the child for each adaptation to a given intellectual space, and can then gradually lead the child to emerge from it, to face a wider space, with exciting new opportunities and challenges. The freedom to work at these adaptations at an individual pace solidly grounds the new skills that are gained in the process of adapting. These new skills become new freedoms, which collectively open the gate to the next larger space for the child to grow into. The process continues, and when the child eventually emerges into the space usually called society, and becomes self-sufficient in that space, the child starts to be called an adult.

PEACE THROUGH SELF-FULFILMENT

Maria Montessori lived through the two most terrible wars in the history of mankind, and the causes of war were very much on her mind, especially in the years after the Second World War. She came to believe that the widespread application of her method of education could help lead the world towards peace.

Montessori believed that her method enables children to satisfy fully their instinctual and personal developmental needs, and so helps to create fulfilled and well-balanced adults, whose innate goodness can shine forth unimpeded by neurotic ambitions and desires. If her method would spread sufficiently throughout the world, she hoped, millions of adults raised by it would be free from such tendencies as greed and aggression. Then, with the passing of the old generations, threats to world peace would gradually subside and disappear.

The Montessori method may also help promote peace by its study and support of the work of the absorbent mind. If we consider the action of the absorbent mind – that children fully accept, without critique or prejudice, the behaviour and traits of those around them, that children transform themselves by incarnating these ways, and that children place complete faith in the goodness and benevolence of others – we see more than a mechanism for learning, but also children's saint-like charity or spiritual love for people. This love emanates unconsciously from each and every child in each and every family and community in the world. If the Montessori method were widely applied, this love, as embodied in the absorbent mind, would be studied and cultivated rather than ignored and distracted. Perhaps the child's innate spirit of love would also carry over from childhood to adulthood, and eventually affect the way in which adults behaved towards one another.

Lastly, Montessori may have helped promote peace by awakening us to the importance of childhood to society. Children's absorbent minds, by assimilating the language, ideas, customs and manners of society, allow the cultural adaptations of each community to be continuous and built upon, from one generation to the next. In this sense, the absorbent mind makes possible all civilisation and its progress, and provides an ever-recurring bond that holds society together. Whatever their differences, most societies share a reverence for children's innocent affections, trust and generosity. Montessori had great hopes that the study of the child would bring together the world's societies in a common and universally beneficial cause. Indeed, Montessori lived to see her method being followed and pursued, at least to some extent, on every continent on the globe.

2 PRACTICAL ACTIVITIES

INTRODUCTION

Montessori believed that the young child 'at play', whether on the playground, at home, or in pre-school, has most of the same feelings and needs as an adult 'at work'. An adult wants interesting and important work that personally appeals, rather than just busywork or menial chores; an adult wishes to have adequate training, proper tools, and a workplace conducive to concentration; and an adult seeks respect and recognition for work done well. Montessori observed that a child at play similarly desires meaningful activities that may be personally selected; a child wants to be shown clearly how things are done and to be provided with proper materials and space; and a child hopes that concentrated efforts will be fully respected while in progress and admired when finished. An adult's work and a child's play are parallel in product as well as process. Just as the primary goal of adult work is to create from Nature a self-sufficient and tolerant society, so the primary goal of child's play is to create from a baby an independent and compassionate adult. Recognising these parallels, Montessori preferred to call child's 'play', the child's own special 'work'.

Some adults are wary of the Montessori method's apparent 'work' ethic, which they fear may cause their children to miss out on the delights of being young and without responsibilities – delights such as pretending, playing games, acting silly, running around outdoors, scheming with friends, or just doing nothing if they like. These parents suffer from their own adult pressures and anxieties, and decide that the responsibilities of education and work will come soon enough in their young children's lives. They firmly believe that early childhood should be fun and carefree.

Montessori also believed that childhood should be fun and carefree. But from her many years of sensitively observing young children, she developed a different understanding of what a child naturally thinks is fun, and how best to help children be carefree. Montessori observed that running around, acting silly, and playing games only kept children entertained for short periods of time, and that afterwards they were still restless and unsatisfied. She found that when she did not try to impose adult conceptions of relaxation on them, the children had the most fun when their play developed early life skills, and they felt most carefree when they were given the means and the freedom to care for themselves. In other words, children seemed most satisfied by their 'play' when it enabled them to progress in their specially appointed 'work' – the work of building a helpless baby into an independent adult. (When children have been satiated with this work, then like adults who have been hard at work, they want to relax, mess about, play games, or just rest. The Montessori environment provides plenty of opportunity for relaxation too.)

In light of these discoveries, Montessori designed special 'play' activities that provide real-life experience – rather than just fantasy experience – to help the child in the 'work' of creating a well-adjusted adult. In the Montessori environment, the child does not just pretend to be a pioneer or an adventurer, but really explores the world, including its geography, cultures and natural history (see the Culture Activities). The child does not just arrange magnetic numbers on the refrigerator or look at cartoon picture books, but really experiences the satisfaction of calculating, reading and writing (see the Mathematics Activities and Language Activities). And the Montessori child does not just play with dolls or play at Wendy House or at tea parties, but actually cares for his or her person, cleans and maintains the work environment, and learns how to behave in a graceful and considerate manner. These latter activities – care of the person, care of the environment, and social graces – Montessori called the 'Practical Life Activities'.

The Practical Activities are the first activities the child is introduced to in the Montessori environment. This is because they can immediately begin to satisfy the young child's inner and hitherto frustrated desire for skills and self-sufficiency.

The Practical Activities allow the child to try doing what adults all around may be seen doing each and every day – for example, dressing oneself, cleaning the home, and greeting people. In addition to giving the child an opportunity for self-development, these activities provide an orientation to the customs of the child's particular society. The precise contents of the Practical Activities should therefore differ from culture to culture. Although the few Practical Activities described in this book are so universal (e.g. pouring, sweeping, thanking) that they are found in nearly all of the world's societies, the exact methods described here for conducting these activities reflect my local technology and customs (e.g. jugs with handles, dustpans, saying 'thank you'). You will need to adjust the methods described here and add your own activities, to reflect your society's and community's unique habits and customs.

Since the Practical Activities are designed to give the child real-life experience, the materials used to conduct the activities should be real working tools, and not just toy versions of adult tools. For example, the broom for the sweeping activity should have good bristles, and the jugs for pouring should be good quality ceramic. Although these tools are not toys, they generally ought to be child-size, so that they may be properly grasped and put to effective use. Like all Montessori materials, each Practical Activities apparatus has its own special place in the environment, and all the things necessary for any Practical Activity are kept out and accessible for use without adult assistance.

The Practical Activities may be seen to fall into three basic categories: Manipulative Skills, Self-Development, and Care of the Environment. Manipulative Skills, such as pouring, opening containers, handling books, and carrying delicate items, are relatively simple tasks that adults commonly do for a young child, usually because adults want to hurry things along for convenience, but often to allay adult fears of accidental messes. Self-Development includes: grace, which describes how one moves about; courtesy, which concerns how one behaves socially; and personal care, which involves dressing and cleaning oneself. Care of the Environment is a fancy name for housework – work which the young child constantly watches adults do, but is never invited to join in on.

The child conducts the Practical Activities for the sake of working through the processes, rather than for the sake of their results. But if you are directing a group of children, the products of the Practical Activities eventually become useful to the small Montessori community in which the child is working. For instance, the painting table is kept clean by children practising scrubbing a table top, the shelves are kept free of dust, floor mats are neatly put away, no one trips over chairs not pushed in, visitors are politely greeted and seated, and coats neatly hung up are easy to find. The children soon realise that they are responsible for their own environment, which enhances their respect for others and for themselves.

ANALYSING MOVEMENT

For every physical activity, there are probably one or two ways of doing it which are the most effective and efficient. Consider, for example, how you unbutton your coat. Do you grasp the button by one edge, gently stretch the opening with the other hand, and then slide the button out? Or do you use only one hand, pulling the flap up with two fingers while pushing the button out of the hole with your thumb? Perhaps you just tug the two sides of the coat until the button pops through? While some methods for unbuttoning a coat probably cause undue wear and tear, and other methods waste a lot of time, there are in all likelihood one or two methods of unbuttoning a coat which are gentle on the coat and yet swiftly effective. Why doesn't everyone naturally use such a method? Because most people were probably never shown how to unbutton a coat – they struggled with it as a child, and whatever method they ended up with is the one they've been using ever since.

For every Practical Activity, you must discover a method which is both efficient and effective, and then show that method to the child. The best way to discover an ideal method is to practise the activity yourself, extremely slowly, breaking it down into, and writing out, each of your component actions or movements. Eliminate any movements which are destructive or wasteful, and be sure to include all movements that are necessary for success. Practise the method over and over, refining it and streamlining it, until it is the epitome of efficiency. Then underline on your list of movements those essential points which, if overlooked, will probably lead to the activity's failure. When you have practised the method until it feels second nature, and you find yourself employing it automatically in your own daily practical life, then you are ready to present it to the child.

The presentation of every Practical Activity must show each of the activity's component movements clearly and distinctly, stressing the essential movements, all in a graceful but efficient step-by-step operation, which leads to an unqualified success. This may sound like a pretty involved process for teaching a child how, for example, to unbutton a coat, but if someone had done this for me when I was child, it would have saved me a great deal of button-sewing, perhaps made my coats last longer, and prevented a lot of silly struggling in entrance halls.

Some activities are so complex once they've been analysed that they are best presented to the child in stages. When you present just one stage of an activity, it must still lead to an attainable success, and so you should present each stage as a small cycle within the larger cycle of the whole activity.

If a child who was responsive to your presentation attempts the activity independently, but fails to reach the activity's goal or to complete the cycle, then it is probably due to the lack of one of those essential movements. Another presentation is therefore necessary, and this second presentation should make especially clear and distinct the essential movements that the child inadvertently missed the first time around.

Following this Introduction is a long but by no means comprehensive list of Practical Activities that you may wish to analyse and present. Feel free to add other daily life activities that you think would be useful to a person in your community or society. So that you will better understand what is meant by 'analysing the movements' in an activity, this chapter also includes

descriptions of five Practical Activities that I have analysed into
component movements and then built into what I consider to be
efficient and effective methods. The first four activities are each
followed by a list of *Essential Movements*. If you find the methods
that I have worked out for these five activities to be odd or
peculiar, then by all means perform your own analyses. The
simplest of these activities, POURING BEANS BETWEEN TWO JUGS, is
analysed into very fine movements, to show you just how detailed
such an analysis can be. The chapter ends with an additional pair
of Practical Activities – two special Self-Development exercises to
which every Montessori child should be exposed.

A LIST OF PRACTICAL ACTIVITIES

Manipulative Skills:

1) Opening and closing boxes
2) Opening and closing lids of jars and biscuit tins
3) Opening and closing various types of doors and cupboards
4) POURING BEANS BETWEEN TWO JUGS, pouring water, and
   pouring water through a funnel
5) Folding and unfolding cloths
6) Lifting, carrying and putting down a delicate object
7) Lifting, carrying and putting down a tray with objects on it
8) Carrying a floor mat
9) Unrolling and rolling up a floor mat
10) Sitting on the edge of an unrolled floor mat
11) Lifting, carrying and putting down a chair
12) With a chair at a table, lifting it away from the table, sitting
    on it, getting up from it, and placing it back under the table
13) Using scissors and handing scissors to someone
14) HANDLING A BOOK
15) Handling and playing a record.

Self-Development:

1) Washing hands and face
2) Brushing and combing hair
3) Braiding (using nylon cords) and plaiting (hair)
4) Dressing Frames (BUTTONING, lacing, buckling, using press
   studs, tying bows, using a zip)
5) Tying a tie
6) Polishing shoes
7) Brushing lint from clothes
8) Folding clothes
9) Hanging clothes on a hook
10) Hanging clothes on a hanger
11) Saying 'please' and SAYING 'THANK YOU'
12) Drawing a person's attention before speaking
13) Gracefully climbing and descending stairs

14) Giving way to others at a doorway
15) Asking permission to get past in a small space
16) Greeting friends and greeting strangers
17) Offering a seat to a visitor
18) Offering refreshments to a visitor.

Care of the Environment:

1) Dusting
2) SWEEPING SAWDUST
3) Washing a table surface
4) Polishing furniture
5) Polishing brass objects
6) Polishing windows or mirrors
7) Washing cloths
8) Laying a table
9) Making a bed
10) Washing and drying dishes and cutlery
11) Stacking dishes and sorting cutlery
12) Drawing and opening curtains and blinds
13) Watering plants
14) Arranging flowers in a vase.

Pouring Beans between Two Jugs

Aim   To help the child develop co-ordination, self-sufficiency, and the following Manipulative Skills: carrying a tray with objects on it; pouring with either hand; and lifting and placing down a delicate object. To enable the child to pour drinks and to become involved in cooking and mealtime activities.

Materials   One small, rectangular tray, on which are kept two small ceramic jugs, placed on opposite sides of the tray, with their handles facing outward and their lips facing each other. The jug on the right side of the tray is about two-thirds full of small dry beans – ideally haricot beans, alternatively lentils.

Preparation   – Ensure that there are sufficient beans in the jug
– Check that the jug with the beans is on the right.

Presentation
(with a detailed
analysis of
movement)

1) Name the Pouring Beans tray, show where it is kept, and place it on a table, ensuring that the jug with the beans is still on the right side of the tray.
2) Seat the child to your left.
3) Say, 'I'm going to show you how to pour the beans. Watch me, and then you can have a turn.'
4) Raise your hand on the side of the full jug to the level of the tray.
5) Extend that hand's index and middle finger forward.
6) Slowly place these extended fingers next to the full jug's handle.

7) Wrap these two fingers around and through the handle, so that they are pointing towards yourself.
8) Place the same hand's thumb on top of the handle, and grip the handle gently.
9) Now raise your other hand to the level of the tray.
10) Extend this hand's index and middle fingers forward, with the palm facing towards your other arm.
11) Slowly place these extended fingers between the two jugs.
12) Gently hold the tips of these extended fingers against the full jug, a little below the lip, but not touching the lip.
13) Grip the full jug between the handle and your still extended fingers, and lift the jug straight up, until it has reached the height at which your extended fingers are level with the top of the other, empty jug.
14) Now move the full jug towards the other until your two extended fingers are almost touching it, and slowly rotate the handle of the full jug up and over those fingers, while centring its lip over the top of the empty jug.
15) Continue rotating until no more beans are heard to fall.
16) Rotate a little further and see that no more beans fall.
17) Slowly reverse the rotation, keeping the two extended fingers in the same place in the air, until the now empty jug is upright.
18) Slowly move the now empty jug to above its initial resting place.
19) Gently lower the empty jug onto the tray.
20) Carefully release your two extended fingers from the empty jug, slowly withdraw this hand towards yourself, and place it on your lap.
21) Lift your other hand's thumb off the top of the empty jug's handle.
22) Slowly remove that hand's fingers from the handle, move your hand away from jug, withdraw it to yourself, and place it on your lap.
23) Look over the tray for spilled beans.
24) If you see any spilled beans on the tray:
    a) Focus your attention on one spilled bean.
    b) Raise to the level of the tray the hand which is closest to the side of the tray on which the bean lies.
    c) Extend this hand's thumb and index finger towards the bean.
    d) Slowly direct your thumb and index finger, slightly separated, towards the bean, going around (and not over) the jug if the bean is behind it.
    e) Place the tips of your thumb and index finger on either side of the bean, and rest the tips gently on the tray.
    f) Grasp the bean between the tips of your thumb and index finger.
    g) Raise the bean slowly to a height just above the tops of the jugs.

h) Slowly move your hand until the bean is centred above the full jug.
i) Release the bean, letting it fall into the full jug.
j) Holding your hand at the same height, withdraw it towards yourself.
k) Focus attention on another spilled bean on the tray.
l) If this bean is on the same side of the tray as the last, repeat steps (c) through (k). If this bean is on the other side of the tray, lower your raised hand to your lap, and repeat steps (b) through (k).
m) Repeat steps (b) or (c) through (j) until no more spilled beans can be seen on the tray, taking care to look behind the jugs.
25) Pour the beans back into the first jug, repeating steps (4) through (22) with opposite hands. Then repeat steps (23) and (24).
26) Invite the child to try the pouring, first into the left jug, and then back into the right jug. Then invite the child to work with the jugs in the same way, now or later, independently.

Essential Movements
– Applying equal pressure when lifting the full jug, in order to keep it level before pouring
– Raising the full jug high enough before pouring
– Rotating the full jug without knocking its lip against the other jug
– Centring the lip of the full jug over the empty jug while pouring
– Pouring slowly
– Releasing fingers from the jug's handle without getting them caught
– Finding spilled beans that might be behind the jugs.

Buttoning

Aim
To help the child develop co-ordination, and gain independence by learning how to get dressed and ready to go out, how to make oneself warmer or cooler as appropriate, and how to care for one's personal appearance. To introduce the skill of buttoning in an activity that is entirely independent of the pressure and anxiety of getting dressed while adults are waiting.

Material
The Dressing Frame for Buttoning, which is a square wooden frame on which are tacked two slightly overlapping, rectangular flaps of cloth. The flaps are each tacked along one side, on opposite edges of the frame. Where the two flaps overlap, one flap has a column of five large buttons equally spaced, and the other flap has five matching buttonholes. When the two flaps are buttoned together, they entirely cover the space inside the frame. (DIY hint: make the flaps from the front of an old shirt, and sew the cut ends to a square cardboard frame.)

– Ensure that all the buttons on the Dressing Frame are done up.   **Preparation**

1) Name the Dressing Frames, show which frame is for   **Presentation**
Buttoning, and bring that frame to a table.
2) Seat the child to your left.
3) Place the frame in front of yourself on the table, so that the
upper flap of cloth – that is, the flap with the buttonholes – is
on your right side.
4) Say, 'I will show you how to unbutton and button again.
Watch me, and then you can have a turn.'
5) Pinch the right side of the furthest button, between your
right thumb and index finger, with the thumb on top.
6) Pinch the left edge of the upper flap of cloth, directly
adjacent to the far button, between your left thumb and
index finger, with the thumb on top.
7) Very gently pull the pinched edge of the cloth to the left,
simultaneously directing the left edge of the button down
towards the table surface, until the left edge of the button
slips into the button hole.
8) Release your right hand's pinch on the button as your left
hand lifts the pinched edge of the cloth towards the right,
causing the button to slip through the buttonhole.
9) Continue to lift the pinched edge of the cloth towards the
right, to expose the unbuttoned button, and then lay the flap
back down so that the button hole rests above the button.
10) Repeat steps (5) through (9) for each of the next four
buttons, from far to near.
11) Now pinch the far left corner of the flap with the buttonholes,
between one hand's thumb and index finger, pinch the near
left corner of that flap between the other hand's thumb and
index finger, and lift the flap with both hands over the right
edge of the frame, laying it on the table top.
12) Repeat step (11) with the flap with the buttons, lifting it with
both hands over the left edge of the frame.
13) Observe the frame open and empty, and tell the child that
the frame is now 'unbuttoned'. Say, 'Now I will button the
frame again.'
14) Pinching the corners of each flap as before, replace the flaps
across the middle of the frame, first the flap with the buttons,
then the flap with the buttonholes.
15) Pinch the left edge of the flap with the buttonholes, adjacent
to the far buttonhole, between your right thumb and index
finger, with the index finger on top.
16) Raise this pinched edge slightly to expose the button
underneath.
17) Pinch the left edge of the far button between your left thumb
and index finger, with the thumb on top.
18) Place the fleshy tip of your right index finger against the
buttonhole, and place the right edge of the button into the
buttonhole against this finger tip.

19) Release your right thumb from its pinch of the flap, and pinch instead the right edge of the button through the buttonhole, grasping it between your right thumb and index finger.
20) Release your left hand's pinch of the button, and instead pinch the left edge of the upper flap of cloth, adjacent to the far buttonhole.
21) Very gently pull the edge of the upper flap to the left, while very gently pulling the button to the right, until the left edge of the button emerges through the buttonhole. Release your left hand's pinch of the flap, but continue to hold the button with your right thumb and index finger.
22) Place your left thumb beneath the left edge of the button, and against the cloth at the left edge of the buttonhole, and gently press down towards the table surface, to ensure that the button is completely through the hole.
23) Place both hands in your lap, and observe with the child the furthest button now re-buttoned.
24) Repeat steps (15) through (23) for each of the next four buttons, from far to near.
25) Invite the child to try unbuttoning and re-buttoning just the furthest button. Then invite the child to work through the entire frame, now or later, independently.

Essential Movements

When unbuttoning:
– Pulling the edge of the upper flap to the left very gently
– Simultaneously directing the button downwards and pulling the edge of the flap towards the left
– Lifting the flap all the way off the button
– Undoing the buttons in order, from far to near.

When buttoning again:
– Closing the flap with the buttons first, and then the flap with the button holes, so that it rests on top
– Starting with the furthest button, doing them up in order, and not skipping any
– Matching each button to its corresponding buttonhole
– Putting the tip of your index finger just against the buttonhole, without pushing it through
– Pinching the button through the buttonhole to draw it through
– Drawing the button all the way through the buttonhole
– Depressing your thumb beneath the button, to ensure that the button went through the buttonhole completely.

Sweeping Sawdust

Aim To help the child gain independence by learning how to care for one's home and workplace – in particular how to sweep up dry spills, dirt and dust on a floor. To integrate earlier practical skills, such as dusting and carrying full containers. To foster concentration, by causing the child to pursue a series of separate activities towards a single goal. In having the child draw a circle into which to sweep, to introduce the technique of envisaging the result of one's work before setting about it. To show the need for organisation when beginning a complex task. In requiring that all sprinkled particles of sawdust are found and swept, to help make the child's visual perception more acute.

Material

An area of floor that is not carpeted.

A broom with a short handle appropriate for a child's height, and with strong, even, good-quality bristles.

A dustpan and brush, easy for a child to grasp.

A small, hand-held mop, dampened daily with water.

A small container filled with a cup of large-grain sawdust.

Another small container with one or more pieces of blackboard chalk in it.

(Although it is not necessary, it is helpful for all the above objects to be the same colour, so that they are clearly associated with the Sweeping Sawdust activity.)

A wastepaper basket in the room, with an opening larger than the mouth of the dustpan.

Preparation

– Ensure that the mop is damp.
– Check that the container has about one cup of sawdust in it.
– Locate a space on the uncarpeted floor at least as wide as the broom handle is long, and at least twice as long as the broom handle, through which other people will not want to pass during the activity, and near which runs a wall or other divider.
– Check that the broom and brush are clean, and that the dustpan is empty and clean.
– Check that at least one piece of chalk is in the container for chalk.

Presentation

1) Name the various materials that are used for Sweeping Sawdust, and show where they are kept.
2) Point out the floor space selected by you in the *Preparation*, and tell the child that you will show how to sweep this part of the floor. Say, 'First I'll sweep it. Watch me closely, and then you can have a turn.'
3) Bring all the materials, one at a time, to the selected floor space. Near the 'entrance' to the space, place each object directly against the wall (or other divider) in the following order from left to right: sawdust container, chalk container, broom, dustpan, brush and mop. The broom handle and mop handle may be leaned upright against the wall, and all the other objects should be placed flat on the floor and against the wall. Special care must be taken to place the first and left-most object, the sawdust container, in a spot against

the wall where it is unlikely to be accidentally kicked or tipped over by a passer-by.

4) Observe, with the child, the order of the things against the wall. Then lift the sawdust container with two hands and carry it to the far end of the chosen floor space.

5) Stand facing the far end of the floor space, hold the sawdust container with one hand, and reach into the container with your free hand. Grasp a large pinch of the sawdust between your thumb and fingers, extend that hand outwards towards the end of the floor space, and then allow the sawdust to sprinkle to the floor, while slowly moving your hand back and forth. Look behind yourself, and take one small step backwards towards the entrance of the floor space.

6) Repeat step (5) until you reach the centre of the selected floor space. Then, take a decidedly larger pinch of the sawdust, almost a small handful, and sprinkle it onto the floor there. Continue repeating step (5) with small pinches of sawdust, as previously, until you reach the entrance to the space.

7) The total amount of sawdust you will have spread onto the floor in steps (5) and (6) is about four tablespoons. Return the sawdust container to its place against the wall.

8) Carefully lift the chalk container with one hand. Select a piece of chalk with the other, and hold it between that hand's thumb, index finger and middle finger. Return the chalk container to its place along the wall.

9) Focus on, and draw the child's attention to, the square foot or so within the designated floor space which appears to have the greatest concentration of sawdust on it. (If step (6) was done correctly, this small area will be roughly in the centre of the floor space.)

10) Slowly walk up to that spot, careful to step only on the cleanest spots on the floor.

11) Bend over and draw a chalk circle on the floor around that square foot or so of concentrated sawdust. (The ideal diameter of this circle is slightly greater than the width of the mouth of the dustpan.)

12) Slowly walk back to the entrance to the space, carefully stepping only in the cleanest spots, as before.

13) Lift the chalk container with your free hand, gently place the piece of chalk back into the container, and return the container to its place along the wall.

14) Grasp the broom handle with both hands, one hand in the middle and the other hand near the top of the handle, and lift the broom from its place against the wall, taking care not to knock it against the chalk container. Go just outside the entrance to the floor space.

15) Facing the entrance to the space, stand behind the broom, hold its brush away from you and downwards, and place its bristles gently against the floor at the entrance to the space, about a foot outside the area sprinkled with sawdust. Sweep

the sawdust in the entrance area towards the chalk circle, using very short, firm thrusts and leaving no sawdust behind the broom's bristles.

16) Using the same short pushing motions, sweep into the chalk circle all the sawdust that is between the entrance area and the circle. Each time a path of sawdust has been pushed into the circle, gently raise the bristles of the broom several inches off the floor, still holding it above the circle, and give it one or two shakes downward, to shake the sawdust off.

17) Next, sweep into the chalk circle any sawdust that lies to the right or the left of the circle, by standing just outside the area sprinkled with sawdust, and using the same pushing motions with the broom. Remember to shake the bristles over the circle again to loosen any clinging sawdust.

18) Lastly, sweep into the chalk circle all the sawdust from the area beyond the circle, stepping only in areas that have already been cleared of sawdust. As before, stand just outside the area sprinkled with sawdust, and use the same pushing motions with the broom. Again shake the bristles to make any clinging sawdust fall into the chalk circle.

19) Carefully check the entire floor space outside the chalk circle for any remaining bits of sawdust. If you find any, sweep it into the circle using the pushing technique. Look over the floor space once more, and return the broom to its place, leaning it against the wall.

20) Lift the dustpan by its handle, holding it with its mouth facing towards your other hand. With that other hand, pick up the brush by its handle, holding it with its bristles facing down. Walk to the chalk circle.

21) Lower the dustpan to the floor so that the front edge of its mouth just touches the chalk circle and its body is outside the circle. Then, leaving the dustpan's mouth touching the floor at the chalk circle, raise the back end of the dustpan about two inches off the floor.

22) Very gently place the bristles of the brush on the floor just outside the chalk circle, on the opposite side of the circle from the dustpan.

23) Using sideways motions of the brush, push a single path of sawdust towards the mouth of the dustpan, and then into the dustpan, stopping when all the brush's bristles are resting on the lower lip of the dustpan.

24) Slowly turn the bristles of the brush towards the inside of the dustpan, and very gently tap the bristles upwards against the upper edge of the mouth, causing any clinging sawdust to fall off onto the lower lip.

25) Lift the brush completely out of and off the dustpan. Slowly lift the dustpan off the floor, and tilt it back so that any sawdust on its lower lip slides into the mouth.

26) Repeat steps (21) through (25), but start off with the dustpan mouth touching a different point on the chalk circle.

27) Repeat step (26) until all the sawdust in the circle has been brushed into the dustpan.

28) Using the brush, gently sweep back into the chalk circle any sawdust that may have been inadvertently spread outside the circle during steps (21) through (27). Then repeat steps (21) through (25) once more.

29) Carrying the dustpan tilted back, with its mouth facing somewhat upwards, and still carrying the brush in your other hand, walk slowly to the room's wastepaper basket. Lower the dustpan until its mouth is just inside the rim of the basket. Then suddenly turn the back of the dustpan upwards, causing the sawdust inside to fall into the wastepaper basket. With the brush in your other hand, lightly brush into the wastepaper basket any sawdust clinging to the lip of the dustpan.

30) Return the dustpan and brush to their places against the wall.

31) With one hand, lift the small, damp mop by its handle.

32) Place the mop's head anywhere on the chalk circle, and with gentle, short, back-and-forth rubbing motions, erase the chalk circle. Work your way around the circle until no chalk marks remain on the floor.

33) Return the mop to its place against the wall.

34) All the materials and the floor space should now be just as they were at the start of the activity, except that there will be less sawdust in the sawdust container. At this point, invite the child to try Sweeping Sawdust independently, now or later, spreading sawdust on and sweeping the same floor space. When the child is done with Sweeping Sawdust for the day, ensure that all materials and the floor space are clean, and if they are not, point it out to the child to correct.

Essential Movements

– Placing the materials along the wall in their correct order
– Placing the sawdust container where it won't be knocked over by a passerby
– Only sprinkling pinches of sawdust, and not big handfuls
– After each sprinkling of sawdust, looking behind yourself before stepping backwards
– Not sprinkling the sawdust outside the selected floor space
– Drawing the chalk circle where there is the highest concentration of sawdust
– Drawing the circle large enough to contain all the sawdust that will be swept, but only slightly larger in diameter than the mouth of the dustpan
– Always standing on the opposite side of the sawdust from the chalk circle, and sweeping by pushing motions only
– Shaking the broom's bristles over the circle to remove clinging pieces of sawdust
– Spotting all the bits of sawdust to sweep

– Tilting the dustpan slightly downwards when brushing in, and tilting it back at all other times
– Moving the full dustpan about slowly
– Brushing sawdust off the lip of the dustpan into the wastepaper basket
– Erasing the chalk circle when the sweeping is done.

Handling a Book (Presentation to a Group)

Aim

To help the child gain co-ordination and self-sufficiency in learning how to handle things gracefully. In particular, enabling the child to look at books without adult help – at home, at school, or in a library. More specifically, to help the child learn a gentle and graceful way to take a book off a shelf, to carry a book, to open a book's cover, to turn its pages, and to replace a book on a shelf that has bookends. To help prepare the child for Language Activities. To give the child experience in group learning situations.

Materials

A child-size table and chair.

A shelf with five or more hardcover books with printed spines, in good condition, preferably with interesting pictures or illustrations inside.

Two heavy, non-decorative bookends to hold the books upright on the shelf, or if the shelf is in a constructed bookcase, one bookend to prop the books up against the inner wall of the bookcase.

If you have a group of children, a number of child-size chairs.

Preparation

– Place the child-size table and chair in front of the bookshelf
– Ensure that the seat of the chair is under the table, and that it faces away from the bookshelf
– Stand at least five hardcover books together on the bookshelf, using the bookend or bookends, ensuring that the books are all upright and have their spines facing out.

Presentation

1) Call a group of children. (The following is a suggested procedure for calling a group, but be flexible to accommodate the needs of particular children. If you are working with only one child, simply invite the one child to sit next to you at a table.)
   a) Decide which children need to attend the presentation. In the case of Handling a Book, all participants should have been in the Montessori environment a minimum of three months. Invite any such child who has no experience of handling books, or has had some difficulty in attempting it. Also include in the group at least one child who has had the presentation before, and is successfully working with books; whisper to this child that you need help in showing the other children how to do it.

b) Only invite children who are not occupied with an activity. To get a sufficient number, the group may be called the first thing in the morning, before most children have started their individual work.

c) Allow other children, whom you have not specially invited, to join the group if they wish, but limit the total number to ten. A group presentation given to more than ten children would be difficult for them all to see, and would make it difficult for all of them to feel involved.

d) When inviting a child, stand close and speak privately. Ask the child to bring a chair, and to place it against a particular wall near the presentation table and chair.

e) When several children are seated and waiting along that wall, get them started on some small activity that will occupy them while you are rounding up the others. For example, ask them to touch a certain part of their bodies, leave the group to invite another child; when you return ask them to touch a different part.

f) When all the children you invited have arrived, sit down in front of the row of chairs along the wall, and sing a song or do a finger-play rhyme with them, giving an opportunity to any uninvited children who may simply wish to be in a group, to join in. Welcome these children to the group. If ten have joined, but others still want to, ask these others to please come to another group at a particular time, later in the day. Make a mental note of these children so that they can be specially invited to that later group.

g) Ask the children in the group, one at a time, to move their chairs to particular places on the floor in front of the table, chair and bookshelf, thereby arranging them in a semi-circle facing the table and chair. Be sure that the semi-circle does not block access to the bookshelf for any child.

h) After the semi-circle has been arranged, and you are seated at the child-size table before them, do not begin the presentation itself until all the children are seated and settled in their own chairs.

2) Indicating the books on the shelf, ask the group, 'Do you know what these are? Yes, books. I'm going to show you how to use a book. Please watch me carefully, and when I'm done, those of you who would like to try can have a turn.' (Throughout the following steps, be sure that all the children can see what you're doing.)

3) Walk to the shelf, lean over, and look at the spine of each of the books you arranged there, perhaps touching each spine with your left index finger as you look at it. Then act as though you found one that you would like to read, selecting one in the middle. Indicating that book, say, 'I would like to look at this book.'

4) With your right thumb and index finger, pinch the top end of

the book's spine, and gently pull it downwards, until the book leans out slightly from its space.
) Grasp the spine firmly with your left hand.
) With your left hand, slowly pull the book all the way off the shelf. When the edge of the book opposite the spine appears, grasp it with your right hand.
) Go to the chair at the table, carrying the book between your hands, close to yourself, with its cover facing up. Stand behind the chair.
Very gently place the book flat onto the table surface. Do this by first lowering the book horizontally, cover up, until your fingers touch the table surface. Then, slowly withdrawing your fingers, allow the book to settle silently onto the table.
Adjust the position of the book on the table surface so that its spine is exactly in the centre of the table space in front of the chair, its bottom edge is a few inches from the front edge of the table, and its sides are parallel with the sides of the table.
Silently seat yourself on the chair in front of the book, and sit up straight with your back against the chair's backrest.
Look at the cover of the book if it has a picture or any print on it.
Place your right middle finger against the far right corner of the book's front cover, so that the hard corner pokes slightly into the fleshy tip of your finger.
Slowly raise the cover about two inches by that middle finger, holding the fingers of your left hand against the book's spine to keep it in place on the table.
Slip your right ring finger and little finger beneath the far right corner of the cover.
Then slide your whole right hand, all fingers touching the underside of the cover, from the far right corner towards the inside spine of the book, raising your hand slightly to help push the front cover up.
As the cover is pushed up to a vertical position, place your left hand against the front of the cover, to ease it over as it opens. Guide the cover open between your two hands, until your left hand rests on the table surface.
Gently withdraw your left hand from under the cover, allowing the cover to settle silently onto the table surface. If something is printed inside the cover, look at it.
Place the tip of your right middle finger on the far edge of the far right corner of the right-hand page. Lift that corner about an inch by raising that finger.
Slip your right middle finger beneath the raised corner, and gently pinch it from above with your right thumb on top.
Feel that you have grasped only one sheet of paper by delicately rubbing the corner between your thumb and middle finger. If two or more sheets have been pinched, release both fingers and repeat steps (18) and (19) until only one sheet has been pinched.
Still gently pinching the sheet in its far right corner, slowly

raise the sheet in a wide arc to the left, your hand passing over the top edge of the book, and aiming for its far left corner.

22) As the sheet turns over, release your pinch of the sheet's corner, and allow the sheet to fall into place on the left.

23) Place two fingers of your left hand, palm downwards, on the crease between the pages, at the near end of the crease.

24) Place the fingers of your right hand just beyond your left hand on the crease.

25) Applying a slight but gentle pressure, slide your right two fingers straight up the crease to the far edge of the book.

26) Release your hands from the book and place them in your lap.

27) Observe with interest what appears on the exposed pages.

28) Repeat steps (18) through (27) several times.

29) Say, 'I think I've finished looking at this book.'

30) Slide the fingers of your left hand, palm up, under the near edge of the front cover of the book, and with your left thumb, grasp the bottom of the exposed page.

31) Lift the front cover over towards the right, and as it reaches the vertical position, place your right fingers against the surface of the exposed left page, to help hold the pages in place as the book is closed.

32) Continue turning the cover until it is completely turned over and your right fingers and left thumb are inside the closed book. Slowly withdraw your right fingers and left thumb, allowing the book to shut silently.

33) Get up from the chair, and push it in under the table.

34) Place your left fingers under the spine of the book, and your right fingers under the right edge of the back cover, and grasp the book with your thumbs on top.

35) Go to the bookshelf, carrying the book between your hands, holding it, cover up, close to yourself. Stand before the bookshelf (remembering not to block the children's view of what you're doing).

36) Visually locate the space where the book was taken out, and place the closed book's bottom right corner on the shelf just in front of that space, still supporting the book by its spine with your left hand.

37) Open the space for the book a little wider with your right fingers, and gently ease the book into its space, releasing your left hand's grasp of the spine. Push in the book's spine so that it is lined up with the other books.

38) Place one hand on each bookend, and push them towards each other to straighten the books. If there is only one bookend, gently push it with one hand towards the books, forcing them up against the inside wall of the bookcase.

39) Return to the table and stand next to it.

40) Say, 'In a minute, anyone who would like to try handling a book can have a turn, but please wait until I call your name.'

41) Invite each child in turn, by name. (The following are some suggestions about doing this.)
   a) First invite the child who had seen the presentation before and who is experienced in handling books.
   b) Do not invite the children in the order in which they are seated.
   c) If any child you invite does not wish to try, don't say anything or show any disappointment; just invite the next child.
   d) If a child, when trying it, misses some *Essential Movement*, then when the child is done, compliment some correct aspect of the child's attempt, and immediately repeat the entire presentation.
   e) Thank each child warmly after trying.

42) Dismiss the group. (The following is a suggested procedure for dismissing a group of children after a presentation.)
   a) Say, 'Now I'd like you to close your eyes and think of what work you're going to do when you leave the group. When you know what work you'll do, open your eyes, sit as quiet as you can, and when you're very quiet I'll call your name. Then you can come and whisper to me what your work will be. Now close your eyes and think.'
   b) Ensure that each child chooses some appropriate activity. Discuss inappropriate choices in whispers with the child.
   c) If a child cannot think of anything, offer a choice of two activities.
   d) When a child comes and whispers to you an acceptable activity, whisper back, 'Fine. Please take your chair back with you.'
   e) After the entire group has been dismissed, put away the materials, and check that the children are doing what they whispered.

Essential Movements

- Pulling the book off the shelf with your left hand, so that the front cover faces you when you are carrying it and when you place it on the table
- Carrying the book with two hands
- Putting the book on the table before sitting down
- Making no sound when laying the book down, opening the cover or closing the book
- Before turning a page, gently feeling the corner to ensure that you have grasped only one sheet
- Gently rubbing along the crease to help keep the exposed pages open
- Pushing the chair under the table after getting up
- Not picking up the book while still seated, but only after standing up
- Finding the vacant space on the shelf when re-shelving the book
- Straightening the books by pushing the bookend(s).

Saying 'Thank You'

Aim To help the child gain independence by learning how to behave courteously with people, without adult intervention. In particular, to help the child learn to say 'thank you' when receiving a thing or a compliment from someone. To give the child additional experience in group learning situations.

Material A box containing about twenty similar but not identical buttons. A ball, easy for a young child to hold.

Preparation – Place a chair for yourself in an appropriate place for a group presentation, and put the materials for Saying 'Thank You' next to the chair.

Presentation
1) Call the group. (See step (1) of HANDLING A BOOK for suggestions on how to call a group. Arrange the children's chairs in a circle, with your chair included in it. Seat the oldest child in the group next to you. If you are working with only one child, simply invite the one child to bring a chair and sit next to you.)
2) Say, 'We're going to practise saying "thank you".'
3) Take one button out of the box and place it in the hand of the older child sitting next to you. Whisper to that child, 'Please hand me the button.'
4) Receive the button, look very surprised and pleased, admire the button appreciatively, and say slowly and clearly, so the whole group can hear: 'thank you'.
5) With an affected air of benevolence, slowly hand the button back to the same child, who should say 'thank you'. (If the child does not say anything, whisper, 'Please say "thank you".')
6) Take the box in one hand, get up from your chair to the inside of the circle, and walk up to each child in random order, handing to each one a button, and pausing to hear 'thank you'. (If one or two children do not say 'thank you', do not bring attention to it. If a number of children say nothing, then go and sit down again, and repeat steps (3) through (5).) Continue until each child in the group has received a button, except those children who clearly did not wish to take part. Return to your chair.
7) Hold the open box out in front of the older child sitting next to you, and when that child drops in the button, look appreciative and say, 'thank you'. Get up again and go to each child in the group, in a random order, holding out the box to each child. Each time a button is dropped into the box, look into the child's eyes and say 'thank you' with sincerity. (If a button accidentally drops outside the box, still say 'thank you', pick up the button, and drop it into the box yourself.) Return to your chair when all the buttons are collected.

8) Place the box beneath your chair, and pick up the ball with two hands.

9) Hand the ball to that same older child sitting next to you, who should now automatically say 'thank you'. (But if the child says nothing, motion for it to be handed back, and say 'thank you' when you receive it. Then hand the ball to the older child, hopefully hearing 'thank you' in response.)

10) Say, 'Please hand the ball to -------', naming the child on the other side of the one holding the ball. This second child should say 'thank you' to the first. Then say, 'Please hand the ball to -------', naming the next child around the circle, who should also say 'thank you'. Continue prompting the passing of the ball around the circle. Stop speaking when the children hand the ball to the next child without any prompting. Speak up again if any child just sits with the ball for more than a moment.

11) When the ball has gone all the way around, and is held by the other child next to you, look very surprised that it has come back. Look at the ball fondly when it is handed to you, and say, with a sense of finality, 'thank you'. Place the ball under your chair.

12) Whisper to that older child seated next to you, 'Please say "thank you" after I have spoken.'

13) Say out loud, looking admiringly at this older child, 'You look very nice today, -------', naming the child. The child should now, as asked, say 'thank you'. (If no 'thank you' is forthcoming, repeat step (12), and then say, 'I think you have lovely hair, -------'.)

14) Say to a child in the group who is sitting up straight, 'You are sitting on your chair very nicely, -------', naming the child. This should elicit a 'thank you' from the child. Say to a different child who is wearing a brightly coloured shirt, 'I like the shirt you are wearing today, -------', naming the child. Again, 'thank you' should be the child's response. In random order, give each child in the group a different compliment, each time pausing for the 'thank you' response. Be sure to name the child being complimented, so that it is clear whom you mean, and look at the child sincerely when you say it. (If one or two children do not say 'thank you', do not make a fuss about it. If a number of children say nothing, repeat steps (12) and (13).)

15) If the children appear comfortable with the activity so far, continue as follows. Again compliment the older child sitting next to you, and wait for the 'thank you'. Say to this older child, 'Please say something nice about ------- to (her)/(him)', naming the next child around the circle. The older child compliments that child, who responds with 'thank you'. Now say to the latter child, 'Please say something nice about ------- to (her)/(him)', naming the next child around the circle. Continue this around the circle. Stop speaking when

the children compliment the next one around the circle without any prompting. Speak up again if the compliments stop. When the last child in the circle, sitting on your other side, compliments you, say 'thank you'.

16) Dismiss the group. (See step (42) of HANDLING A BOOK for suggestions on how to dismiss a group. When each child comes to whisper to you, say, 'Thank you for being in the group.')

Walking on the Line

Theory   Walking is an essential aspect of being human, and it is universal among humans. Whereas different cultures have developed different uses for the vocal chords and the hands, people in all cultures walk nearly the same way. Walking is universal because it is a biologically-given skill.

Montessori described four stages through which a child develops the equilibrium necessary for walking. In the first stage, from about six months to nine months of age, the child perfects sitting, which starts the process of supporting the head in an erect position. In the second stage, from about nine months to one year of age, the child can stand erect, but moves on four limbs. At this stage, however, the child, when lifted, can make walking movements on tip-toe. In the third stage, from one year to about fifteen months of age, the child can place both feet flat on the ground, and can walk if helped a bit. By the fourth stage, from fifteen months on, the child begins to walk without help.

This stage-by-stage, rapid acquisition of equilibrium for walking is accompanied by a rapid development of the cerebellum, and the sudden purposeful use of the hands.

Montessori postulated that the evolution of the human species paralleled this early development of equilibrium in the child. As the pre-human primates began to walk erect, rather than with the aid of forelimbs, the curve of the spine was probably able to support a larger brain, and the hands were probably first freed for purposeful use. In this picture of evolution, walking erect was essential to the formation of intelligent, technological humankind.

At eighteen months of age, walking skills are further expanded and combined with the use of the hands. The child aims to strengthen the now erect body, and pushes heavy objects about or tries to walk while carrying them. When climbing, a child of this age uses both hands to pull the rest of the body up, and to aid the shifting equilibrium. At two years, this synthesis of hand usage and walking is nearly complete, and the child can walk and hold things with certainty. The two-year-old also runs, establishing a new, higher level of equilibrium.

By two-and-a-half years of age, as the use of the hands is applied to activities which make the child ever more independent, walking becomes a tool for exploration. (You may recall that the sensitive period for 'co-ordination of movement' begins at this age.) A two-and-a-half year old loves to take long walks, sometimes for hours, often posing challenges to the equilibrium along the way, but other times just wanting to look and explore the world around.

The child may first enter the Montessori environment at about this age, and this is an appropriate time to begin the process of perfecting and refining the equilibrium and the hands/feet co-ordination skills earlier created. This opportunity is provided by the activity Walking on the Line.

Walking on the Line helps perfect walking by giving the child progressive challenges to its normal use, first in keeping it moving in a straight line, then in maintaining its relation to another person's movements, then in requiring a greater and greater steadiness. The activity refines muscular co-ordination in requiring an exact placement of the feet, first on the line, then heel-to-toe. Later it combines feet co-ordination with the control of hand and arm motions, to prevent a bell from ringing, a weight from swinging, and a glass of water from spilling. The activity helps foster the correct use of the spine, which naturally results from a greater mental emphasis on equilibrium, thereby improving the child's posture and general physiology. Walking on the Line builds up to a systemic exercise of the entire body, which directly facilitates mental harmony, and so is calming and relaxing despite the degree of concentration required. When you are conducting the activity, you may notice that as each child's personal concentration grows, this inner harmony is extended to the group, and all the children on the line become more integrated in their movements. In other words, the community becomes united when its members are whole, busy, and internally balanced. In this way, Walking on the Line creates a small instance of the kind of peace Montessori believed could be achieved in society at large, if children were to grow up with their developmental needs fulfilled.

Materials

The outline of a large ellipse, or a rectangle with very rounded corners, at least ten feet long and eight feet wide, painted on the floor in an open space.

A table situated in the centre of the outline, on which are placed: flags; small weights made of Plasticine wrapped in cloth, each attached to a one-foot piece of string; small, plastic glasses filled nearly to the brim with water; bells with handles; and small, flat-bottomed baskets.

A source of quiet, calming music, with a weak or imperceptible rhythm, which is played during each session of walking.

Stages

(Each of the following stages of Walking on the Line are conducted as a group activity, as described, once a day, throughout the period indicated. After all children reach stage (2), they may each progress through the remaining stages at their own pace. You will need to remember what stage each child is at, in order to provide the correct challenge. Each daily session should last about fifteen minutes. Before you start a session, clear the space to expose the entire painted outline on the floor, and put your materials on a table in the middle of it. To signal to the children that a session of Walking on the Line is beginning, don't announce anything – just put on the music. New children will understand what's going on simply by observing. After fifteen minutes of the activity, indicate the end of the session by turning the music off again.)

1) For the first several months of Walking on the Line, the children should just follow the painted outline at their own pace, placing their feet only on the line, and all going in the same direction. Faster children may leave the line temporarily to overtake slower ones.

2) For the next few months, the children should continue to walk with their feet only on the line, but should also each maintain a constant distance between themselves and the child directly in front.

3) For the next few months, each child should walk 'heel-to-toe' on the line, placing each foot forward so that its heel touches the foot behind, still maintaining a constant distance from the child in front.

4) For the next few months, you should hand the children something from the materials table in the middle of the outline, while they are walking heel-to-toe, at a constant distance from the other children on the line. Stand next to the table, pick up one of the objects on it, and walk alongside one of the participating children. Fully raise the child's arm so that it extends straight forward, and place the object in the child's extended hand. Start a child off holding just the flag. Later, hand the child the weight, held by its string, and tell the child that it should not be allowed to swing during the walking. When the weight has been mastered, hand the child the bell, and say it must remain silent during the walking. Lastly, hand the child one of the nearly-full glasses of water, which of course should not spill or drip during the walking.

5) For the last few months of a child's experience with Walking on the Line, hand the child two items to hold as in stage (4), one in each hand, while still walking heel-to-toe, and maintaining a constant distance from the child in front. Then later, give the child one object to hold and a basket to balance on top of the child's head. Finally, give the most experienced child two objects to hold as well as the basket to balance.

Being Silent

Theory   Just as the two-and-a-half year old entering the Montessori environment is ready to perfect early equilibrium skills, a child at this age is also ready to refine general motor skills. And the ultimate control of movement is to create absolute immobility, the most obvious sign of which is 'silence'.

As the control of muscles throughout the body, the ▰▰▰▰of silence is a positive, rather than negative, activity. As a creative effort, it requires great concentration, which, like WALKING ON THE LINE, centres and harmonises the urges and reflexes of the body, leading to calmness and serenity. Also like WALKING ON THE LINE, the creation of silence can be a community endeavour, in which each child perceives the importance of his or her smallest actions to the work of the group.

Montessori came across the idea of the Being Silent activity when one day a small baby, sleeping and still, was brought into her classroom, and the children were greatly impressed by the superiority of the infant's stillness and delicacy of movement. This provided inspiration for the perfection of their own control of movement, and Montessori devised 'Being Silent' to provide an opportunity for this perfection to develop.

For most children, becoming still and silent suddenly opens up a whole new world of subtle, interesting sounds, which were previously covered by the child's own noises and motions. They first notice their own internal noises – heart beats, breathing, stomach churns and gurgles – and they become acutely aware that their insides are alive and moving of their own accord. This may awaken the child's intellectual interest in the internal workings of the body. Secondly, the children notice outdoor sounds never before perceived – the machines operating to keep the building warm, cars and planes far away, workmen down the road, and many subtle sounds of Nature, which change through the year.

Finally, being silent can suggest to a child, in an intuitive way, the significance of an individual's presence in the world. Because it is like trying to be 'not there', creating silence reaches the edge of a deep metaphysical precipice, from which the child can momentarily peer into the bottomless space of non-existence. Tottering there, the child affirms in contrast to that emptiness the fullness and tangibility of his or her own body – heart beating and chest swelling with life. With this new awareness of self-existence, the silence then lets the outer edges of perception reach in from a far-off distance – bird sounds and rumbles and unidentifiable clicks and cries from the far edges of the world – and the child feels a smallness, but solidity, in the midst of a vast expanse. This relation of the self (as one being) to the whole universe (as all Being) is the essence of spirituality. So, for some children, the Being Silent activity will be a mystical experience, too.

In sum, Being Silent gives each child a sense of participation in a communal effort, an opportunity to refine early motor skills, an expanded observation of things inside and outside that are not usually perceived, and for some children an entrance into the realm of spirituality.

Materials   A 'silence board', which has a very tranquil, peaceful picture or design on one side, and has the word 'silence' printed on the reverse side. The picture side of the 'silence board' remains in plain sight all day long in the environment; it may be hung on the wall like a normal picture.

Indirect Preparation

a) When calling the register, or the children's names for any reason, only begin when the room is quiet, speak very quietly, and stop completely whenever anyone is making unnecessary noises. If some children are talking or whispering, speak even more quietly, or perhaps whisper, and everyone will be quieter themselves in order to hear.

b) Before any group activity begins, and the group is momentarily silent in expectation, pause and let the children hear that silence, closing your eyes, perhaps, for emphasis.

c) In showing or asking for any movement in any activity, say, 'See how quietly we can. . .', which is essentially asking for greater control.

d) Provide a quiet area of the environment where children can look at books, be alone, or just rest or contemplate.

e) In games and songs, pause for silence to emphasise surprise or anticipation, or use silence as a desirable effect to be achieved.

Presentation

1) Call a group of children (see step (1) of HANDLING A BOOK for suggestions).

2) Assess the feeling of the group. Only proceed with the Being Silent activity if all the children in the group are happy and secure.

3) Show the tranquil picture on the 'silence board', and say, 'Let's see if we can keep every part of our bodies perfectly still. Our feet perfectly still. Our hands perfectly still, and our heads and middles.' Pause for about ten seconds. 'Did you hear that? We made something very special. We made "silence".'

4) Turn the 'silence board' around and show the word printed on it. Explain, 'This says "silence". Whenever we see the board turned to "silence", let's all make silence together.' Turn the board back to the picture side.

5) Say, 'Now everyone get really comfortable in your chairs.' Make motions to show that you are getting comfortable. Turn the 'silence board' to the side with 'silence' on it, and be very still.

6) Wait several moments, perhaps as long as a minute or two, and after complete silence has been achieved for say twenty seconds, whisper, 'Now listen for a gentle voice to call you by name, and come join me when it calls.' Step very quietly to the far side of the room or into an adjacent room.

7) Whisper the children's names in random order – however, leave an older, more experienced child for last. Wait until each called child has joined you, and has sat down on the floor near you, before calling the next name. If no one

responds to a name that you call, or if the wrong child comes, simply continue and repeat the name a bit later.

8) After everyone has joined you, dismiss the group in a calm and ordered fashion (see step (42) of HANDLING A BOOK for a suggested method).

9) One day, the following week, during a group session, indicate the 'silence board' and say to the entire group, 'Tomorrow I am going to turn over the silence board when you are all working. It will say "silence". When you see the board turned to "silence", go quietly to a seat at a table and become silent. Don't tell anyone else that you've seen the board – let them discover it for themselves.'

10) The next day, while the children are fairly busy, but not when they are very noisy, turn the 'silence board' around to say 'silence', without announcing it or calling attention to it. Sit down at a table and become perfectly still, looking at the children. If any of them speak to you, do not answer them (unless of course it's an emergency). Some children will begin to notice, and they too will fall silent, and gradually the silence will spread. When all the children have become silent, and have stayed that way for a minute or two, move very quietly to the far side of the room, or into the adjacent room, and whisper the children's names in random order, to join you there, as in steps (6) through (8).

11) Repeat steps (9) and (10) every few weeks, and sometimes just do step (10) without announcing it the day before. When new children join the Montessori environment, repeat the presentation as in steps (1) through (8).

3 SENSORIAL ACTIVITIES

INTRODUCTION

Think for a moment of what a baby's sense experience of the world must be like. For example, think of a typical one-year-old in a living room with the usual modern furnishings, including a television, a record player, an older sibling's electronic game, a dog, a collection of large plastic toys, games with pieces, puzzles and dolls.

In such an environment, amid the whirl of family activity, wild and fleeting images, colours, noises, rhythms and movements incessantly bombard the child's senses. The available field for experience is intensely visual and auditory; touch is either forbidden or confined to smooth unbreakable plastic, temperatures are constant, smells are masked, and taste is of necessity guarded against. But even the realm of sights and sounds is largely a mystery, as brightly patterned, irregularly shaped objects flash, beep and even speak, for no apparent reason. Usually, several things are going on at once, and attempts on the child's part to get involved are likely to be discouraged or manipulated with a heavy hand. The one-year-old's concept of such an environment is at centre a 'humming and buzzing confusion'.

Gradually, the young child will begin a struggle to discern the structure and inter-relationships of these everyday sense perceptions, in an effort to understand the world and to adapt to it with appreciation and confidence.

The primary purpose of the Sensorial Activities is to help the child in this effort to sort out the many and varied impressions given by the senses. The Sensorial Activities help the child do this in four ways: they are specially designed to develop, order, broaden and refine sense perception. The activities 'develop' the child's senses through exercises that gradually build up from simple to complex perceptual challenges. The child's sense perceptions are given 'order' because the activities identify a single perceptual quality, disclose a range of discrete differences in the quality, and explore patterns in those differences. The child's perception of the world is 'broadened' when the Sensorial Activities awaken certain sense experiences that were previously unexplored, such as the feel of shapes or the smell of spices. And the Sensorial Activities 'refine' sense perception because they allow the child to experience and concentrate on particular qualities in perfect clarity and isolation.

The materials used in the Sensorial Activities are quite unlike anything else that the child has ever encountered in the way of playthings. Most toys are designed to be attractive to the adults who purchase them. The sensorial materials are specially designed so that children will be attracted to them. This means, first, that they are made of substances that young children, with their pre-technological disposition, are intuitively fond of: wood, grains, straw, cotton, silk, wool and stone. Second, the materials are made in manageable and attractive dimensions, fashioned for easy handling by child-size hands and arms, and designed with classic and harmonic proportions. Third, the materials are clear and simple in appearance, with pure enamel colours selected from nature, and neat elemental forms. The clear and simple appearance of the sensorial materials is a great relief to a typical child like the one discussed above, who is unceasingly burdened with garish and frenzied stimuli.

Each apparatus for the Sensorial Activities consists of a set of objects which, experienced together, evidence a single perceptual quality, such as 'colour' or 'taste'. This experience of a single quality occurs because each object in the set is identical in all respects except that one quality. If the quality is quantifiable, it varies regularly and, where possible, mathematically, from object to object in the set, so that an evenly graded series is apparent. At least one Sensorial Activity is provided for every quality that can be perceived by each of the human body's sense faculties: the visual sense (which perceives size, shape, composition, pattern and colour), the auditory sense (perceiving loudness and pitch), the tactile sense (which perceives texture), the baric sense (perceiving weight), the thermic sense (which perceives temperature or heat absorption potential), the gustatory sense (perceiving tastes), the olfactory sense (perceiving scents and odours), and the stereognostic sense (which perceives form through tactile and muscular impression, combined with movement).

In presenting each Sensorial Activity, the Montessori director reveals the structure that can be found in sense experience, in steps that parallel the principle of 'three stage learning'.

The first presentation of a Sensorial Activity identifies a particular quality and generally defines its range and limits, by introducing the two most contrasting units of material, such as the loudest and softest SOUND BOXES, or the roughest and smoothest TACTILE TABLETS. If the quality is unquantifiable, then it is simply identified by a selection of typical stimuli. This constitutes the first stage of 'three stage learning' because it simply presents the components and extremes of the quality to the absorbent mind.

Once these loosely-associated sensations are presented, the director provides exercises to group sensations which are clearly related or similar. With some Sensorial Activities, this means matching pairs of identical or complementary units of the material; with other activities, it means sorting a mixture of units into three or four categories. In discovering how the component phenomena are related, they are more firmly bound as a family of phenomena, subsisting as a unified idea – that idea simply being the presence of the quality. This clearly parallels the second stage of 'three stage learning', which connects previously absorbed phenomena and makes of them a unified concept.

Later exercises show that the variations in certain qualities may occur in patterns. In these exercises, the child places the units of material, one by one, in the order which evidences a measured increase or decrease in the degree of the quality. For many Sensorial Activities, the gradation found in the material is mathematically regular (increasing linearly, geometrically, or exponentially), giving the child indirect preparation for later work in the Mathematics Activities. Some of these exercises may also involve comparing units of the material to degrees of the quality observable in actual things in the room. So this third stage of 'three stage learning' gives context to each sensation of the quality, by establishing its relative degree and comparing it to the degree of the quality in everyday things.

In sum, the Sensorial Activities demonstrate that certain sensations can be associated as a quality, related to other instances of that quality, and in some cases quantified as a degree of that quality. After experience with the Sensorial Activities, the child's incessant deluge of sense perceptions will appear inherently structured and susceptible to comprehension.

As with all other Montessori activities, the key to involving the child is to provide precisely the right level of challenge for the child's level of development. For the Sensorial Activities, this challenge must be both physical and mental, since sense perception is an embodied power, depending upon a person's physical as well as mental faculties. The Sensorial Activities present two physical challenges (applying the senses acutely and accurately manipulating the materials) and two mental challenges (exercising both memory and judgement when matching, grouping and ordering the materials). To meet these combined challenges, the child is drawn to repeat a Sensorial Activity many times over, and is thereby repeatedly impressed with the necessary integration of mind and body in perception.

To help the child feel challenged, and to indicate to you

whether the child is being challenged, every Sensorial Activity is designed with a built-in feedback to show when errors have been made. As with most Montessori activities, this feedback is inherent in the materials, and does not come from you, so that the child remains independent of your oversight, and develops an inner, personal incentive to practise and improve. For some of the sensorial materials, like the CYLINDER BLOCKS, this 'control of error' is a physical impediment which does not allow completion of the activity when a mistake has been made along the way. For other materials, another of the body's senses is used as a check; for example, in the case of the BARIC TABLETS, a colour difference between tablets of different weight is apparent when the blindfold is removed. For a few of the sensorial materials, like the SOUND BOXES, the only inherent 'control of error' is the quality itself, making the point that there is not always an absolute answer when it comes to perception, and the best we can do is improve and refine our perceptual skills.

Because the Sensorial Activities involve certain bodily faculties, you should be aware that inordinate difficulties with particular materials may indicate previously unnoticed handicaps in the child, such as a hearing impairment or colour blindness. Some such handicaps, when detected at this early age, can be successfully corrected; for other defects, appropriate work can be initiated to help prevent later intellectual or social repercussions.

Finally, the Sensorial Activities can have a moral and spiritual importance for the child. A very young child, like the baby discussed earlier, who has not yet organised sense experience, sees the world as consisting of lively, responsive 'things', which behave like fountains of impressions, spouting changing sensorial stimuli in response to playful proddings. There is a moral danger, at the point in the child's early psychic development when structure is first being applied to sense perceptions, that these thriving companions will be turned into lifeless repositories of dull existence, attended by a determinate set of functions or characteristics, which can be negated and replaced at whim by the indifferent observer. This 'objectification' of things, both living and inanimate, can result when they are identified and classed only in terms of their service to people (e.g. 'we grow plants for eating, keeping warm, and building homes') or are described as isolated pockets of existence with alterable attributes (e.g. 'this is a rock; it is rough, heavy, grey and hard to break'). The child learns from such lessons that the unsympathetic manipulation of things (as well as living creatures) is not only possible but expected, and the child is hardened to the wonderment of endless exploration which guides a baby's interactions with things. As a result, the world is narrowed to a place full of 'objects' to be possessed for our vanity, altered for our pleasure, or destroyed for our convenience.

Montessori's Sensorial Activities introduce the child to a

structured comprehension of the world in a different way. The child is not led by the activities away from the baby's world of lively thing-friends, but is only given the skills to clarify and order the sensorial gifts that may be received from them. The activities' enlargement of sensorial sensitivity increases the child's respect and awe for the things which are the source of those sense impressions. Rather than leave the child feeling that a thing is easily defined and manipulated, the Sensorial Activities make the child aware of the endless avenues available for exploring the thing in its infinite depth and fullness.

In this spiritual aspect of the Sensorial Activities, we can see one of the far-reaching differences between the Montessori approach and conventional teaching methods. Note that the Sensorial Activities isolate a single perceptual quality by making each object in a set identical in all respects except one. Conventional teaching methods commonly introduce a quality in just the opposite way; that is, the quality of interest is usually identified as the one most obvious quality which a group of otherwise unrelated objects have in common. For instance, to introduce the colour 'blue', a conventional teacher will gather together a blue flower, a blue toy truck, a blue cloth, and a blue pencil, all of which vary in shape, material, size, texture and weight, but have nearly the same colour. Though it might seem that Montessori's approach is nothing more than a pedagogical mirror-image of the conventional method, it is actually conveying an entirely different message to the child. The focus in the Sensorial Activities in not on objects, but on the phenomenon of colour as an experience. In Montessori's materials, the things themselves have no practical significance, and they have no uses or functions outside the exercise; the quality is simply presented, explored and related to the child's actual experience of the environment. In the conventional teaching method, the focus is instead on the objects, which do have uses or functions outside the exercise, and which are shown to 'possess' various qualities, including the one under study. The point made by the conventional teaching is not that you can experience colour, but that a number of objects may all possess the same quality. In brief, the conventional teaching method perpetrates the 'objectification' of the child's world by subordinating experience to objects, while Montessori's approach introduces the quality as a facet of the child's experience, leaving 'things' free of the limitations and manipulations of human definition, preserving for the child a sense of their mystical depth and liveliness.

Three Stage Lesson

To apply the principle of 'three stage learning' to teaching a child the names of things, qualities or symbols.   **Aim**

In the Sensorial Activities, the Three Stage Lesson is used to   **Uses** teach the names of qualities and their various degrees. For Practical and Cultural Activities, it is used to introduce the names of the implements and materials the child is using. The Three Stage Lesson occurs in the Mathematics Activities when the child learns the names of symbols used to represent quantities and functions. For the Language Activities, it is used to help the child associate written symbols with sounds, and in certain exercises, to increase the child's vocabulary.

General Description   Select three different things, qualities, or symbols from the set which you intend the child to learn (in this discussion we will presume they are 'things'), and place them on a mat, isolated from all other objects. (A Three Stage Lesson may also be done with two or four things, but three is the optimum number.) Ask the child to 'listen to what these are called'.

STAGE ONE simply presents and associates the experience of the three things with their names:

(a) Isolate on the mat and attentively experience one of the three things, as fully as possible (e.g. if it is a solid shape, look at it and feel it; if it is a tool, examine it and pretend to use it; if it is a tone, make it sound and listen to it; if it is a Sandpaper Letter, feel and trace its shape). Immediately after, face the child and say the thing's name very clearly out loud.

(b) Repeat step (a) again for the same thing, and then say 'you try', inviting the child to copy you. The child should experience the thing in just the same manner, and then immediately afterwards, say its name. If the child does not imitate you exactly, repeat step (a) a third time and again invite the child to copy you.

(c) Experience, name, and invite the child to experience and name each of the other two things, as in steps (a) and (b).

(d) Repeat steps (a) and (b) a few times for each of the three things, in random order.

STAGE TWO challenges the child to recognise the three things by their names, requiring that the things and their names be mentally paired and the pairs distinguished from one another:

(e) Clearly say the name of one of the three things and invite the child to indicate, by some movement or action, which thing you have named (e.g. say 'please point to the "square"' or 'please hand me the "spoon"'). If you asked that the thing be handed to you or otherwise removed from the surface you're working on, return it to a different spot.

(f) Repeat step (e) for each of the other two things.

If the child errs, and points out a thing which you did not name, do not show any hint of disappointment or disapproval, but continue with the requests, to see whether it was just a careless mistake or if it was instead due to an incorrect association of things and names. If it was the latter, then smoothly slip into a round of STAGE ONE, and cheerfully announce the end of the lesson, having left the child with an impression of the correct associations.

(g) Repeat step (e) several times for all three things on the mat, selecting them in random order, and varying the requested action (e.g. 'point at', 'turn over', 'pick up', 'hand me') to maintain the child's interest. After each request is fulfilled, be sure to return any removed thing to a different spot. Continue until the child's recognition of each of the three things by their names appears to be automatic and nearly instantaneous.

STAGE THREE allows the child to make use of, give mental context to, and verify the associations just learned, by naming the thing which you indicate:

(h) Use one of the movements described above to indicate one of the three things on the mat (e.g. pick it up and hand it to the child), ask the child 'What is this called?', and show enthusiastic appreciation for the answer. Repeat this for each of the three things on the mat, selecting them in random order, until they have each been named by the child several times, varying your indicating action to maintain the child's interest. Return any removed thing to a different spot.

If the child errs, and names a thing incorrectly, do not show any hint of disappointment or disapproval, but continue asking names to see whether it was just a careless mistake or if it was instead due to some confusion. If it was the latter, then smoothly slip into several rounds of STAGE TWO, and afterwards, try STAGE THREE again.

If the child declines to say any of the names at all, but was able to carry out the indicating movements in STAGE TWO correctly, then do not insist, as the child may simply not be ready to speak. Do other Three Stage Lessons until the child feels more confident about speaking, and occasionally ask the child to help teach a younger one the names of something that the first child knows very well.

Sample Presentation

The following presentation illustrates a typical Three Stage Lesson, in this case to teach the names of the three primary colours found in the second box of the Colour Tablets (see exercise (6) of the Sensorial Activity called COLOUR TABLETS):

STAGE ONE
- Invite a child who has had experience pairing the twenty-two tablets in Colour Tablets Box 2 to place Box 2 on a table mat. Sit with the child at the table.
- Put Box 2 on the far right corner of the mat, remove one tablet of each of the three primary colours (red, blue and yellow), and place these three tablets on the mat. Close the box.
- Isolate the red tablet on the mat in front of the child, point to it, and say 'red' in a slow, clear voice. Invite the child to repeat.

– Point again and say 'red'. Prompt the child's repetition with a glance. If the child is not pronouncing the word properly, repeat until the pronunciation is correct, or nearly so.
– Repeat the above for the yellow tablet, and then the blue tablet, and then repeat a few times for all three tablets, in random order.

STAGE TWO
– Place the three tablets within easy reach of the child.
– Ask the child to 'please hand me the yellow tablet', emphasising the word 'yellow'. When the child does this, excitedly say 'thank you!' and return the yellow tablet to a different spot on the mat.
– Repeat this request for the blue tablet, and then the red one.
– Ask the child, 'Will you please point to the blue tablet?', emphasising the word blue. After the child points to it, show excitement that the child knew which tablet to point to.
– Repeat this request for the red tablet, and then the yellow one.
– Ask the child to 'please place the red tablet here', pointing to a spot near you on the mat. After the child does this, say 'thank you!' and place the tablet back within reach of the child, but in a different spot.
– Repeat this request for the yellow tablet, and then the blue one.
– Continue to ask the child to indicate a named colour by some movement or action, always returning a moved tablet to within the child's reach, but in a different spot. Name them in a random sequence, and vary the requested actions in an amusing way (e.g. 'gently touch your elbow to the blue tablet' or 'smell the yellow tablet').

STAGE THREE
– Isolate and point to the red tablet and ask the child, 'What colour is this tablet?' When the child answers 'red', show pleasure and excitement that the child can name a colour.
– Repeat the question for the blue and then the yellow tablet.
– Pick up the blue tablet, and ask its colour. Say 'thank you' for the answer. Hand the red tablet to the child and ask this tablet's colour, and again say 'thank you'. Continue in this way for several rounds of the three colours, continuing to vary the movement that indicates which tablet you wish the child to name, and continuing to show appreciation for the child's new-found knowledge.

SIGHT

Cylinder Blocks
Aim   To help develop the child's visual discrimination of size. Indirectly, to prepare the child for writing, through the handling

of the cylinders by their knobs. Indirectly, to prepare the child for later work in Mathematics, through observation of the regular differences in the cylinders.

Four rectangular wooden blocks, into each of which is drilled a row of ten cylindrical wells or sockets, in each of which rests a precisely fitted wooden cylinder with a small spherical knob on top. The cylinders and their corresponding wells vary in diameter and/or height from 5.5 centimetres (cm) to 1.0 cm, in increments of 0.5 cm. Block 1 cylinders are all 5.5 cm tall, and decrease in diameter from 5.5 cm to 1.0 cm. Block 2 cylinders decrease in both diameter and height from 5.5 cm to 1.0 cm for both. Block 3 cylinders decrease in diameter while increasing in height, ranging from 1.0 cm tall and 5.5 cm in diameter to 5.5 cm tall and 1.0 cm in diameter. Block 4 cylinders are all the same diameter (2.5 cm), and decrease in height from 5.5 cm to 1.0 cm.
   A smooth wooden board, about two feet square.

– Name the Cylinder Blocks and show where they are kept.
– Select and name Cylinder Block 1, and show the child how to carry it with a hand wrapped around each end.
– Gently place the block on a table, without a table mat, so gently that you do not make a sound.
– Remove the cylinders in random order, lifting each by its knob from above, holding the knob between your thumb, index finger and middle finger (the same fingers used to write with a pencil). Gently and silently place each cylinder, after it is removed, upright on the table surface between yourself and the block, in a random arrangement. Place each cylinder down so gently that no tap is heard as the cylinder touches the table top. After they are all removed, pause, and with the child, look over the ten mixed-up cylinders standing on the table.

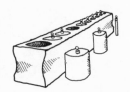

– Selecting either the thickest or thinnest cylinder, lift it by its knob, and without holding it next to any of the wells to compare, visually determine which well it would fit into best. Replace this cylinder in its correct well in one graceful and careful movement. The cylinder should not knock against the edge or sides of the well, and no tap should be heard as the cylinder touches the bottom. Repeat with the other extreme in thickness or thinness. Continue in random order, replacing each cylinder in its well. Occasionally pause to examine visually which cylinder should go into which well, without actually holding the cylinders next to the wells. Continue until all the cylinders have been returned to the block.
– Offer the child a turn.

(1) The child works with Cylinder Block 1 as in the presentation.
(2) The child works with each of the four Cylinder Blocks singly, as in the presentation, using Block 4 last.
(3) The child works with any two blocks simultaneously,

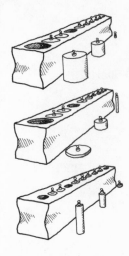

arranged on the table in a 'V' shape open to the front, using combinations with Block 4 last.

(4) The child works with any three blocks simultaneously, arranged in a triangle on a low table, or placed on the smooth board on a floor mat.

(5) The child works with all four blocks arranged in a square on a low table or placed around the board on a floor mat.

(6) Give Three Stage Lessons on the following relative terms for the visual perception of size.

Use only two opposites in each lesson, as follows: using the second thickest and second thinnest cylinders from Block 1, introduce 'thick' and 'thin'; using the second largest and second smallest cylinders from Block 2, show 'large' and 'small'; using the second tallest and second shortest cylinders from Block 4, introduce 'tall' and 'short'; and using the second deepest and second most shallow wells in Block 4, show 'deep' and 'shallow'.

Later, give lessons on the comparatives and superlatives of the above terms (except 'shallow'): use two cylinders near either end of Blocks 1, 2 or 4, or two wells near the deep end of Block 4, to teach the comparatives (e.g. 'thick' and 'thicker'); and use the three cylinders at either end of Blocks 1, 2 or 4, or the three wells at the deep end of Block 4, to teach both the comparative and superlative (e.g. 'small', 'smaller' and 'smallest').

Pink Tower

Aim To help develop the child's visual discrimination of differences in three dimensions. To help develop the child's fine muscular co-ordination. Indirectly, to prepare the child for later work in geometry through the general observation of the geometrically regular differences in the size of the cubes' edges, faces and total volumes. Indirectly, to prepare the child for the concept of numbers, in demonstrating the unit difference in distance between the edges of the ten successively larger cubes.

Material Ten pink wooden cubes varying in size from one cubic centimetre to one cubic decimetre, and differing equally in all dimensions by increments of one centimetre.

Presentation – Name the Pink Tower and show where it is kept.

– Ask the child to spread a floor mat. Show how to carry the cubes singly, lifting each with one hand, holding it from above, and show how to place them in a random arrangement on the mat. (When carrying larger cubes, use your other hand to support the cube underneath. Obviously the child will need to do this for smaller cubes than you will.)

– Look over the cubes intently, select the largest cube, and compare it with one or two other cubes near in size, holding it next to them to be sure it is the largest. Then place it down gently in an isolated spot on the mat.

- Look over the remaining cubes intently, select the next smaller cube, and compare it with one or two others near in size to be sure it is the largest one remaining on the mat. Then carefully place it, without a noise, in one graceful movement, exactly centred on top of the isolated largest cube.
- Again look over the remaining cubes intently, again select the next smaller cube, and place it, as before, exactly centred on top of the other two cubes.
- Continue in the same way to build a consistently narrowing pink tower, always selecting the next smaller cube, and occasionally comparing it with one or two cubes near in size to be sure that it is the largest one remaining on the mat. Each time a cube is placed, show the child that you are satisfied and pleased with the progress you are making. (If the child appears anxious to try placing a cube, say, 'Let me finish the whole tower, and then you can have a turn.')
- With the child, excitedly examine the completed tower, from all sides, and from above.
- Dismantle the tower, gently removing the cubes one by one, lifting each cube with one hand holding it from above (and for the larger cubes, also supporting it from underneath), placing them again in a random arrangement on the mat.
- Offer the child a turn.

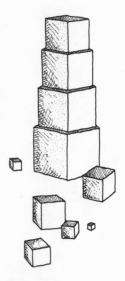

(1) The child builds the Pink Tower exactly as in the presentation.   **Exercises**

(2) Begin with the cubes placed in a random arrangement on a floor mat. Build the tower so that the same corner of each cube is perfectly aligned with the others, all the way up, giving the tower two flat sides and two steeply stepped sides. Build the tower in a place on the mat which allows the child to see one flat side and one stepped side. Two or three times during the building process, gently feel with fingers of both hands down the two adjacent, flat sides of the tower, to confirm the perfect alignment of the cubes. When the tower is complete, view it from all sides and from above.

Say that you're now going 'to do something special with the tower'. Take the smallest cube from the top, and place it gently on the lowest step of the tower. Slide the little cube gently across one ledge, then around the corner and gently across the other ledge. Place the cube on the next higher step and repeat. Continue up the tower, sliding the little cube across the ledges at each step, and then replace the cube at the very top of the tower.

(3) Give Three Stage Lessons on the following relative terms for the visual perception of size.

Use the second or third largest cube together with the second or third smallest cube to reinforce the concept of 'large' and 'small'.

Later, give lessons on the comparatives and superlatives of these terms, using two of the largest cubes to teach 'large' and its comparative 'larger', and two of the smallest cubes to teach 'small' and its comparative 'smaller'. Then use the three largest or smallest cubes to teach both the comparative and superlative (e.g. 'large', 'larger', 'largest').

(4) (Activities like this one, and the two that follow, which are conducted over a distance, are especially good for a restless child who has had experience with the material, or they can be done with a number of children.) Place two floor mats at a considerable distance. Arrange the cubes of the Pink Tower randomly on one of the mats. Select and pick up the largest cube, walk with the child to the other mat, and place that cube down on it. Ask the child to return alone to the first mat and bring 'the next cube' to place on the largest one. Continue asking until the tower is built, sending the child back and forth between the mats.

(5) Arrange two mats and the Pink Tower cubes as at the start of exercise (4). Select and pick up any cube, walk with the child to the other mat, and place the cube down on it. Ask the child to return alone to the first mat and bring 'a cube that is larger' (or 'smaller'), without taking the first cube back to compare. Either retain both cubes at the second mat, or ask the child to return one to the first mat. Repeat as long as the child is interested.

(6) Later, repeat exercise (5), but ask for 'the cube which is the next larger' or 'the next smaller'.

Brown Stair

Aim   To help develop the child's visual discrimination of differences in two dimensions. To help develop the child's muscular co-ordination. Indirectly, to prepare the child for later work in geometry through the general observation of the geometrically regular differences in the size of the prisms' edges, faces, and total volumes. Indirectly, to prepare the child for the concept of numbers, in demonstrating the unit difference in height and width between the ten successively thicker prisms.

Material   Ten brown, wooden, rectangular prisms, square on two ends. The prisms all have the same length (20 cm), but vary in thickness by equal increments, from 10 cm x 10 cm on each end to 1 cm x 1 cm on each end.

Presentation   – Name the Brown Stair and show where it is kept.

– Ask the child to spread a floor mat. Show how to carry the prisms singly, lifting each with one hand, holding it from above, and show how to place them in a random arrangement on the mat. (When carrying thicker prisms, use your other hand to support the prism underneath. As with the PINK TOWER, the child will need to do this with thinner prisms than you will.)

– Look over the prisms intently, select the thickest prism, and compare it with one or two other prisms near in size, holding it next to them to be sure it is the thickest on the mat. Then place it down gently in an isolated spot towards the far edge of the mat, with the square ends facing left and right.

– Look over the remaining prisms intently, select the next thinner prism, and compare it with one or two other prisms near in size to be sure it is the thickest remaining on the mat. Then carefully place this prism, without letting go of it, an inch or two in front of, and parallel to, the first prism; then, continuing the same graceful movement, gently slide the second prism up against the first, so that their ends are exactly even.

– Continue to build the stair towards the front of the mat, always selecting the next thinner prism, and occasionally comparing it with the one or two prisms near in size to be sure that it is the thickest one remaining on the mat. Each time a prism is placed, show the child that you are satisfied and pleased with the progress you are making. Two or three times during the building process, gently feel with fingers of both hands along the aligned ends of the prisms in the stair, to confirm their perfect alignment. (If the child appears anxious to try placing a prism, say, 'Let me finish this whole stair, and then you can have a turn.')

– With the child, excitedly examine the completed stair, from all sides, and from above.

– Dismantle the stair, gently removing the prisms one by one, starting with the thinnest one, lifting each prism with one hand holding it from above (and for the thicker prisms, also supporting it from underneath), again placing them in a random arrangement on the mat.

– Offer the child a turn.

Exercises

(1) The child builds the Brown Stair exactly as in the presentation.

(2) Begin with the Brown Stair completely built as in exercise (1). Take the thinnest prism, and place it gently against the inside corner of each step, starting with the highest and furthest step, and working towards yourself. Each time, ensure that the ends are evenly lined up, observe the stair's appearance, and feel the evenness of all the aligned surfaces, especially the filled-in step. When finished, replace the thinnest prism at the front end of the stair.

(3) Give Three Stage Lessons on the following relative terms for the visual perception of size.

Use the second or third thickest prism together with the second or third thinnest prism, to introduce the idea of 'thick' and 'thin'.

Later, give lessons on the comparatives and superlatives of these terms, using two of the thickest prisms to teach 'thick' and its comparative 'thicker', and two of the thinnest prisms to teach 'thin' and its comparative 'thinner'. Then use the three thickest or thinnest prisms to teach both the comparative and superlative (e.g. 'thick', 'thicker' and 'thickest').

(4) Place two floor mats at a considerable distance. Arrange the prisms of the Brown Stair randomly on one of the mats. Select and pick up the thickest prism, walk with the child to the other mat, and place that prism down on it. Ask the child to return alone to the other mat and bring 'the next prism' to place against the thickest one. Continue asking until the stair is built, sending the child back and forth between the mats.

(5) Arrange two mats and the Brown Stair prisms as at the start of exercise (4). Select and pick up any prism, walk with the child to the other mat, and place the prism down on it. Ask the child to return alone to the first mat and bring 'a prism that is thicker' (or 'thinner'), without taking the first prism back to compare. Either retain both prisms at the second mat, or ask the child to return one to the first mat. Repeat as long as the child is interested.

(6) Later, repeat exercise (5), but ask for 'the prism which is the next thicker' or 'the next thinner'.

Red Rods

Aim   To help develop the child's visual discrimination of differences in one dimension. To help develop the child's muscular co-ordination. Indirectly, to prepare the child for later work in geometry through the general observation of the geometrically regular differences in the rod's lengths, faces, and total volumes. Indirectly, to prepare the child for the concept of numbers, in demonstrating the unit difference in length between the ten successively longer rods.

Material   Ten red, wooden rods of equal thickness, square (2.5 cm x 2.5 cm) on each end, varying in length from 1 metre to 10 cm, by 10 cm increments.

Presentation   – Name the Red Rods and show where they are kept.
– Ask the child to spread a floor mat. Show how to carry the rods singly, holding each horizontally with two hands. (If space does not permit, hold each rod vertically.) Show how to place them in a random but roughly parallel arrangement on the mat. After placing each rod on the mat, feel the full length of the rod with both hands, stretching your arms to reach the ends of the long ones, and holding your arms together when touching the ends of the short ones.
– Look over the rods intently, select the longest one, and compare it with one or two other rods near in size, holding it next to them to be sure it is the longest on the mat. Then place it down gently in an isolated spot towards the far edge of the mat, with the square ends facing left and right.

– Look over the remaining rods intently, select the next shorter rod, and compare it with one or two other rods near in size to be sure it is the longest remaining on the mat. Then carefully place it on the mat an inch or two in front of, and parallel to, the first rod, with the left square ends roughly lined up; continuing the same graceful movement, gently and carefully slide the second rod up against the first, so that the left ends are exactly even.
– While holding your left fingers against the aligned left ends, run the index and middle fingers of your right hand along the top of the crevice where the two rods meet, sliding them from the left to the right, thus experiencing a tactile impression of their lengths.
– Continue to build the rod stair towards the front of the mat, always selecting the next shorter rod, and occasionally comparing it with one or two rods near in size to be sure that it is the longest one remaining on the mat. Each time a rod is placed, show the child that you are satisfied and pleased with the progress you are making. Also, each time a rod is placed, gently feel with your fingers, as above, along the crevice between the last rod in the stair and the rod just placed, to gain a tactile impression of their lengths. Two or three times during the building process, very gently feel with the fingers of your left hand down the flat left edge of the rod stair, to confirm the perfect alignment of the rods. (If the child appears anxious to try placing a rod, say, 'Let me finish this whole rod stair, and then you can have a turn.')
– With the child, excitedly examine the completed rod stair, from all sides, and from above.
– Dismantle the stair, gently removing the rods one by one, starting with the shortest one, lifting each rod with two hands holding it from above, placing the rods again in a random but roughly parallel arrangement on the mat.
– Offer the child a turn.

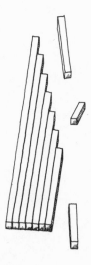

Exercises

(1) The child builds the Red Rods stair exactly as in the presentation.
(2) Begin with the Red Rods stair completely built as in exercise (1). Take the shortest rod, and place it gently in the inside corner of each step, starting with the right-most and furthest step, and working towards yourself. Each time, ensure that the shortest rod is perfectly placed, observe the stair's appearance, and feel the evenness of the two now coinciding right ends. When finished, replace the shortest rod at the front of the stair, aligned on the left.
(3) Give Three Stage Lessons on the following relative terms for the visual perception of size.

Use the second or third longest rod together with the second or third shortest rod, to introduce the idea of 'long' and 'short'.

Later, give lessons on the comparatives and superlatives of

these terms, using two of the longest rods to teach 'long' and its comparative 'longer', and two of the shortest rods to teach 'short' and its comparative 'shorter'. Then use the three longest or shortest rods to teach both the comparative and superlative (e.g. 'long', 'longer' and 'longest').

(4) Place two floor mats at a considerable distance. Arrange the Red Rods randomly, but roughly parallel, on one of the mats. Select and pick up the longest rod, walk with the child to the other mat, and place that rod down on it. Ask the child to return alone to the first mat and bring 'the next rod' to place against the longest one. Continue asking until the rod stair is built, sending the child back and forth between the mats.

(5) Arrange two mats and the Red Rods as at the start of exercise (4). Select and pick up any rod, walk with the child to the other mat, and place the rod down on it. Ask the child to return alone to the other mat and bring 'a rod that is longer' (or 'shorter'), without taking the first rod back to compare. Either retain both rods at the second mat, or ask the child to return one to the first mat. Repeat as long as the child is interested.

(6) Later, repeat exercise (5), but ask for 'the rod which is the next longer' or 'next shorter'.

Colour Tablets

Aim To help develop the child's perception of colours, including differences in hues and intensities. Indirectly, to prepare the child for later technique work in the visual arts.

Material Three boxes, with lids, containing small rectangular plastic tablets, in vivid enamel colours, with white plastic edge-guards on the narrow ends. Colour Tablets Box 1 contains six such tablets: three matching pairs of red, yellow and blue – the three primary hues. Colour Tablets Box 2 contains twenty-two tablets: eleven matching pairs of red, yellow, blue, green, orange, purple, pink, brown, white, grey and black. Colour Tablets Box 3 contains, in separate compartments, nine sets of seven tablets each; each set shows seven different intensities of one hue.

Presentations (1) Colour Tablets Box 1
  – Name the Colour Tablets, show where they are kept, and name Box 1.
  – Ask the child to spread a table mat, and show how to carry Box 1 to the table, how to open the lid, and how to lift out the tablets, handling them by their white edges only. Place all six tablets in a random arrangement in the centre of the mat.
  – Select one tablet and isolate it near the front of the mat.
  – Intently examine the isolated tablet, and then carefully look over the remaining tablets in the centre of the mat, excitedly finding the tablet which is the same as the isolated one.

- Compare the two matching tablets by holding them close, and with evident satisfaction isolate the pair side-by-side in a far corner of the mat, arranging them so that they look like the Roman numeral 'II', with their white edges touching.
- Repeat the matching for the other two pairs, placing the matched pairs in the same corner of the mat, in a column of 'IIs' running towards the mat's near edge. When finished, say, pointing to the pairs from far to near, 'These two tablets are the same colour; these two are the same colour; and these two are the same colour.'
- Replace all six tablets in a random arrangement in the centre of the mat, and offer the child a turn.

(2) Colour Tablets Box 2
- Introduce and name Box 2.
- Ask the child to spread a floor mat, show how to carry Box 2 to the mat, and how to open the lid.
- Take out the three pairs of tablets which are the same as those in Box 1 (the red, blue and yellow pairs), and place them in a random arrangement in the centre of the mat, again handling them by their white edges only. Invite the child to do the pairing with these six tablets, as demonstrated in presentation (1), placing the column of three pairs in a far corner of the mat.
- Take out from the box another three pairs of tablets – the green, orange and purple ones – and place them in a random arrangement in the centre of the mat.
- Select one of these six new tablets and isolate it near the front of the mat. Examine this tablet, look over the other five, find the matching one, closely compare the matched tablets, and with satisfaction place the pair at the front end of the column of the first three matched pairs.
- Invite the child similarly to pair the four tablets remaining in the centre of the mat.
- Mix all six pairs in a random arrangement in the centre of the mat, and invite the child to pair them all in a column.
- When the child has finished, and if the child wishes to continue, take out from the box another three pairs of tablets – the pink, brown and grey ones – and place them in a random arrangement in the centre of the mat.
- Match one pair as before, invite the child to pair the four tablets remaining, then mix all nine pairs in the centre of the mat and invite the child to pair them all in a column.
- When the child has finished, and if the child still wishes to continue, take out from the box the remaining two pairs – the black and white ones – and place them in a random arrangement in the centre of the mat.
- Invite the child to pair these four tablets, then mix all eleven pairs in the centre of the mat and invite the child to pair them all in a column.

– When the child is finished, proudly view with the child the
column of eleven pairs of matched tablets, and say, 'these two
tablets are the same colour', as you point to each pair down
the column.

– Replace all twenty-two tablets in a random arrangement in
the centre of the mat, and invite the child to do the entire
matching independently.

(3) Colour Tablets Box 3
– Introduce and name Box 3.

– Ask the child to spread a floor mat, show how to carry Box 3
to the mat, and how to open the lid.

– Take out any one set of seven tablets, all different intensities
of one hue, and place them in a random arrangement in the
centre of the mat.

– Say, 'let's start with this one', selecting the darkest of the
seven tablets, comparing it with one or two of the other dark
tablets, and then isolating it near the front edge of the mat,
placed so that it looks like the Roman numeral 'I'.

– Find the next lighter tablet among the remaining six,
compare it with one or two others of similar intensity to be
sure it is the darkest, and place it to the right of the first
selected tablet, arranging them so that they look like the
Roman numeral 'II', with their white edges touching.

– Find the next lighter tablet among the remaining five,
compare it with one or two others of similar intensity to be
sure it is the darkest, and place it to the right of the first two
selected tablets, arranging them so that they look like the
roman numeral 'III', with their white edges touching.

– Continue until all seven tablets have been placed in a row,
left to right from darkest to lightest. Observe, with the child,
the resulting pattern.

– Replace these seven colour tablets in a random arrangement
in the centre of the mat, and offer the child a turn.

– When the child is finished, show the child how to return the
tablets in their graded order to their compartment in the box.

Exercises   (1) The child pairs tablets from Box 1, on a table mat, as in
presentation (1).

(2) The child pairs tablets from Box 2, on a floor mat, as at the
end of presentation (2).

(3) The child selects and grades any one set of seven tablets
from Box 3, on a floor mat, as in presentation (3).

(4) The child combines two sets of tablets from Box 3 in a
random arrangement in the centre of a floor mat. Then,
selecting one tablet at a time, the child grades all fourteen
tablets by intensity while separating them by hue, so as to
build two graded rows of seven. (It does not matter whether
the child first grades all of one hue and then all of the second
hue, or instead takes turns between the hues, adding the
next lighter tablet to each row in turn.)

(5) The child combines all nine sets of tablets from Box 3 in a random arrangement on one floor mat, and lays a second floor mat beside it. The child finds the darkest tablet of each hue, comparing it carefully with other tablets of the same hue to be sure it is the darkest, and then places these nine tablets in a circle on the second mat, with the corners of the white edge-guards touching. Then selecting one tablet at a time, the child grades the remaining fifty-four tablets by intensity while separating them by hue, forming a star-shaped pattern of graded rows, decreasing in intensity from the centre outward. (It is easiest to do this by repeatedly selecting the darkest nine tablets, and placing them in their appropriate rows.)

(6) Give Three Stage Lessons on the following terms for hue, three at a time, using the colour tablets in Box 2: 'red', 'yellow', 'blue', 'green', 'orange', 'purple', 'pink', 'brown', 'white', 'grey' and 'black'. (See the Sample Presentation of the Three Stage Lesson.)

(7) Give Three Stage Lessons on the following relative terms for colour intensity, using the tablets in Box 3.

Remove from Box 3 one of the sets of seven tablets, which show seven intensities of one hue. Use the second darkest tablet together with the second lightest tablet to give a lesson on 'dark' and 'light'. Repeat this lesson with the second darkest and second lightest tablets from a different set of seven from Box 3.

Later, give lessons on the comparatives and superlatives of these terms, using the second and third darkest tablets from a set of seven to teach 'dark' and its comparative 'darker', and the second and third lightest tablets from that set to teach 'light' and its comparative 'lighter'. Then use the three darkest tablets and three lightest tablets from that same set to teach both the comparative and superlative (e.g. 'dark', 'darker' and 'darkest'). Repeat these lessons with a different set of seven from Box 3.

(8) Give Three Stage Lessons on the nine hues found in Box 3, using the one colour tablet from each set of seven that has the medium intensity (neither the three lightest nor the three darkest), and giving their precise names (e.g. 'auburn', 'maroon', 'chartreuse', 'lavender').

(9) Lay two floor mats at a considerable distance. Place one tablet from each pair in Box 2 on one mat, and place their matching tablets on the other mat, both in random arrangements. Stand with the child at one of the mats, isolate one of the tablets on the mat, show it to the child, and ask the child to bring 'the same colour tablet from the other mat', without taking the first tablet there. Compare the child's choice to the first tablet, show appreciation for a correct match, and ask the child to return the second tablet to the distant mat. Repeat as long as the child desires.

(10) Invite a child who has learned the names of the colours in

Box 2 to lay a floor mat, and place Box 2 on it. Take out of the box three tablets of different colours, and place them widely spaced on the mat. Ask the child to find an object in the room which is the same colour as one of these tablets – naming that colour – and to place that object next to its matching tablet on the mat, or if the object is immovable, to place the tablet next to it. When this is done, show appreciation, ask the child to return the objects and to replace the three tablets in the box. Repeat with three new colours as long as the child is interested.

(11) Lay two floor mats at a considerable distance, and place Box 3 on one of them. Take the single darkest tablet of each set out of the box, put these nine tablets in an isolated pile, and place the other fifty-four tablets out on the mat in a random arrangement. Carry the nine darkest tablets to the other, distant mat. Isolate one of these nine tablets on that mat, show it to the child, and ask the child to return alone to the first mat and bring 'the next tablet' to place against the isolated one. Repeat until that set of seven is graded, sending the child back and forth between the mats. If the child is interested, grade another set in the same way. If you continue until all nine sets are graded, invite the child to arrange the nine graded rows into the familiar star pattern (as in exercise (5)).

(12) Lay two floor mats at a considerable distance, and place Box 3 on one of them. Take all sixty-three tablets out of the box and place them in a random arrangement on the mat. Select one of the medium-intensity tablets, and carry it to the other, distant mat. Then ask the child to return to the first mat alone and bring a tablet which is 'the same colour but darker', without taking the first tablet back to compare. Show the original tablet again, and next ask the child to return to the first mat alone and bring a tablet which is 'the same colour but lighter'. Return all three tablets to the first mat. Repeat with a new medium-intensity hue as long as the child shows interest.

(13) Later, repeat exercise (12), but ask for the tablet which is the 'next darker' or 'next lighter'.

(14) Repeat exercise (10), but using Box 3 instead of Box 2.

Geometric Cabinet

Aim   To help develop the child's visual and tactile perception of the shapes of two-dimensional figures. To introduce, through the Geometric Cabinet Cards, the general function of symbols. Indirectly, to prepare the child for writing, through the handling of the insets by their knobs, and through the acquisition of visual and muscular familiarity with the movements essential to forming letters. Indirectly, to prepare the child for later work in Mathematics, through the observation of, and manipulative discrimination between, regularly varied shapes, and through learning the names for these shapes.

Material

A wooden, rectangular Presentation Tray, on which are resting six thin, natural-colour squares of wood, in two rows of three. Three of the squares have a large space cut into them. Into the far left square is cut a slightly smaller square; into the near centre square is cut a circle; and into the far right square is cut an equilateral triangle; the other three squares are not cut at all. Each side of the square, the diameter of the circle, and each side of the triangle, are all approximately the same length. Resting in each cut-out space is a thin wooden 'inset', the exact shape and size of the space. Each inset is painted blue and has a small, white wooden knob at its centre. The surface of the tray is also painted blue, which is visible when the insets are lifted out of their cut squares or 'frames'. Resting on top of the Presentation Tray is a dark wooden lattice, the cross beams of which form thick dark borders for each of the six squares in the tray.

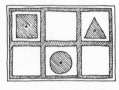

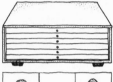

A wooden Geometric Cabinet, with six shallow drawers. Like the Presentation Tray, each drawer is a blue-painted tray with six thin natural wood squares covering it, into which are cut spaces of various shapes, with fitted insets painted blue and their knobs painted white. Unlike the Presentation Tray, the drawers have no lattices on them. In two of the drawers, the top and third from the top, only the four corner squares have cut-out frames with insets; in the other four drawers, all six squares are cut-out frames with insets. The shapes found in each drawer, from the top drawer in the cabinet (Drawer 1) to the bottom drawer (Drawer 6), are as follows: (For drawers 1, 2, 3 and 5 the shapes are named in the order they occur in their drawer, from left-to-right in the back row and then left-to-right in the front row.)

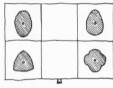

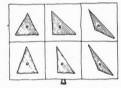

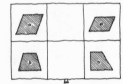

Drawer 1: ellipse, oval, curvilinear triangle, quatrefoil;
Drawer 2: equilateral triangle (the same as in the Presentation Tray), right-angle isosceles triangle, obtuse-angle isosceles triangle, acute-angle isosceles triangle, right-angle scalene triangle, obtuse-angle scalene triangle;
Drawer 3: rhombus, parallelogram, trapezium, trapezoid (as these last two are defined in the UK; in the US, their definitions are the reverse);
Drawer 4: square (the same as in the Presentation Tray), and five successively narrower rectangles;
Drawer 5: pentagon, hexagon, heptagon, octagon, nonagon, decagon;
Drawer 6: circle (the same as in the Presentation Tray), and five successively smaller circles.

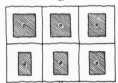

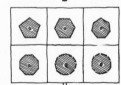

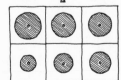

A small wooden shelf unit with three open shelves, on which are stored three sets of thin, white, square Geometric Cabinet Cards. Each of the three sets contains one card for every shape found in the Geometric Cabinet. The thirty-two cards on the upper shelf bear solid blue representations of the shapes; the thirty-two cards on the middle shelf bear thick blue outlines of the shapes; and the thirty-two cards on the lower shelf bear thin blue outlines. All the cards are exactly the same size as the square wooden frames in the drawers of the Geometric Cabinet, and all the representations are exactly the same size and shape as the insets.

(DIY hint: If you are going to make this material yourself, do not attempt the cabinet. Cut the frames and insets out of stiff corrugated cardboard. For each tray, cut another piece of cardboard, the size of six frames. Glue the frames in position to the trays. Paint the insets and the spaces on the tray where they rest blue. For the knob at the centre of each inset, poke a small hole and glue in a 1.5 cm piece of wooden dowel, about the same diameter as a pencil.)

Presentation   – Name the Geometric Cabinet and the Presentation Tray (which may be stored on top of the Cabinet), and show where they are kept.

– Ask the child to spread a table mat. Show how to carry the Presentation Tray and gently place it on the far portion of the mat, leaving about six inches of the mat in front.

– (The following presumes that you are right-handed; if not, reverse the 'right/left' directions.) Seat the child on your left. Slowly and gracefully lift one of the insets out of its frame by grasping the little white knob between the thumb, index finger and middle finger of your left hand, and hold the inset vertically in front of you, over the mat, with its blue side facing the child. With the fleshy tips of your right hand's index and middle fingers, slowly and intently feel the entire edge of the inset in one continuous movement, starting at the near bottom corner and moving clockwise, as seen from the blue side. Gently place the inset down on the mat, and with the same fingers as before, feel the entire inside edge of the space in that inset's frame, in one continuous movement, starting at the far left corner, and again moving clockwise. Pick up the inset again and feel its edge, as before, and by your facial expression show that you have affirmed that the shape of the inset feels the same as the shape of the space in its frame. In one smooth, continuous movement, replace the inset in its frame.

– Repeat this exact process for the other two shapes in the Presentation Tray.

– Invite the child to feel each of the three insets and frames, exactly as you just did.

– (If the child is unable to feel the insets and frames properly, conclude the presentation, and repeat the presentation from the start another day, emphasising the motions which the child had difficulty with; if the child feels the insets and frames properly, continue the presentation as follows.) Remove each inset from its frame, placing them in a random arrangement on the mat in front of the Presentation Tray. Select one of the insets, lift it by its knob with your left fingers, feel its edge as before, and visually examine the inset and the three empty frames. Then feel the inner edge of the space in the frame which appears to match the inset, feel the inset again, and in one smooth movement place it in its frame. Select a second inset, repeat the process, and repeat it again with the third inset.

– Offer the child a turn at putting all three insets on the mat, and at correctly replacing them in their frames as above.

Exercises

(1) The child independently works with the Presentation Tray, as in the presentation, feeling and replacing each inset singly, and then putting all three shapes on the mat and replacing them.

(2) Show the child how to remove, carry and replace drawers in the Geometric Cabinet, and create activities which practise this. Then invite the child to work with the top drawer, treating it just like the Presentation Tray in exercise (1). On another day invite the child to work with the second drawer, and so on with each drawer in succession. Afterwards, the child may work with any of the drawers in the cabinet, at will, performing only the second half of exercise (1), that is, putting all the insets on the mat and replacing them.

(3) Teach by Three Stage Lessons, the full name (as given above in the *Material* section) for the shape of each inset in the Geometric Cabinet. Later, teach by Three Stage Lessons the family names of the shapes, by drawer (except Drawer 1): Drawer 2 contains triangles; Drawer 3 contains quadrilaterals; Drawer 4 contains rectangles (the square is a kind of rectangle); Drawer 5 contains polygons; and Drawer 6 contains circles.

(4) Show the child how to arrange two or more drawers on table mats (or on a floor mat, if table space does not permit), and how to put all the insets on the mat in a random arrangement and then replace them, feeling their edges and their frames, as above. Invite the child to work with two, then three, four, five and finally all six drawers in combination.

(5) Name the Geometric Cabinet Cards, and show the child how to remove, carry and replace each pile of cards on its shelf. Place the top pile of cards, the ones with solid representations, face up on a floor mat near the Geometric Cabinet. Remove Drawer 1 from the Cabinet, and place it on the mat. Invite the child to remove one of the insets, examine it, place it on the mat, and then turn the cards over one at a time, to find the one card which best matches the inset. Direct the child to remove that card from the pile, isolate it in a far corner of the mat, and place the inset directly on top of it, with the inset and its representation

coinciding precisely. Restore the cards in one upright pile. The child similarly finds the card which best represents each of the other insets in Drawer 1, and later repeats the activity for each of the other five drawers, in succession.

Later, the child sets up the activity with any one drawer, and independently finds the card which best represents each inset.

(6) Lay down three adjacent floor mats. Place the pile of Geometric Cabinet Cards with solid representations in one corner of one mat. Invite the child to examine the top card, and then to find the inset which it appears to represent by looking through the drawers in the cabinet. Direct the child to place the matched pair in a far corner of the mats, with the inset on top of the card, precisely coinciding with its representation. The child similarly finds the inset represented by each of the other cards in the pile.

Later, the child sets up the activity and independently finds the inset that appears to be represented by each card.

(7) The child repeats exercises (5) and (6) using the set of cards with thick outlines.

(8) The child repeats exercises (5) and (6) using the set of cards with thin outlines.

(9) Place one (or several) drawer(s) from the Geometric Cabinet on a floor mat nearby. On another floor mat a considerable distance away, spread out, face up, in a random arrangement, the cards from each of the three piles of Geometric Cabinet Cards which correspond to the insets in the selected drawer(s). Invite the child to pick one inset from the drawer, examine it and remember its shape, put it down on the mat, and then go to the distant mat and bring back the three cards which best represent the inset's shape. The child fits the inset to the image on each of the cards to check the match, and then returns the cards to the distant mat. Invite the child to continue playing independently or with you suggesting which inset to pick.

(10) Repeat exercise (9), but purposely leave out one of the three cards which correspond to one of the insets in the chosen drawer(s). Tell the child that for one of the insets, one of its three cards is missing, and invite the child to try to discover which inset this applies to, by repeatedly playing through the matching as before. (The child who plays this several times will be able to tell which card is missing by simply looking them over.)

Constructive Triangles

Aim   To introduce to the child the concept that visual images may be combined to create different visual images. Indirectly, to prepare the child for later work in Mathematics, by demonstrating the principle that all plane geometrical figures constructed with straight lines may be conceived as being composed of triangles.

Two boxes containing matching pairs of thin wooden **Material**
Constructive Triangles of various types, with each triangle
painted, on one side, a bold enamel colour. In Box 1, each
triangle has a thick, black line drawn along one edge; for each
matching pair, this line is drawn along the same edge on both. In
Box 2, the triangles do not have any lines on them.

– Box 1 contains: two yellow equilateral triangles with the black
line along one edge; two green right-angle isosceles triangles
with the black line along the 'hypotenuse'; two yellow
right-angle isosceles triangles with the black line along one of
the 'sides' (i.e. not along the 'hypotenuse'); two green
right-angle scalene triangles with the black line along the longer
of the two 'sides'; two yellow right-angle scalene triangles with
the black line along the shorter of the two 'sides'; two grey
right-angle scalene triangles with the black line along the
'hypotenuse'; and a pair of smaller red triangles, one a
right-angle scalene (the remaining two angles being 65
degrees and 25 degrees) and the other an obtuse-angle
scalene (the three angles being 115 degrees, 40 degrees
and 25 degrees), with the longer 'side' of the first the same
length as the longest edge of the second, and the black line
on each drawn along these two matching edges.

– Box 2 contains: two blue right-angle scalene triangles; two blue
right-angle isosceles triangles; two blue equilateral triangles;
and a pair of smaller blue triangles identical in shape and size to
the two red triangles in Box 1.

Three packets of thin-cardboard Triangle Cards. One packet
contains twenty equilateral triangles, another packet contains
twenty right-angle isosceles triangles, and the third packet
contains twenty right-angle scalene triangles.

(DIY hint: Make the Constructive Triangles from coloured
matboard, draw the black lines with a thick marker, and store
them in cardboard boxes.)

(1) Constructive Triangles Box 1 **Presentations**
  – Name the Constructive Triangles, introduce Box 1, and place
  Box 1 on a floor mat.
  – Remove from the box the two yellow equilateral triangles, the
  two green right-angle isosceles triangles, and the two grey
  right-angle scalene triangles. Place the triangles of each pair
  close together but not touching, with their black line edges
  closest and the black lines parallel.
  – Hold one yellow equilateral triangle steady with one hand
  and run the index finger of your other hand along the black
  line. Repeat with the other yellow equilateral triangle.
  – In one smooth movement, gently push the two yellow
  equilateral triangles together so that the edges with the black
  lines are touching and exactly coinciding.
  – Holding both yellow triangles steady with one hand, run the
  index finger of your other hand along the crevice where they
  meet, between the two black lines.

- (Throughout the Constructive Triangles activity, if you form a new shape that has already been named in a Three Stage Lesson in the Geometric Cabinet activity, the child may spontaneously recognise it, and say, 'That's a -------.' If not, then at this point, simply tell the child the shape's name – in this case, say, 'This is a parallelogram.')
- Repeat the above process with the two green right-angle isosceles triangles (which will form a 'square') and then the two grey right-angle scalene triangles (which will form a 'rectangle').
- Separate the three pairs of triangles, arranging them as they were at the start of the presentation, and offer the child a turn in forming the three new figures from the triangles.

- (If the child is unable to feel and match the triangles properly, conclude the presentation, and repeat the presentation from the start another day, emphasising the motions which the child had difficulty with; if the child does feel and match the triangles properly, continue the presentation as follows.) Place the first six triangles aside or put them back in the box, and remove from the box the two yellow right-angle isosceles triangles, the two green right-angle scalene triangles, and the two yellow right-angle scalene triangles. Arrange them and repeat the merging process as above, which will form three 'parallelograms'.
- Separate these three pairs of triangles and offer the child a turn at feeling and merging them.
- Place this second set of six triangles aside or put them back in the box, and remove from the box the small red right-angle scalene triangle and the small red obtuse-angle scalene triangle. Place them close on the mat as with the other pairs, then feel their black-lined edges and move them together as above, forming a 'trapezium' (called in the US, a 'trapezoid').
- Separate these two triangles, and invite the child to make the red trapezium.

(2) Constructive Triangles Box 2
- Name Box 2, and place it on a floor mat.
- Remove from the box the two right-angle scalene triangles. Construct five different shapes (two different parallelograms, two different isosceles triangles, and a 'kite' shape), only putting together edges of equal length.
- Offer the child a turn at forming these different shapes.

- Repeat the process with the two right-angle isosceles triangles (which can form a square, two parallelograms, and two triangles), then with the two equilateral triangles (which can only form a rhombus), and lastly with the two smaller triangles (which can only form a trapezium as in presentation (1)), always just putting together the edges of equal length. Offer the child a turn after demonstrating each pair.

(3) Triangle Cards
- Name the packets of Triangle Cards, select the packet with the right-angle scalene triangles, and empty it out on a floor mat.
- Experiment arranging the cards in regular patterns, such as a pinwheel, a polygon and a diagonal checkerboard. (Do not name these shapes.)
- Undo your patterns, and offer the child a turn.
- On other days, try each of the other packets, offering the child a turn after demonstrating some possible designs.

(1) The child works independently with the triangles in Box 1 exactly as in the presentation.

Exercises

(2) The child works independently with the triangles in Box 2 as in the presentation.
(3) Teach the child, by Three Stage Lesson (also using two figures the child knows), the name of the new shape created in exercise (2): 'kite'.
(4) The same as exercise (2), but after constructing a new figure with two triangles, the child turns over one of the two triangles to show its natural, unpainted side, and notes how the figure changes, if at all.

(5) The child works independently with any of the packets of Triangle Cards, as in presentation (3).
(6) The child combines the triangles from two, and then three, packets of Triangle Cards, and continues to experiment with them, creating regular patterns that utilise more than one type of triangle.

Square of Pythagoras

To reinforce further the concept of combining visual images to create new images. Indirectly, to prepare the child for Group 4 Mathematics work, by providing a full sensorial experience of the operation of a multiplication table.

Aim

A large, shallow box with ten compartments, each holding a set of plastic tiles of a particular colour. The smallest set consists of one small square; the other sets consist of a square and matching pairs of rectangles. The colours of the sets and the dimensions of their plastic tiles, in centimetres (cm), are:

Material

- In red, one 1 x 1 cm square
- In green, one 2 x 2 cm square and two 1 x 2 cm rectangles
- In pink, one 3 x 3 cm square, two 1 x 3 cm rectangles, and two 2 x 3 cm rectangles
- In yellow, one 4 x 4 cm square, two 1 x 4 cm rectangles, two 2 x 4 cm rectangles, and two 3 x 4 cm rectangles
- In pale blue, one 5 x 5 cm square, two 1 x 5 cm rectangles, two 2 x 5 cm rectangles, two 3 x 5 cm rectangles, and two 4 x 5 cm rectangles

– In grey, one 6 x 6 cm square, two 1 x 6 cm rectangles, two 2 x 6 cm rectangles, two 3 x 6 cm rectangles, two 4 x 6 cm rectangles, and two 5 x 6 cm rectangles

– In white, one 7 x 7 cm square, two 1 x 7 cm rectangles, two 2 x 7 cm rectangles, two 3 x 7 cm rectangles, two 4 x 7 cm rectangles, two 5 x 7 cm rectangles, and two 6 x 7 cm rectangles.

– In brown, one 8 x 8 cm square, two 1 x 8 cm rectangles, two 2 x 8 cm rectangles, two 3 x 8 cm rectangles, two 4 x 8 cm rectangles, two 5 x 8 cm rectangles, two 6 x 8 cm rectangles, and two 7 x 8 cm rectangles

– In navy blue, one 9 x 9 cm square, two 1 x 9 cm rectangles, two 2 x 9 cm rectangles, two 3 x 9 cm rectangles, two 4 x 9 cm rectangles, two 5 x 9 cm rectangles, two 6 x 9 cm rectangles, two 7 x 9 cm rectangles, and two 8 x 9 cm rectangles

– In orange, one 10 x 10 cm square, two 1 x 10 cm rectangles, two 2 x 10 cm rectangles, two 3 x 10 cm rectangles, two 4 x 10 cm rectangles, two 5 x 10 cm rectangles, two 6 x 10 cm rectangles, two 7 x 10 cm rectangles, two 8 x 10 cm rectangles, and two 9 x 10 cm rectangles.

Preliminary Presentation

– Name the Square of Pythagoras box, show where it is kept, ask the child to spread a floor mat, and place the box on the mat.

– Show the child what is in the box, how the tiles in each compartment are stacked (from largest on bottom to smallest on top), and how the smaller tiles, which are in smaller sets, are kept in the smaller compartments.

– Show how to remove one set of tiles at a time, how to place the tiles of one set in a row (from largest to smallest going left to right), how to reconstruct the set into a stack of diminishing size, and how to replace the stack in its proper compartment. Invite the child to practise these manipulations on the white set, then on one larger set and one smaller set.

– Take, from the bottom of the largest stack – the orange set – just the square tile, and place it on the mat. Then take each successively smaller square from the bottom of each of the other sets, and build on top of the orange square a somewhat flat pyramid, centring each new square on the last. Only build up to the pale blue colour, and offer the child the task of finishing it. Admire and examine the resulting pyramid with the child, and return the squares to the bottom of their compartments.

Presentation

– Ask the child to lay a floor mat and to place on it the Square of Pythagoras box. Also, if you have a smooth board or other flat surface, about 60 x 60 cm, place it on one side of the mat.

– Ask the child to build the flat pyramid from the squares, as in the Preliminary Presentation, near one edge of the mat.

– Take the top square from the pyramid – the small red one – and put it in the near left corner of the work space (the mat itself, or the board if there is one).

– Find the compartment with the green set, take out the top two pieces – two green rectangles – and place them on the mat, one with a narrow end against the right side of the red square, and the other with a narrow end against the far side of the red square. Then take the green square from the pyramid, and place it in the corner formed by the green rectangles. Show the child that the edges of these tiles line up and that their collective shape is a larger square.

– Find the compartment with the pink set, take the top two pieces – the thinnest pink rectangles – and place them on the mat extending to the right and afar from the green rectangles. Place down the thicker pink rectangles, extending to the right and afar from the green square. Then take the pink square from the pyramid, and place it in the corner formed by the pink rectangles. Again show the child that the edges of these tiles line up and that their collective shape is a yet larger square.

– Find the compartment with the yellow set, take the top two pieces – the thinnest yellow rectangles – and place them on the mat extending to the right and afar from the thinner pink rectangles. Place down the next thinner yellow rectangles, extending to the right and afar from the other pink rectangles. Place down the last, thickest yellow rectangles extending to the right and afar from the pink square. Then take the yellow square from the pyramid, and place it in the corner formed by the yellow rectangles. Show the child that the edges of all the tiles still line up and that their collective shape is a still larger square.

– Continue to create a successively larger square by adding the successively larger sets of tiles, always first placing the top, thinnest rectangles from each compartment's stack, and the top square from the pyramid last, building in two directions towards the upper right corner of the construction. From the pale blue set onwards, invite the child to participate, placing some tiles. Be sure that the edges of the tiles butt against the adjacent tiles as completely as possible.

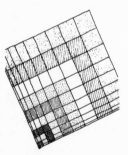

– Build together for a couple of sets, and allow the child, when ready, to carry on alone. The child may finish the construction with the largest orange set, or may stop building after placing down any complete set.

– Together examine as much of the Square of Pythagoras as is built.

– Disassemble the construction, one colour at a time, starting with the square of each set. As you remove the pieces of each set, hand them to the child to stack and replace in their compartment properly.

(1) The child independently builds the Square of Pythagoras, as in the presentation.

(2) One day, say to a child who has had much experience with exercise (1) and who has just finished building the square, 'I'd like to show you something new we can do with the

Exercises

Square of Pythagoras.' Remove any one of the middle sets of tiles (one colour entirely) from the construction, starting with the thinnest rectangles and working towards the square, and stack it properly on the mat. Then, again starting with the thinnest rectangles and working towards the squares, slide all the other sets towards the front left corner of the construction, removing and setting aside on the mat any pieces which no longer fit, in order to close the L-shaped gap and again make a large solid square. Examine the new square construction with the child, and note the relationship of the 'set aside' tiles to the completely removed set. Repeat the above process, removing another middle set, closing up the gap, and setting aside pieces which no longer fit, so as to remake the square. Invite the child to remove a set as described, and then to remove each of the remaining sets, re-making the square each time, until no more sets remain. Help the child return the properly sorted and stacked tiles to their compartments.

Henceforth, the child independently builds, and then diminishes, the Square of Pythagoras, as just described.

(3) Starting with all the sets of tiles in the box, remove one of the middle-size sets from the box and spread out its tiles on the mat. Isolate that set's square in front of you. Then, using that set's various rectangles, construct other squares, identical to the first square in size, accomplishing this in as many different ways as possible. Afterwards, replace this set in the box, remove another, and invite the child to match the second set's square by combining its various rectangles. Later, the child performs this activity independently.

One day, show the child how to place out all the squares in a column from largest to smallest, and to the right of each its matching rectangle constructions.

(4) Starting with all the sets of tiles in the box, remove the largest, orange square from the box and place it on the mat. Combine tiles of any size and colour to construct a square which matches the orange one in size. (For example, place down the grey square, and place the two second-to-largest grey rectangles on adjacent sides of it. Then place the yellow square in the corner formed by the grey rectangles.) Explore with the child the many ways to combine various tiles to build a square the same size as the orange one.

Working with the child, repeat this process of creating multi-coloured squares out of various rectangles, to match successively smaller squares from the box, all the way down to the pink square.

Later, the child conducts this activity independently.

Binomial and Trinomial Cubes

Aim   To develop further the child's visual perception of three-dimensional patterns. Indirectly, to prepare the child for later work in Mathematics, especially algebra, through the cubes' visual representation of the following algebraic formulas: for the binomial cube, $(a+b)(a+b)(a+b) = aaa + 3aab + 3abb + bbb$; and for the trinomial cube, $(a+b+c)(a+b+c)(a+b+c) = aaa + 3aab + 3aac + 3abb + 3bbc + 3acc + 3bcc + 6abc + bbb + ccc$.

Material

The Binomial Cube, a wooden box with a cover and two adjacent hinged sides, containing eight wooden blocks, painted in bold enamel colours, that fit together to form a cube with the same pattern on each side and also in the middle (when the cube is opened along any plane). This pattern is: a square divided by two off-centre lines (one vertical and one horizontal) into two squares (one larger than the other) in opposite corners and two rectangles (of equal size) in opposite corners; the larger square is red, the smaller square is blue, and both rectangles are black.

The Trinomial Cube, a larger wooden box with a cover and two adjacent hinged sides, containing twenty-seven wooden blocks, painted in bold enamel colours, that fit together to form a cube with the same pattern on each side and also in the middle (when the cube is opened along any plane). This pattern is: a square divided by four off-centre lines (two vertical and two horizontal) into three squares (of three different sizes) and six rectangles (of three different sizes); the three squares run diagonally, largest to smallest, from one corner of the face to the opposite corner; the largest square is red, the middle square is blue, the smallest square is yellow, and all six rectangles are black.

Presentations

(1) Binomial Cube
- Name the Binomial Cube and show where it is kept.
- Ask the child to spread a table mat, and show how to carry the box (holding it from below) to the table, how to open and remove the box's lid, and how to lower the two adjacent hinged sides gently towards yourself.
- Remove the blocks singly and place them on the mat in the following arrangement: make two columns; place in the left column, from far to near, the red cube and the three red and black rectangular prisms; place in the right column, from far to near, the blue cube and the three blue and black rectangular prisms.
- Say, 'Now we'll build the Binomial Cube.' Gently place the red cube in the far inside corner of box (opposite the hinged sides).
- Gently place the three red and black prisms around the red cube, with one of the red faces of each prism touching a red face of the cube.
- Gently place the blue and black prisms against the red and black prisms, with only black faces touching black faces.
- Gently place the blue cube in the blue-faced corner made for it by the three blue and black prisms.

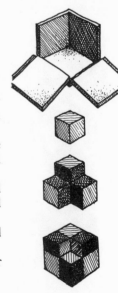

- Close the hinged sides and replace the top of the box, noting that the patterns on the constructed Binomial Cube inside are the same as the patterns showing on the faces of the box.
- Open the box again, remove and arrange the blocks in two columns as before, and offer the child a turn at building the Binomial Cube.

(2) Trinomial Cube

- Name the Trinomial Cube and show where it is kept.
- Ask the child to spread a table mat, and show how to carry the box (holding it from below) to the table, how to open and remove the box's lid, and how to lower the two adjacent hinged sides gently towards yourself.
- Remove the blocks singly and place them on the mat in the following arrangement: make four columns; place in the left column, from far to near, the six all-black rectangular prisms; place in the next-to-the-left column, from far to near, the red cube, the three tall red and black rectangular prisms, and then the three short red and black rectangular prisms; place in the second-from-the-right column, from far to near, the blue cube, the three tall blue and black rectangular prisms, and then the three short blue and black rectangular prisms; and place in the right column, from far to near, the yellow cube, the three tall yellow and black rectangular prisms, and then the three short yellow and black rectangular prisms.

- Say, 'Now we'll build the Trinomial Cube', emphasising the 'tri' sound.
- Invite the child to build the Binomial Cube, as in presentation (1), in the far inside corner of the box (opposite the hinged sides).

- Gently add the short red and black prisms by placing one of the red faces of each prism against the red faces on the Binomial Cube.
- Gently add the all-black prisms by placing them so that they touch only the black faces on the construction.

- Gently add the short blue and black prisms by placing one of the blue faces of each against the three exposed sides of the blue cube.
- Gently add the tall yellow and black prisms, each with its black sides touching only black on the construction, and each with one yellow face touching an inside surface of the box.

- Gently add the short yellow and black prisms by matching up a yellow face on each prism with one on the construction, leaving a three-sided, yellow-faced corner.
- Gently place the yellow cube in the yellow corner.

- Close the hinged sides and replace the top of the box, noting that the patterns on the constructed Trinomial Cube inside are the same as the patterns showing on the faces of the box.
- Open the box again, remove and arrange the blocks in four

columns as before, and offer the child a turn at building the Trinomial Cube.

(1) The child independently builds the Binomial Cube in its box as in presentation (1).

(2) The child builds the Binomial Cube in exactly the same way, but outside the box, with the empty box placed aside.

One day, after the cube is built outside the box, show the child that all the cube's faces have the same pattern on them. Turn the cube around to show that the back faces are the same. Place both hands around the cube and lift it, to show that the bottom has the same pattern too. After placing the cube back on the mat, show the child that even the six 'inside' faces have the same pattern, by splitting the cube three ways (horizontally, vertically, and back-to-front), exposing both 'inside' faces with each split.

Later, the child builds the Binomial Cube outside its box and independently examines all its possible faces.

(3) Show the child how to build the Binomial Cube in two layers, and then place the layer with the blue cube (holding it by wrapping your hands around it) on top of the layer with the red cube.

Later, the child does this independently.

(4) The child independently builds the Trinomial Cube in its box as in presentation (2).

(5) The child builds the Trinomial Cube in exactly the same way, but outside the box, with the empty box placed aside.

One day, after the cube is built outside the box, show the child that all the faces have the same pattern on them. Turn the cube around to show that the back faces are the same. Place both hands around the cube and carefully lift it, to show that the bottom has the same pattern too. After placing the cube back on the mat, show the child that even the twelve 'inside' faces have the same pattern, by splitting the cube three ways (horizontally, vertically, and back-to-front) into three layers each time, exposing both 'inside' faces with each split.

Later, the child builds the Trinomial Cube outside its box and independently examines all its possible faces.

(6) Show the child how to build the Trinomial Cube in three layers, then place the layer with the blue cube (holding it by wrapping your hands around it tightly) on top of the layer with the red cube, and the layer with the yellow cube on top of the layer with the blue cube.

Later, the child independently builds three separate layers of the Trinomial Cube and puts them together to make the complete cube, although the child should put them together piece by piece, rather than by trying to lift each layer in its entirety.

TOUCH

Blindfold

Aim   This is not a Montessori activity in itself, but a preparation for performing activities exclusively involving touch or the stereognostic sense. It is used to focus the child's concentration on these senses, by blocking the one sense most commonly relied upon.

Material   A washable cloth rectangle and a piece of soft elastic, sewn together to form a small blindfold. A pile of soft, disposable facial tissues folded lengthwise. Also, a pair of child's sunglasses.

Presentation   – Sit down at a table next to the child, with the cloth blindfold and two folded tissues.
– Place the tissue against the inside of the cloth and place the blindfold on yourself, emphasising the fun in not being able to see what's around you, and showing through jokes and play that things do not go away just because they can't be seen.
– Place the other tissue inside the blindfold and offer the child a turn.
– If the child is afraid of wearing the blindfold, pleasantly conclude the activity, and try the following presentation another day:
   Sit down at a table next to the child, with the pair of children's sunglasses and one folded tissue. First invite the child to wear the sunglasses, happily talk about how good they look and how these are just like the sunglasses grownups wear. Then show how they can be worn with the tissue inside them.
– If the child is still unwilling, do not insist, pleasantly conclude the activity, and try it again in a few months. If it then still makes the child insecure, simply show the child how to hold one's eyes shut for a long period of time.
– Whichever technique the child is comfortable with (the blindfold, the blocked sunglasses, or simply shutting one's eyes) is thereafter used in the activities whenever the 'blindfold' is called for.

Tactile Sense

Sensitising the Fingers

Aim   This is not a Montessori activity in itself, but a preparation for performing activities involving the tactile sense. It is used to increase the sensitivity of, as well as to clean, the finger tips, prior to handling tactile materials.

Material   A small vacuum flask (e.g. a small Thermos bottle). A number of plastic bowls and face-flannels. An absorbent drying cloth. A source of warm water.

The flask, which is filled each morning and afternoon with warm water, is always kept in an accessible place, along with the drying cloth and several of the bowls and face-flannels. **Preparation**

– Before beginning a tactile Sensorial Activity, name the 'materials for Sensitising the Fingers', and show where they are kept. Tell the child, 'We must always sensitise our fingers before doing any touching work.' **Presentation**
– Go to the place where the materials are kept, open the flask, select one bowl, pour about a half-inch's depth of warm water into the bowl, and re-close the flask tightly.
– Dry any drips with the drying cloth next to the flask.
– Carefully carry (or if the child has had experience with stage (4) of WALKING ON THE LINE (see Practical Activities), invite the child to carry) the bowl to a table with chairs, and ask the child to return to the materials and bring back one face-flannel.
– Be seated with the child at the table.
– Hold all of one hand's fingers (including the thumb) in the warm water for about fifteen seconds, and repeat with your other hand.
– Afterwards, pick up the face-flannel and dry your fingers thoroughly, rubbing hard with the cloth on each finger tip and on the tip of your thumb.
– On each hand, squeeze your thumb tightly against each of your other fingertips in turn.
– On each hand, rub the thumb vigorously against each of your other fingertips in turn.
– Carry the bowl to a sink (or used water container) and empty it, dry any drips on the table with the drying cloth, put the face-flannel with the soiled cloths, pour more warm water into the bowl, collect a new face flannel, and repeat the entire process from the beginning, but this time, the child's fingers are to be sensitised. For one hand, you should physically guide the child's movements: gently hold the child's hand, place the child's fingers in the water, rub them with the flannel, and press and rub them together. Then invite the child to sensitise the other hand without your help.

Touch Boards

To help awaken the child's tactile perceptual skills. Generally, to aid the child's fine motor control by cultivating a lightness of touch, which also indirectly prepares the child for writing. **Aim**

Two small, rectangular wooden boards, each with a length twice its width, and with pieces of medium-grain sandpaper glued to one side. Board 1 has a square of sandpaper on one half of its **Material** surface; the other half is varnished smooth. Board 2 has five strips of sandpaper, alternating along the length of the board with four smooth varnished areas.

(DIY hint: Use smooth, coloured matboard instead of wood for the boards.)

Presentation

– Name the Touch Boards 1 and 2, and show where they are kept.
– Sensitise your fingers and ask the child to do the same (see SENSITISING THE FINGERS).
– Invite the child to spread a table mat and to place Boards 1 and 2 on it.
– Position Board 1 directly in front of you on the mat, with its smooth side on the left.

– With your eyes averted (perhaps looking towards the child), lightly brush the tips of the fingers of one hand over the smooth non-sandpaper surface, pulling your hand towards yourself, from far to near. Show that you are relaxed but gently controlling the movement.
– Again with your eyes averted, lightly brush the tips of the fingers of the same hand over the sandpaper surface, pulling your hand towards yourself, from far to near. Show mild surprise at, and interest in, the new, different texture.
– Repeat, touching the smooth side, and then the rough side.
– Place Board 1 in front of the child, and offer a turn.
– (Continue the same presentation, or start another day at this point:) Position Board 2 in front of you, with the strips running far and near.

– With eyes averted as before, lightly brush the tips of just the index and middle fingers of one hand over the left-most strip of sandpaper, pulling your hand towards yourself, from far to near. Exhibit a gentle control in keeping your index and middle fingers only on the strip.
– Again with your eyes averted, lightly brush these same fingers, in the same way, over the smooth area just to the right of that sandpaper strip. Show delight in the difference in texture.
– Repeat with the next rough strip, and then the next smooth area, moving across the board to the right, looking pleased with the contrasts in texture with each change.
– When you have felt all the strips, place Board 2 in front of the child, and offer a turn.

Exercises

(1) The child works independently with Touch Boards 1 and 2, as in the presentation.
(2) Give a Three Stage Lesson, using Touch Board 1, on the relative terms 'rough' and 'smooth.' With Board 2, just feel the strips and say 'rough' or 'smooth' appropriately, as you feel the strips, and invite the child to repeat.

Tactile Tablets

To refine the child's tactile sense.   **Aim**

In an open wooden box, five matching pairs of wooden   **Material**
rectangular tablets, each with sandpaper covering one side. The
five pairs vary in the degree of roughness of their sandpaper,
ranging from heavily granular to grainy smooth.
   (DIY hint: Use smooth, coloured matboard instead of wood for
the tablets.)

- Name the Tactile Tablets, show where they are kept, and place   **Presentation**
  them on a table mat.
- Sensitise your fingers and ask the child to do the same (see
  SENSITISING THE FINGERS).
- Place the box of tablets in the far right corner of the mat.
- Select from the box one of the pair of roughest tablets, and
  position it in front of yourself, lengthwise far to near. With your
  eyes averted, lightly brush the tips of the fingers of one hand
  over the tablet's sandpaper surface, pulling your hand towards
  yourself, from far to near. Show that you are relaxed but gently
  controlling the movement, and show interest in the texture you
  are feeling. Feel the tablet a second time in the same way.
- Invite the child to feel the tablet in the same way.
- Place this tablet near the left edge of the mat.
- Select from the box one of the pair of smoothest tablets, position
  and feel it as above, invite the child to feel it, and place it near
  the other tablet on the left side of the mat.
- Repeat with one tablet from each of the remaining pairs,
  making a randomly arranged group of five different tablets on
  the left side of the mat.
- Remove the other five tablets from the box, tell the child that
  'these are the same as the first five tablets', and place them in a
  randomly arranged group on the right side of the mat.
- Select any one tablet from the left group, positioning it in front
  of yourself, and select any one tablet from the right group,
  positioning it just to the right of the first tablet.
- Averting or closing your eyes, feel the left tablet of this pair,
  touching it as before, and then feel the right tablet of this pair. If
  they feel different, place the right tablet of the pair in the box, to
  isolate it.
- Still with eyes averted or closed, select another tablet from the
  group on the right, and compare the textures of this pair, the
  left one first and then the right one. Again, if the pair does not
  match, isolate the tablet on the right by placing it in the box.
- Repeat, with eyes averted or closed, until the selected tablet
  from the right group feels the same in roughness or smoothness
  as the tablet from the left group. Show great satisfaction at
  having found the match, saying, 'These tablets feel the same.'
  Invite the child to feel them to verify the match. Isolate this

matched pair at the centre of the far edge of the mat. Return the rejected tablets, the ones in the box, to the group on the right.
- Ask the child to select a new tablet from the left group. Then you repeat the pairing process as above. Continue to pair until all the tablets are in matched pairs, placed in a column of pairs running towards yourself down the centre of the mat. After each matching pair is found, invite the child to feel and verify the match. Also, after each pair is placed in the column, feel each matched pair in turn, down the column, and ask the child to do the same.
- After the child has felt the completed column of matched pairs, from far to near, separate the pairs again into randomly arranged left and right groups of five different tablets each.
- Invite the child to pair the ten tablets, reminding the child to avert or close eyes during the pairing.

Exercises
(1) The child independently pairs the Tactile Tablets, as in the presentation.

(2) The same as exercise (1), but the child wears the blindfold when feeling and matching the tablets. (This is more challenging than it sounds, despite the averting or closing of eyes in the presentation as in exercise (1), because of the need to picture mentally the changing arrangement of the materials on the mat. You should practise this exercise with the blindfold many times before showing it to the child.) Sit with the child using the blindfold for the first time, to promote a feeling of security.

(3) Show the child how to grade one set of five different Tactile Tablets, as follows.

Place five different tablets in random order in a row running left and right along the front edge of the table mat. Averting or closing your eyes, feel each tablet in the row and locate the roughest. If two seemed similar, compare them again. Remove the roughest tablet from the row, invite the child to feel it, and place it along the far edge of the table mat, somewhat to the left side.

With eyes averted or closed, feel each of the remaining four tablets in the row, and again locate the roughest. Invite the child to feel it, place this second chosen tablet just to the right of the first one, along the far edge of the mat. Feel the roughest tablet, and then the second roughest one, and invite the child to do the same.

Keep finding the next roughest tablet of the ones remaining at the front edge of the mat, building a graded row at the far edge, with both you and the child feeling the sequence left to right each time you add a new tablet.

Leaving your graded row in place along the far edge of the mat, take the other five tablets out of the box, and place them in a random order in a row running left and right along the front of the mat. Invite the child to grade these five in the same way, with eyes averted or closed, in a row just in front of yours. When this is done, show the child how to check the new graded row against your graded row, by feeling them.

Later, the child independently grades one set of five different Tactile Tablets, as above.

(4) The child independently grades the Tactile Tablets as in exercise (3), but uses the blindfold when feeling the tablets, repeatedly selecting the roughest, and placing out the graded row.

(5) Give Three Stage Lessons on the comparatives and superlatives of 'rough' and 'smooth'. Use the next-to-roughest tablet with the roughest tablet to teach 'rough' and its comparative 'rougher', and the next-to-smoothest tablet with the smoothest tablet to teach 'smooth' and 'smoother'. Then, to teach the superlative, use the three roughest tablets (i.e. 'rough', 'rougher', 'roughest') and use the three smoothest tablets (i.e. 'smooth', 'smoother', 'smoothest').

(6) Place one set of five different Tactile Tablets on a table mat, and the other matching set on a table mat a considerable distance away. Ask the child to wear the blindfold, and hand the child a tablet to feel. Take the tablet after the child has felt it and place it back amongst the other tablets on the table mat. Instruct the child to remove the blindfold and to go to the other mat to find the tablet which matches the one just felt. When the child brings that tablet, show the one you had selected, and invite the child to compare them. Repeat as long as the child enjoys it.

(7) Arrange the tablets and mats as at the start of exercise (6). At one of the two mats, invite the child to feel any one tablet. Then ask the child to go to the other mat and bring 'a rougher one' or 'a smoother one'. The child checks the selected tablet against the first one, and reports whether it is rougher or smoother, as requested.

(8) The same as exercise (7), but ask for the tablet which is 'the next rougher one' or 'the next smoother one'.

Fabrics

Aim

Further refinement of the child's tactile sense.

Material

Two small, flat, square boxes, each containing six identical pairs of square pieces of six different fabrics. Each square is about 10 cm by 10 cm, and all are the same neutral colour (e.g. off-white). Box 1 has heavy fabrics clearly contrasting in texture: linen, velvet, cotton flannel, tweed, ribbed corduroy, and polyester. Box 2 contains fine cloths, varying only slightly in texture: nylon, silk, very fine cotton, fine cotton/synthetic blend, acetate and rayon.

Presentation

– Name the Fabrics Boxes and show where they are kept.

- Ask the child to spread a table mat. Put Fabrics Box 1 in the far right corner of the mat.
- Sensitise your fingers and ask the child to do the same (see SENSITISING THE FINGERS).
- Select from the box of fabrics one of the two tweed cloths, and hold it with both hands, each side of the square gently grasped between the thumb and the other fingers. Avert your eyes, and lightly rub your fingers and thumb against the cloth as you are holding it.
- Hand the tweed cloth to the child, to feel in the same way.
- Place the tweed cloth near the left edge of the table mat.
- Select from the box one of the two velvet cloths, avert your eyes, hold and feel it as you did the tweed cloth, hand it to the child to feel in the same way, and place it on top of the tweed cloth on the left side of the mat.
- Repeat with one of each of the remaining pairs of cloths in the box, making a pile of six different cloths on the left side of the mat.
- Remove the remaining cloths from box, and place them in a pile near the right edge of the mat, saying, 'These feel the same as the ones we just felt.' Leave the box open.
- Say, 'I will try to match the cloths by feeling them.'
- Avert or close your eyes, select any one cloth from the left pile, and place it in front of yourself on the mat. Then select any one cloth from the right pile, and place it on the mat just to the right of the first cloth.
- With your eyes still averted or closed, feel the left of the two cloths, holding it with both hands as before, and then the right of the two. If they feel different, isolate the cloth on the right by putting it into the box.
- Select another cloth from the right pile, compare these two, the left one first and then the right one, and isolate the right one in the box if they feel different.
- Repeat until the selected cloth from the right pile feels the same as the one from the left pile. Show great satisfaction at having found the match, saying, 'These cloths feel the same.' Invite the child to feel them to verify the match. Isolate this matched pair at the centre of the far edge of the mat. Return the rejected cloths, the ones in the box, to the pile on the right.

- Ask the child to select for you a new cloth from the left pile. Then repeat the pairing process as above. Continue to pair, until all the cloths are in matched pairs, placed in a column of pairs running towards yourself down the centre of the mat. After each pair is matched, invite the child to feel and verify the match. Also, after each pair is placed on the column, feel each matched pair in turn, down the column, and ask the child to do the same.
- After the child has felt the completed column of matched pairs, from far to near, look at the mat again or open your eyes, and check the pairing visually, saying, 'yes, these are the same' for

each matched pair down the column. Separate the pairs again into randomly arranged left and right piles of six different cloths each.

– Invite the child to pair the twelve cloths independently, in the same way, with averted or closed eyes.

(1) The child pairs, as in the presentation, the cloths in Box 1.
(2) The child pairs, as in the presentation, the cloths in Box 2.
(3) The child repeats exercises (1) and (2), but wears a blindfold.
(4) If the child is interested, teach the names of the various cloths in Fabrics Boxes 1 and 2 by Three Stage Lessons, three cloths at a time, with no blindfold on either of you.
(5) Place one set of six different cloths from Box 1 on a table mat, and the other set on a table mat a considerable distance away. Ask the child to wear the blindfold, and hand the child a cloth to feel. Take the cloth after the child has felt it and place it back amongst the other cloths on the table mat. Instruct the child to remove the blindfold and to go to the other mat to find the cloth which matches the one just felt. When the child brings that cloth, show the one you had selected, and invite the child to compare them. Repeat as long as the child has fun.
(6) The same as exercise (5), but using the cloths from Box 2.

Thermic Sense

Thermic Bottles
To help awaken and refine the child's thermic sense.

A wooden box with a lid, divided into eight narrow, vertical compartments, each containing a cylindrical metal bottle with a screw cap and a ring handle on top. Each compartment is lined with insulation – for instance, a knitted cosy. One of the bottles has a pink spot painted on its screw cap top.

(DIY hint: For the bottles, you can use any set of eight small, metal, water-tight containers with fitted lids, such as those little assorted tea tins you can buy as gifts. Steel or tin is preferable to aluminium, since the former are better heat conductors. Paint all the tins and lids the same colour with oil-based paint, and paint a pink spot on one of the eight lids. A cardboard container, with corrugated cardboard dividers as insulation, will do well for the box.)

Thermic Bottles must each be filled with water at a particular temperature, and this must be done just before they are used, since if they are left on a shelf, they will all be room temperature before long. To be prepared in advance for when a child wishes to work with the Thermic Bottles, keep containers of water around the room at the appropriate temperatures, as follows. Keep a plastic jug of water in the refrigerator (10 degrees Centigrade (C) or less, but not frozen), keep another jug of water anywhere in the room out of the sun, such as in a cupboard (approximately 22 degrees C), and keep a third pitcher of water on a window sill in the sun in the summer, or near a heat source or radiator in the winter (about 35 degrees C). For the high temperature (approximately 50 degrees C), you will simply need access to a hot water tap. When a child is ready to work with the Thermic Bottles, fill two bottles with 10 degree C water, two bottles with 22 degree C water, two bottles (one of which is the bottle with the pink mark) with 35 degree C water, and two bottles with 50 degree C water (making sure these hot bottles are not so hot that they burn). Close the bottles tightly, dry them thoroughly, and place them in the lined compartments of their box, arranged in order of temperature from one end of the box to the other, with matching ones side-by-side. Close the box, place it in its spot on the shelf, and refill the three jugs around the room.

Presentation
– Name the box of Thermic Bottles and show where it is kept.
– Ask the child to spread a table mat. Place the box in the far right corner of the mat and remove the box's lid.
– Holding the insulation so that it stays in the box, remove the bottle with the pink top from the box, lifting it by its ring (or if it is a DIY bottle, by its corner edges), and place it upright in front of yourself near the front edge of the mat.
– Gracefully grasp the bottle with all of one hand (wrapping your fingers and thumb around it, and pulling it gently against your palm), without lifting or moving it. Release this gentle grasp after two or three seconds.
– Invite the child to feel the bottle in exactly the same way.
– Say, 'This one', pointing to the bottle's pink top, 'is special – we always need to feel this one first.' (This pink-top bottle is felt before feeling any other, because it will help restore the surface of the skin to its natural temperature after trying a very hot or very cold bottle, and will serve as a kind of sensory 'reference' to make the child's experiences of the other temperatures more distinct.)
– Remove one of the 10 degree C bottles as above, and place it in the centre of the mat. Feel the pink bottle first, and then the 10 degree C bottle with the same hand. Invite the child to do the same.
– Repeat with one of the 50 degree C bottles.
– Remove each of the other bottles, at random now, making sure that you feel the pink one first each time, and that you feel the other bottle with the same hand that held the pink one. Carry the bottles by their ring handles (or their corner edges), remember to offer the child a turn, and place all the bottles but the pink top one in a mixed-up group in the centre of the mat, close but not touching each other.
– Pause, looking excited about seeing all these interesting bottles

on the table. Make sure the pink-top bottle is still isolated in front of you, near the front edge of the mat. Select a bottle from the mixed-up group, and place it to the right of the pink top one. Feel the pink one, and then the selected one with the same hand. If they are not the same, invite the child to feel the pink one and then the other, and isolate the selected one in the front right corner of the mat. Try another bottle from the mixed-up group, isolating it as before if it is different from the pink one, and repeat this testing until you find the bottle that feels the same temperature as the pink-top bottle.

– When a match is found, excitedly say, 'These are the same!' Invite the child to verify that they feel the same, but this time instruct the child to hold one bottle in each hand. Place this matched pair, which is now the 'reference pair', in the front left corner of the mat, and return the ones isolated in the front right corner to the mixed-up group in the centre of the mat.

– Select a bottle at random from the group, place it in front of yourself, and try to find its match amongst the group. But now, when comparing two bottles, do not feel them both with the same hand; instead, first feel the 'reference pair' in the front left corner with both hands, one bottle in each hand, and then feel the selected bottle and its prospective match with two hands, one bottle in each hand. If you decide they are different, invite the child to verify this, by feeling the bottles in the same way. Be sure to keep the initially selected bottle on the left, and the prospective match on the right. As before, isolate in the front right corner of the mat those prospective matches which do not match.

– When a match is found, say, 'These are the same!' Invite the child to verify the match, and place the newly matched pair behind the 'reference pair' on the left side of the mat.

– Repeat the matching process until all the bottles are paired and placed in a column of pairs running behind the 'reference pair' towards the far left corner of the mat. Feel each pair again, feeling the 'reference pair' first each time, moving from the front of the column to the back, and ask the child to do the same.

– Mix up the bottles in the centre of the mat again, isolate the pink one in front, and offer the child a turn at pairing. The child should start with finding and isolating the 'reference pair' by feeling with one hand, and should then find the remaining matches by feeling with two hands.

– Afterwards, if the child wishes to work with the materials further, empty and refill the bottles from their jugs (and the hot water tap), since by this time the temperature differences between them may have considerably diminished. Tell the child that in order to work with the Thermic Bottles, you, the adult, must first get them ready by filling them.

(1) The child requests you to prepare the Thermic Bottles, and pairs them independently, as in the presentation.

(2) Prepare the Thermic Bottles and tell the child you will do

Exercises

something new with them. Then show how to grade one set of bottles with four different temperatures. The method for grading is as follows.

Place one set of four different-temperature bottles, including the pink-top bottle, in the centre of the mat. Position the pink one directly in front of yourself.

Find the one that is hotter than the pink one, by comparing the pink one with bottles selected from the group, feeling with one hand as in the first stage of exercise (1). Place this hotter one to the right of the pink one, return the rejected, cooler bottle(s) to the middle of the mat, and invite the child to feel first the pink one and then the hotter one.

Now select one of the two cooler bottles, and place it to the left of the pink bottle. Feel these three bottles in a row, from right to left, the hotter one, the pink one, and then the cool one, and invite the child to do the same. Replace this cool bottle with the other cool one and repeat. Decide which cool bottle is closer in temperature to the pink one, saying, 'this one is closer to the pink bottle', and place it to the immediate left of the pink bottle. Place the remaining coolest bottle to the left of that.

Now check the grading, feeling the entire row of four bottles from right to left, starting with the hottest and ending with the coolest, and ask the child to do the same.

Slide this row, preserving its sequence, to the back edge of the mat, and place the other four bottles in the middle of the mat. Find, by pairing, the one equivalent to the pink one, substitute the pink one for it in the middle of the mat. Invite the child to grade these four bottles as above.

When done, the child may check the new sequence against the old sequence by feeling, with two hands, the pairs of equivalent bottles in the two rows.

Later, the child independently grades one set of four different Thermic Bottles, including the pink one.

(3) The child repeats exercises (1) and (2), but when you prepare the Thermic Bottles for grading, make the temperature differences less, so as to make the exercises more challenging. This can be done by filling each bottle one third from the 22 degrees C (room temperature) jug before filling them the rest of the way from their usual jugs (and the hot water tap).

(4) Using one set of bottles of four different temperatures (as in exercise (2), but not (3)), introduce by a Three Stage Lesson the following relative terms for the perception of temperature 'hot', 'warm', 'cool' and 'cold'.

Thermic Tablets

Aim To help the child develop a special facet of the thermic sense, which allows one, by touch alone, to distinguish between materials with different capacities to conduct heat. Dense minerals, such as stone, steel or copper, conduct heat very well and feel cool to the touch, since they draw heat off our skin rather than reflect it back. Porous, organic materials, such as rubber, wood or felt, conduct heat poorly and feel warm to the touch, since they reflect body heat back against our skin, rather than draw it off. Surfaces that feel cool to the touch are generally perceived to be different in composition from surfaces that feel warm.

Material

A wooden box with a lid, divided into four compartments, each of which contains an identical pair of tablets, all the same size and shape, each pair made of a particular material. One pair is stone, one pair is metal, one pair is wood, and the last pair is very thick wool felt.

Presentation

– Name the box of Thermic Tablets and show where it is kept.
– Ask the child to spread a table mat. Place on the mat the blindfold with two folded tissues, and put the box of Thermic Tablets on the right side of the mat.
– Select from the box one of the stone tablets and place it in front of yourself. With your eyes averted (perhaps looking at the child), place the palm of one hand down flat upon the stone tablet, hold it there for a few seconds, and lift it off again.
– Invite the child to feel the tablet in the same way.
– Move the stone tablet to the left side of the mat, placed lengthwise far and near.
– Select from the box one of the felt tablets, feel it as above, invite the child to feel it, and place it on the left side of the mat, next to the stone tablet, also running lengthwise far and near.
– Repeat with one of the metal tablets and one of the wooden tablets, making a neat row of four different tablets on the left side of the mat.
– Remove the remaining four tablets from the box, tell the child that 'these are the same as the first four tablets', and place them in a similar neat row on the right side of the mat, though not in the same order.
– Avert your eyes, place your left palm on the left-most tablet in the left row, and place your right palm on the left-most tablet in the right row. Concentrate, for a moment, on the thermic sensation of the two tablets. If one feels cooler or warmer than the other, say, 'These feel different.' Lift each hand slightly off its tablet, leave your left palm over the same left-most tablet, and move your right palm one tablet over in the right row. Now lower your palms and compare the thermic sensation of these two tablets. Continue until your right palm is on a tablet of the same thermic quality as the left-most tablet in the left row, and say, 'These feel the same.' Look back at the mat and place the two matching tablets side-by-side at the centre of the far edge of the mat. Invite the child to feel the two tablets to verify their thermic equivalence, placing one palm on each.
– Place your left palm on the left-most of the three tablets

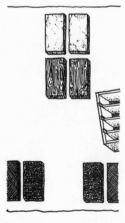

remaining in the left row, and repeat the pairing process. Place the newly matched pair in front of the other pair, and invite the child to feel both pairs in the column, from far to near.

– Repeat the pairing until all eight tablets are in four matched pairs in a column of pairs down the centre of the mat.

– Feel all four pairs, from far to near, and invite the child to do so.

– Visually separate the pairs into their left and right rows, each row in a different order, and invite the child to repeat the pairing process with averted eyes.

– Afterwards, again separate the tablets into two rows, and repeat the process yourself with the blindfold on, going right through without inviting the child to verify your matchings. Remove the blindfold and examine how well you sorted. (Your sorting should, of course, be perfect.)

– Invite the child to try the pairing with the blindfold on, but do not pressure a reluctant child.

Exercises

(1) The child independently pairs the Thermic Tablets as in the presentation, with or without the blindfold. After some experience without the blindfold, encourage the child to try it with the blindfold. Sit with the child using the blindfold for the first time, to promote a feeling of security.

(2) Using one set of four different Thermic Tablets, give a Three Stage Lesson on the names of the materials they are composed of: 'stone', 'metal', 'wood' and 'felt'.

(3) Place one set of four different Thermic Tablets on one table mat, and the other set on a table mat a considerable distance away. Wearing a blindfold at one of the mats, the child places a palm on a tablet you have isolated at the front edge of the mat. Still wearing the blindfold, the child is led (by you or another child) across the room to the other mat, and places a palm on each of the tablets on this mat until finding the one that gives the same thermic sensation as the first. The child then removes the blindfold and brings the selected tablet back to the first mat to make a visual comparison. Invite the child to return the selected tablet and play again.

(4) Lead a blindfolded child around the room, briefly placing the child's palm against various smooth surfaces, inviting guesses on whether each surface is made of stone (e.g. a concrete floor), metal (e.g. one of the METAL INSETS), wood (e.g. a MOVABLE ALPHABET box), or felt (e.g. a table mat).

Stereognostic Sense

Geometric Solids

Aim   To develop the child's stereognostic sense, which creates a mental picture through touch. To help make the child more aware of the basic shapes found in the cultural environment. Indirectly, to prepare the child for later work in Mathematics, especially geometry, by identifying solid shapes and exploring the relationships between their plane and curved surfaces.

A large wicker basket (about 30 cm in diameter) containing the Geometric Solids, which are nine solid wood shapes, each painted in enamel royal blue. The Geometric Solids include one each of the following shapes: rectangular prism, triangular prism, cube, cone, pyramid (tall with a square base), cylinder, sphere, ovoid, and ellipsoid. The long solids (everything but the cube and sphere), are about 6 cm in width and 10 cm long or tall; the cube and sphere are about 6 cm in width and diameter, respectively.

Also in the basket are three stands, one each for the curved-surface Geometric Solids (i.e. the sphere, the ovoid and the ellipsoid). Each stand is a thick piece of natural-finish wood with a large cut-out space the shape of a lengthwise slice of each of the three solids (i.e. the spaces are a circle, an oval, and an ellipse). The stands can be used to support a curved solid whenever it is placed on a flat surface.

A wooden box with a lid, containing nine Geometric Solids Bases, which are wooden tablets with thick blue outlines painted on one surface, comprising the following plane figures: three squares (6 x 6 cm), two circles (6 cm in diameter), two rectangles (6 x 10 cm), one equilateral triangle (6 cm on each side), and one tall isosceles triangle (6 cm across the base). The Bases correspond in size to the plane sides of the Geometric Solids which they match in shape.

An opaque square of fine fabric (about 70 cm square; a woman's dark-coloured silk scarf would do).

Two shallow trays and a wide-mouth container of extremely fine grain sand, enough to cover the surface of one tray about 1 cm deep.

(1) The Stereognostic Experience
  - Name the basket of Geometric Solids, show where it is kept.
  - Ask the child to spread a floor mat, and place on the mat the basket containing the solids.
  - Show the child how to experience, stereognostically, three contrasting shapes, as follows.
  - Lift the cube from the basket, avert your eyes (perhaps looking at the child), hold the cube with both hands, and make your palms and fingers conform to the surfaces, edges and corners of the cube, turning it to compare the various sides, holding and pressing with parallel palms the opposing planes, and so on, until you have fully perceived the cube's shape. Place the cube on the mat and invite the child to feel it in the same way.
  - Repeat this activity with the cone, curving your palms and fingers around it, tracing your fingers around and putting your palm flat against the base, following with one whole

hand the gradual tapering towards the point, and so on. Place the cone on the mat, offering it to the child to feel.

– Repeat this activity with the sphere, emphasising with rolling palms the uniformity and continuity of the curve, gently brushing the regularity of its surface, and so on. Afterwards place the sphere on its stand on the mat and ask the child to feel it too.

– Then, for as long as the child sustains an interest, feel each solid in the basket in a similar manner, inviting the child to do the same after each one, and then leaving the solid on the mat.

– Carefully replace all the solids in the basket and invite the child to work with them as just presented.

– Later, the child independently takes out the basket to experience the solids stereognostically.

– One day after the child has just finished a round of stereognostically handling the Geometric Solids, ask whether the child can see one of the particular shapes in the basket (e.g. the sphere) somewhere else in the room. (For example, the child might realise that the sphere can be seen in the ball in the corner, or in each little golden bead in the Mathematics activity.) Do this with several of the shapes, and invite the child to explore such comparisons independently, with each of the solids in the basket.

(2) Combining the Shapes

– Ask the child to spread a floor mat and say that you will do something new with the Geometric Solids. Put the basket on the mat.

– Show the child that the solids can be placed together in such a way that their plane surfaces fit and coincide, or partly coincide. Experiment creatively with a few of the solids, to show that there are many possibilities, building upwards, sideways, or holding the solids against one another in ways that won't stand up by themselves. (The child may tend to recognise familiar structures among the combined shapes thereby created (e.g. a house, a rocket), but don't emphasise such modelling as the main purpose of the activity.)

– Invite the child to work independently with the solids in this way.

– Later, the child spontaneously experiments with combining the Geometric Solids as presented.

(3) The Bases

– Ask the child to spread a floor mat and say that you want to show something else that can be done with the Geometric Solids.

– Name the Geometric Solids Bases, show where they are kept, and place them on the floor mat with the basket of Geometric Solids.

– Show the child that you can continue to explore the relationships between the solids, as in exercise (2), by comparing them to, and placing them on and against, the Bases which coincide with their plane surfaces. For each solid with one or more plane surfaces (meaning everything but the sphere, ovoid and ellipsoid), first simply stand the solid in its tallest position on top of the Base which is the same shape as its bottom. Then, leaving the solid on that Base, show how other Bases, the same shape or another shape, can fit against the solid's other plane surfaces. Place as many Bases as will fit against the solid's sides: the cube, for example, will have a square under it and squares against two of its sides; the pyramid, for example, will have a square under it and the isosceles triangle against one of its sides.
– Offer the child a turn, and encourage experimentation, with the child trying different Bases against all the various sides of each of the six solids that have at least one plane surface.
– Then show the child how the curved sides of the cone and cylinder, and none of the sides of the sphere, ovoid or ellipsoid, seem to fit well against any of the Bases. Let the child test this. Point out, then, that the cone, for example, held up next to the isosceles triangle Base, 'has no isosceles triangle on the outside, but does have an isosceles triangle on the inside', and that the sphere, for example, held up to the circle Base, 'has no circle on the outside, but does have a circle on the inside'. Show that the ovoid and ellipsoid also can be seen to have a circle inside, when viewed from their ends.
– Invite the child to experiment independently with the solids and the Bases.
– Later, the child spontaneously puts the Geometric Solids and their Bases out on a floor mat to work with as presented.

(4) Families of Shapes
 – Ask the child to spread a floor mat and to place the basket of Geometric Solids on it. Say that you will now do something new with the solids.
 – Show the child that by feeling the shapes stereognostically, they can be divided into three families: those with only plane surfaces (cube, rectangular prism, triangular prism, pyramid); those with only a curved surface (sphere, ovoid, ellipsoid), and those with some flat and some curved surfaces (cone, cylinder). Place all the solids out on the mat, avert your eyes to emphasise your use of the stereognostic sense, feel each solid to determine which family it belongs to, and place it in an isolated group on the mat with others of that family. Invite the child to feel the solids in each family, and replace them in the basket.
 – Offer the child a turn at sorting the solids into families.
 – Later, the child routinely sorts the solids as presented, after doing exercise (1), (2) or (3).

(5) Naming the Solids
 – After much experience with the above activities, teach the names of the Geometric Solids, three at a time, one from each family, by Three Stage Lesson. In each stage, the child stereognostically feels the solid, rather than just looks at it or points to it, whenever it is identified. Begin each lesson by selecting one from each family, after the child has sorted them one day as in exercise (4). (Again, the names of the nine solids are: cube, rectangular prism, triangular prism, pyramid, cone, cylinder, sphere, ovoid and ellipsoid.)

(6) Stereognostic Perception
 – As the child is learning the names of the Geometric Solids in exercise (5), do the following with the shapes the child has learned so far.
 – Ask the child to spread a floor mat. Place on it the basket of solids. Show where you keep the large, opaque square of fine fabric, and place it on the mat next to the basket. (Remove from the basket, and place in a far corner of the mat, any shapes the child has not yet learned the names of in exercise (5).)
 – Spread the piece of fabric over the basket so that it completely covers its contents. Say, 'I wonder what I can feel in the basket.' Avert your eyes, reach under the cloth with both hands, say for example, 'I think I've got the cube', take it out, look at it, excitedly acknowledge visually that it is the cube, and hand it to the child to feel. Put the cube back in the basket and repeat with a different solid.
 – Invite the child to reach in under the fabric, identify a solid, say what it is, and take it out to look at. Feel the solid that the child brings out, and place it back in the basket, putting it under some of the other solids.
 – After this has been played for a while, request the child stereognostically to find, and take out of the basket from under the fabric cover, a particular solid that you name. (If the child takes out the wrong solid, do not point this out, but allow the child to recognise the shape visually, and realise whether it was wrong or right. If the child is confused in the visual identification of any solid, include it in the next Three Stage Lesson given in exercise (5).) Feel the solid the child brings out, and replace it in the basket. Repeat these requests as long as the child likes.
 – Repeat this presentation, on other days, adding solids the child has newly learned by Three Stage Lesson in exercise (5).
 – Then do the presentation with the child asking you for particular solids to retrieve, steognostically, from under the fabric cover. Let the child feel the solid you have taken out, before putting it back.
 – Later, when the names of all the Geometric Solids have been

learned, the child spontaneously takes out the basket of solids and the fabric cover, and independently identifies each covered solid by feeling it, or finds a particular solid by feeling through them all.

(7) Surface Patterns
   – Invite a child with experience in all the previous Geometric Solids exercises to lay a floor mat and place the basket of solids on it.
   – Name the trays and the container of fine sand, show where they are kept, and place one tray and the container on the mat.
   – Show the child how to empty the sand onto the tray, how to spread the sand evenly over the tray with your fingers, and how to tap the underside of the tray to give the sand a smooth surface.
   – Take one solid from the basket, place it on the sand at one end of the tray, and gently flip (if its surfaces are all planes) or roll (if it has any curved surface) the solid across the tray, leaving a patterned track in the sand. Excitedly examine this pattern with the child.
   – Lift the solid slightly off the tray, shake it and dust it with your fingers to remove all the sand, and place it back in the basket. Smooth the sand again by tapping the underside of the tray, as before.
   – Invite the child to select another solid to try, and repeat the above process. Again closely examine the track with the child.
   – Offer the child a turn.
   – Allow the child to work in this way with each of the solids in the sand, one at a time.
   – When finished, get the other tray, pour the sand from the full tray's corner back into the container, holding them both over the other tray. Pour any spill on the second tray into the container, holding them both over the first tray.
   – Later, the child independently makes tracks in the sand with the Geometric Solids, as above, and when finished, puts the materials neatly away.

Stereognostic Bags

To refine further the child's stereognostic sense. **Aim**

Three cloth bags with cord ties, with contents as follows. Bag 1 **Material**
contains twenty wooden blocks: ten cubes (2.5 centimetres (cm) on each edge) and ten rectangular prisms (2.5 x 5 x 1 cm). Bag 2 contains sixteen buttons: four buttons 3 cm in diameter, four buttons 2.5 cm in diameter, four buttons 1.8 cm in diameter, and four buttons 1.5 cm in diameter; each set of four is a slightly different shape. Bag 3 contains sixteen beads: four small beads

with large holes, four beads the same size as the first set but with small holes, four elongated beads, and four very small beads.
The blindfold with folded tissues.

Presentation   – Name the Stereognostic Bags and show where they are kept.
– Ask the child to spread a table mat, and to bring the blindfold with two folded tissues.
– Place Bag 1 on the mat, untie it, hold its bottom corners, and gently empty the twenty wooden blocks into the middle of the mat. Place the bag in the far left corner of the mat.
– Select a cube, feel it carefully, with two hands, in the manner of the GEOMETRIC SOLIDS (see exercise (1) of that activity), and place it in the front left corner of the mat. Select a rectangular prism, feel it, and place it in the front right corner of the mat.
– Put on the blindfold with a tissue inside it. Pick up one of the blocks in the centre of the mat. Determine stereognostically whether it is a cube or a rectangular prism, feeling it carefully with your fingers. Hold the block with one hand, and with the other hand quickly feel the cube and then the rectangular prism in the front corners of the mat, to remind yourself which is where. Place the new block in the corner with the one it matches.

– Repeat for each block in the middle of the mat, until all the contents of the bag have been sorted into a group of cubes in the front left corner and a group of rectangular prisms in the front right corner.
– Remove the blindfold to check the sorting visually.
– Mix up the blocks again in the middle of the mat, place a cube in the front left corner of the mat, place a rectangular prism in the front right corner, and offer the child a turn at sorting them with the blindfold on.

Exercises   (1) The child independently sorts the contents of Stereognostic Bag 1, wearing the blindfold.
(2) Show the child how to sort the contents of Stereognostic Bag 2, with the blindfold on. Follow the same general process used in exercise (1), except: start by placing one of each kind of button in a widely-spaced row along the front edge of the mat; feel a button from the mixed-up group, with one hand only, and with the other hand quickly touch each of the buttons along the front of the mat to remind yourself which kind is where. After you have sorted them all, mix them again in the centre of the mat, make a row of four types in the front, and offer the child a turn.

Later, the child independently sorts the contents of Stereognostic Bag 2, wearing the blindfold.
(3) The child sorts the contents of Stereognostic Bag 3, with the blindfold on, following the same procedure used in exercise (2).
(4) If a child especially enjoys stereognostic sorting, make up a

special stereognostic bag with four kinds of commonly used coins, to be sorted by the child, with the blindfold on, as in exercise (2).

Mystery Bag

Aim
To give the child an opportunity to apply the stereognostic sense to the exploration and identification of unknowns.

Material
A cloth bag with a cord tie, containing eight small, interesting objects, which you rotate, each week, from a store of about fifty such objects. These objects should be tiny things that the child commonly has contact with, or tiny doll's-house-size versions of familiar large items. (These objects may include, for example: a seashell, a tiny padlock, a coin, a spinning top, a torch light bulb, a small doll's-house furnishing (such as a frying pan or a rolling pin), a doll's tennis racket, a plastic pencil sharpener, a fancy button, a key ring, a large metal screw (with a rounded top and a blunt end), a ribbon, a wooden spool, a nut and bolt, a tiny toy animal.)

Presentation

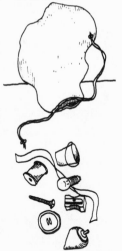

- Name the Mystery Bag, show where it is kept, ask the child to spread a table mat, and place the bag on the mat.
- Position the bag with the open end facing you, and carefully untie its cord.
- Reach one hand into the bag, averting your eyes (perhaps looking at the child), and grasp hold of one object. Excitedly say, 'Oh! I've got something! I wonder what it is!'
- Still holding the object and leaving your hand inside the bag, stereognostically examine the object, showing puzzlement, concentration and then realisation as you say what the object is.
- Remove the object from the bag and look at it to verify your guess.
- Repeat with a second object.
- Invite the child to finish identifying the objects in the bag, in the same way. Sit with the child to share in the surprise and help sustain interest.
- When finished, refill the bag with these eight objects, and offer the child a turn.

Exercise
(1) The child independently works with the Mystery Bag as in the presentation, finding new objects in it every week.

Sorting Grains

Aim
Further refinement of the child's stereognostic sense.

Material
Two trays, each with a bowl in the centre and three small cups in a row along one edge. Each of the six cups contains about fifteen of a particular type of whole dried grain, pea or bean. On one

tray, one cup contains corn kernels, another cup contains dried peas, and the third cup, dried lentils. On the second tray, one cup has uncooked rice, another has whole barley, and the third cup, whole wheat grains.

The blindfold and folded tissues.

Presentation
– Name the trays for Sorting Grains, and show where they are kept.
– Show which tray has the larger grains (like the corn kernels) and which has the smaller grains (like the rice).
– Place the tray with the larger grains on a table, positioned so that the edge with the cups is nearest you. Ask the child to put the blindfold and two tissues on the mat also.
– Sensitise your fingers and have the child do the same (see SENSITISING THE FINGERS).
– Show how to feel each of the grains between your thumb, index finger, and middle finger, and offer the child a turn feeling one grain from each bowl.
– Place about three grains from each cup into the bowl in the middle of the tray, transferring them singly.

– Put on the blindfold with a tissue inside. With one hand, pick up one grain from the bowl, identify it stereognostically, with the other hand quickly feel the three types of grains in the cups to remind yourself which kind is where, and put the grain selected from the bowl into its appropriate cup.
– Repeat the sorting for each grain in the bowl.
– Remove the blindfold to check the sorting visually.
– Again place about three grains from each cup into the bowl in the middle of the tray, transferring them singly. Offer the child a turn at wearing the blindfold and sorting.
– When the child is done, invite the child to check the sorting visually and to fix any mistakes.

Exercises
(1) The child independently sorts the larger grains, wearing the blindfold, as in the presentation, but putting five grains from each cup into the bowl.
(2) The child independently sorts the smaller grains, wearing the blindfold, as in exercise (1).

Visual Work with Blindfold

Aim   To apply the child's newly developed stereognostic sense to familiar activities previously guided primarily by sight.

Materials   The PINK TOWER, RED RODS, BROWN STAIR, CYLINDER BLOCKS and GEOMETRIC CABINET.
The blindfold and folded tissues.

Presentation:
– Ask a child who has had much experience with the four previous stereognostic activities, and much experience with the Sensorial Activities listed above, to get the blindfold and two

folded tissues, as you have something new to show.
- Repeat the presentation for one of the above activities, following exactly the same process as the original presentation, except: put on and continue to wear the blindfold once everything has been laid out for use; and do not, as you had in the original presentation, involve the child in the process.
- Emphasise the importance of organising the material, so that you know exactly where everything is, before putting on the blindfold.
- When you complete the presentation, remove the blindfold and check your work visually.
- After the presentation, invite the child to try the activity with the blindfold. If the child is reluctant to try it, do not insist.
- On other days, do similar blindfolded presentations for each of the activities listed above.

(1) The child conducts exercise (1) of each activity listed above, **Exercise**
in the familiar way, but wearing the blindfold, as in the above presentation.

    Later, the child works blindfolded and stereognostically with most of the other exercises previously done visually with these materials, except those exercises in which the mats are placed at a distance and the GEOMETRIC CABINET exercises using the cards.

Baric Sense

Baric Tablets
To help awaken and develop the child's baric sense.   **Aim**

A wooden box with a lid, containing three sets of six identical **Material**
wooden tablets. Each set of six tablets is made from a different kind of wood, so that the tablets in one set each weigh about 9 grams, the tablets in another set each weigh about 18 grams, and the tablets in the third set each weigh about 27 grams. All eighteen tablets are precisely the same size and shape, and are finished to the same smoothness. Because they are different types of wood, the sets of tablets are also different in colour.

    (DIY hint: If you are cutting the tablets yourself, use balsam, pine and walnut or mahogany, to get the three different weights; these woods are readily available from hobby shops and wood stores.)

- Name the Baric Tablets and show where they are kept.   **Presentation**
- Wash your hands with soap and water (as finger oils will be absorbed by the woods, which can change the weights of the tablets), and ask the child to do the same.

– Ask the child to spread a table mat and to place the blindfold and two folded tissues on it.

– Put the box of Baric Tablets in the far right corner of the mat.

– Remove the six 9 gram tablets singly from the box, placing them in a neat pile (lengthwise far and near) at the front of the mat.

– Remove the six 27 gram tablets singly from the box, placing them in a neat pile (lengthwise far and near) just to the right of the first pile.

– Take a tablet from the 9 gram pile in your left hand, and a tablet from the 27 gram pile in your right hand. Hold each tablet balanced on your fingertips, which are facing upward, keeping your arms relaxed, your palms up, and your thumbs free. Then avert your eyes (perhaps looking at the child), and gently and slightly lift and relax your arms (from the elbow), several times, to perceive, by the slight difference in resistance to your muscles, the relative weights of the tablets.

– Place them on the mat for the child to pick up, and invite the child to feel the weights of the tablets by exactly the same method.

– Now mix up all the tablets, in a random arrangement in the middle of the mat, each tablet flat on the mat. Using your baric sense, sort the tablets into two piles, as follows.

– Avert your eyes and pick up any two of the mixed-up tablets (or ask the child to hand them to you) without your seeing which kind of wood they are, and balance them on your fingers, as before.

– Feel the comparative weights of the tablets.

If the weights feel the same, say, 'These feel the same.' Put one of the tablets back among the mixed-up tablets. Without looking, pick up a different tablet from among them (or ask the child to hand one to you), and again feel the comparative weights of the two tablets in your hands. If they are still the same, return one and select another. Continue ur.'il the two weights feel different.

When you have two tablets whose weights feel different, say, 'These feel different.' Put the lighter one on your left at the front of the mat, and put the heavier one on your right.

– Repeat this random selection and comparative weighing process, thereby sorting, without looking, the mixed-up tablets into a 9 gram pile on the left and a 27 gram pile on the right. Occasionally invite the child to balance and weigh a selected pair after you, to verify your judgement about their relative weights.

– When all the tablets have been placed on one or the other pile, turn your eyes back towards the mat to see how well you have sorted the piles, each of which should contain six of the same colour tablets.

– Again mix up all the tablets, in a random arrangement in the middle of the mat. Invite the child to do the sorting, in the same way, with eyes open but averted.

– Afterwards, again mix up the tablets, and repeat the sorting process with the blindfold on, going right through without inviting the child to verify any of your judgements. Remove the blindfold and examine how well you sorted.
– Invite the child to try the sorting with the blindfold on, but do not pressure a reluctant child.

Exercises

(1) The child independently sorts the 9 gram tablets from the 27 gram tablets as in the presentation, with or without the blindfold. After some experience without the blindfold, encourage the child to try it with the blindfold. Sit with the child using the blindfold for the first time, to promote a feeling of security.
(2) The same as exercise (1), but the child sorts the 9 gram tablets from the 18 gram tablets, putting the lighter tablets on the left and the heavier on the right, as before.
(3) The same as exercise (1), but the child sorts the 18 gram tablets from the 27 gram tablets, putting the lighter tablets on the left and the heavier on the right, as before.
(4) The child simultaneously sorts all three sets of tablets, using a pairing process. Before putting on the blindfold, the child places one tablet from each set on the mat as a 'reference': a 9 gram tablet in the front left corner, an 18 gram tablet at the centre of the front edge of the mat, and a 27 gram tablet in the front right corner. Only one tablet is selected from the mixed-up tablets, and it is then compared to each of the 'reference' tablets, in turn, from left to right. When two tablets feel the same, the randomly selected tablet is put just behind the 'reference' tablet on the mat, eventually making a pile of five matching tablets behind each 'reference' tablet.
(5) Give Three Stage Lessons on the following relative terms for the perception of the weight of things.

  Use a 9 gram tablet and a 27 gram tablet to introduce the terms 'light' and 'heavy'.

  Later, give lessons on the comparatives and superlatives of these terms, using an 18 gram tablet and a 9 gram tablet to teach 'light' and its comparative 'lighter', and using an 18 gram tablet and a 27 gram tablet to teach 'heavy' and its comparative 'heavier'. Then use one from each set of tablets to teach the comparative and superlative: one day teach 'light', 'lighter' and 'lightest'; another day, use the same tablets to teach 'heavy', 'heavier' and 'heaviest'.

HEARING

Sound Boxes

Aim

To help develop the child's auditory sense, especially the perception of the relative loudness or softness of sounds.

Material

Two wooden Sound Boxes, one with a red lid and the other with a blue lid. In each box are six hollow, wooden cylinders with plastic non-removable caps the same colour as the box lid, each cylinder containing a different granular material that makes a different pitch and volume of sound when shaken (e.g. dried whole peas, dried lentils, dried barley, uncooked rice, coarse sand and fine white sand). The contents of the cylinders in one box precisely match those of the other box.

(DIY hint: Instead of the specially-made wooden cylinders, use twelve identical small, plastic, cylindrical containers, such as those in which baking powder, baking soda or yeast are often packaged. For every two containers, put exactly the same amount of one of the above ingredients in each (actually counting the grains or weighing the sand to be sure they match). Permanently glue the lids on each container. Paint all the containers white, the tops of one set of six blue, and the tops of its matching set red. Store them in two cardboard boxes, with their lids painted appropriately.)

Presentation

– Pre-arrange the cylinders in the red Sound Box so that the one with the largest particles (the loudest when shaken) and the one with the finest particles (the softest when shaken) are in positions in the box that you will remember.
– Name the Sound Boxes, show where they are kept, and ask the child to spread a table mat.
– Place the blue Sound Box in the far right corner of the mat, and the red Sound Box in the far left corner.
– Open the red box, place the red lid under the box, locate the loudest red cylinder (in its pre-arranged position), lift it out by its top, and place it on the mat in front of yourself.
– Show the child how to hold the cylinder by its middle between the thumb and fingers of one hand. Hold the cylinder this way a few inches from one ear and give it two sharp shakes downward, listening intently to the sound this makes. Then hold it a few inches from the other ear and again give it two sharp shakes downward, fixing the sound in your memory. Replace the cylinder on the mat.
– Invite the child to shake the loudest red cylinder in precisely the same way and to listen to the sound.
– Place this loud red cylinder on the left side of the mat.
– Locate in the box the softest sounding red cylinder (in its pre-arranged position), lift it out by its top, and place it on the mat in front of you. Shake this softest red cylinder as above, invite the child to do the same, and place it on the left side of the mat near the loudest red cylinder.
– Repeat with each of the other red cylinders, making a group of six randomly arranged red-top cylinders on the mat's left side.
– Now place the blue lid under its box, remove the blue cylinders, tell the child that 'these sound the same as the red ones', and place them in a group on the right side of the mat.

– Select any cylinder from the red group and place it in front of yourself. Then select any cylinder from the blue group and place it just to the right of the red one.

– Shake the red one, as before, and then the blue one. If they sound different in pitch or loudness, place the blue one into the blue-lid box to isolate it.

– Repeat until a blue cylinder is found that sounds exactly the same as the red one, and say, 'These sound the same.'

– Invite the child to shake the matched cylinders, one at a time, to confirm the match.

– Place the matched pair in the centre of the far edge of the mat, with the red one on the left and the blue on the right. Return the blue cylinders in the box to the group on the right.

– Invite the child to select another red cylinder to pair.

– Repeat the pairing process until all the cylinders are in matched pairs. After each pair is found, invite the child to shake and hear them one at a time, and place the pair in front of the other matched pairs, making a column of pairs down the centre of the mat. When all twelve cylinders have been paired, shake each matched pair in turn, one cylinder at a time, from far to near, and invite the child to do the same.

– Separate the six pairs into red and blue groups as before, and offer the child a turn at pairing them.

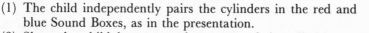

Exercises

(1) The child independently pairs the cylinders in the red and blue Sound Boxes, as in the presentation.

(2) Show the child how to grade one set of six cylinders, as follows.

Begin with the closed Sound Boxes arranged as at the start of exercise (1). Place the red cylinders in a randomly arranged row from left to right at the centre of the mat. Shake each cylinder in the row as many times as needed, in order to determine which is the loudest. If necessary, repeatedly compare two or three that seem close. Remove the loudest cylinder from the row and place it in front of the empty red box next to the left edge of the mat.

Of the remaining five cylinders in the row, again determine which is the loudest, repeatedly comparing if necessary. Place this next loudest cylinder just in front of the first loudest along the left edge of the mat. Hear the loudest, then the second loudest, and invite the child to do the same.

Repeat this process of finding the loudest and adding it to the front of the column along the left edge of the mat, hearing the sequence with the child after each new cylinder is added. Continue until all six cylinders have been graded.

Leave the graded row in place, take the blue cylinders out of their box, place them in a randomly arranged row at the centre of the mat, and offer the child a turn at grading the blue set, in a column along the right edge of the mat, in front of the empty blue Sound Box. When this is done, show the child how to check the sequence of blue cylinders against the sequence of red cylinders, by shaking each corresponding pair in turn (one cylinder at a time) from far to near.

(If the child shows great difficulty grading the six cylinders, give the same presentation another day, but only take out three cylinders of each colour: the loudest, a middle one, and the softest. On other days, repeat the presentation, adding one of the other middle cylinders each time.)

Later, the child independently grades both sets of cylinders, as in the presentation, and checks them against each other.

(3) Give Three Stage Lessons on the following relative terms for the auditory perception of the volume of a sound.

Use the second-loudest blue cylinder together with the second-softest blue cylinder to introduce the concept of 'loud' and 'soft'.

Later, give lessons on the comparatives and superlatives of these terms, using the third-from-loudest blue cylinder with the second-loudest blue cylinder to teach 'loud' and its comparative 'louder', and the third-from-softest blue cylinder with a second-softest blue cylinder to teach 'soft' and its comparative 'softer'. Then use the three loudest red cylinders or the three softest red cylinders to teach both the comparative and superlative (e.g. 'loud', 'louder', 'loudest').

(4) The blue set of cylinders is placed on a table mat, and the red set is placed in a random arrangement on a table mat a considerable distance away. Isolate one of the blue cylinders for the child to shake and hear, and ask the child to leave the blue cylinder where it is and to go alone to the other mat to 'get the red cylinder which sounds the same'. Direct the child to compare the blue cylinder and selected red cylinder, show appreciation for a correct match, and ask the child to return the red cylinder to the distant mat. Repeat as long as the child is having fun.

(5) Arrange two mats and the blue and red cylinders as at the start of exercise (4). Isolate one of the middle-loudness blue cylinders, invite the child to shake and hear it, and ask the child to go alone to the other mat and to bring back a red cylinder that is 'louder' (or 'softer'), without taking the blue cylinder along. The child compares the selected red cylinder to the isolated blue one, you show appreciation for a correct choice, and the child returns the red cylinder to the far mat. Repeat as long as the child likes.

(6) Later, repeat exercise (5), but ask for the red cylinder which is the 'next louder' or 'next softer'.

(7) Stand behind a screen and produce familiar noises with familiar objects, and ask the child to identify the object or activity. Begin with noises that are easily distinguishable (e.g. ringing a bell, knocking on wood, blowing a whistle) and gradually make quieter, more subtle sounds (e.g. cutting paper, yawning, inflating a balloon).

(8) The child sits (or a group of children sit) silently, with eyes closed. While you slowly move a ticking clock through the air, holding it at various heights and positions around the room, the child is asked to point continuously to where the ticking sound is coming from.

Bells

Aim

To help develop the child's auditory sense, especially the perception of tones. Indirectly, to prepare the child for music, since each set of thirteen bells corresponds to one octave of musical notes.

Material

A long wooden board, painted with thirteen black and white stripes in the pattern of a piano keyboard, one octave from C to C. (From left to right, the stripes are coloured: white, black, white, black, white, white, black, white, black, white, black, white and white.) This board is kept on a low table that the child can work at comfortably while standing, and it is situated on the table lengthwise left and right, about 15 cm back from the front edge of the table.

On each of the board's thirteen stripes rests, one in front and one in back, two hemisphere-shaped bells on wooden stems with wooden stands, making two rows, running left and right, of thirteen bells each. The tone of each bell is the same as the tone of the piano note which would correspond to the stripe on which the bell rests. The base of each bell's stand is exactly the width and about half the length of the stripe. The stem and stand of each of the thirteen bells in the back row are painted black or white to match the stripe on which the bell rests. The stems and stands of the thirteen bells in the front row are left their natural brown colour.

A wooden striker, made of a long, thin wooden dowel stuck in the end of a short, thick piece of dowel.

A damper, which is a flat stick with a small piece of thick felt glued on one surface at one end.

Preliminary Presentations

(a) Name the Bells and show the table on which they are kept. Show how to carry a bell in the upright position only, with one hand gripping the stem, and the other hand beneath the base. Say, 'We have to be so careful, because if a bell drops, it will always sound different than it should, and it can never be used again.'

(b) Show how to hold the striker in one hand and the damper in the other (but not yet how to strike a bell). Each is held hanging down, perpendicular to the floor, by the three 'writing fingers' (thumb, index and middle) extended forward.

(c) Show how to strike a single bell isolated on the table, using a free, gentle, but precise wrist movement to swing the hanging striker against the bell's lower rim.

(d) Show how to strike a bell isolated on the table and then hold it up to each ear in turn, until the sound fades. Listen to each of the thirteen brown bells this way, offering the child a turn for each bell.

(e) Strike a bell left in its place on the striped board and show how to stop the sound by gently placing the felt pad of the damper against the bell's lower rim. Listen to each of the thirteen brown bells this way, selecting them in a random order, leaving them in place on the board, and offering the child a turn for each bell.

Presentations (1) Remove from the Bells table, one at a time, each black bell as well as the brown bell directly in front it, and place these ten bells on a table or on a shelf elsewhere in the room.

– Invite the child to stand at the table with the remaining white and corresponding brown bells on the board.

– Select three brown bells contrasting in tone (low C, F and B, for example, which can be identified by their position on the piano keyboard pattern), and place them together, in a mixed up order, in the centre of the space on the table in front of the board.

– Take up the striker, strike the white bell behind one of the three new empty spaces, and listen carefully to the sound. Then strike one of the three removed brown bells. If the tones heard do not match, remove the brown bell just struck to the far right corner of the table.

– Strike the same white bell again, and try a second brown bell.

– Repeat until you find the match. Invite the child to strike each bell of the matched pair. Place the brown bell back in front of its matching white one, and return the rejected brown ones, in the far right corner of the table, to the centre of the space in front of the board.

– Now strike the white bell behind one of the remaining empty spaces, find its matching brown bell as before, and invite the child to strike the matched pair.

– Check that the remaining third pair of bells matches, and replace the last brown one on the board.

(2) Another day, repeat the presentation with three new pairs of clearly contrasting bells.

(3) Another day, do the presentation with another three pairs (re-using a pair used before).

(4) Another day, do the presentation with all eight brown bells mixed up on the front edge of the table.

– Start with any white bell, and match all eight pairs in random order, inviting the child to select which white bell to match next and which brown bell to try. Also allow the child to remove the rejected brown bells to the far right corner, to verify each matched pair, and to put the selected brown bell back on the board in front of its corresponding white one. Except when the child verifies a match, you should continue to wield the striker.

– After you have completed the matching, again remove all eight brown bells (or any lesser number if the child does not seem ready for eight) from the board, place them in a random order in the space in front, and invite the child to pair by the same process, but without your help. When finished, invite the child to check the pairing by a comparison of the tone of each white bell, selected in random order, with the tone of the brown bell in front of it.

(1) When the black bells and their corresponding brown ones are put away, the child goes to the Bells table and independently matches eight or less white bells, in random order, to mixed-up brown ones, as in the presentation.

(2) With the black bells and their corresponding brown ones put away, the child matches all eight white bells, in sequence from left to right (low tone to high tone), to mixed-up brown ones. The matching follows the same process as exercise (1), except: it is started with the extreme left white bell and continues along the board to the right; after each matched brown bell is returned to the board, the child strikes every brown bell on the board from left to right and lastly the next white bell to be matched.

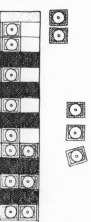

(3) With the black bells and their corresponding brown ones put away, show the child, as follows, how to mix up the remaining eight brown bells, and then grade them, using only the ear as a guide.

Place the eight brown bells in a random arrangement in the space in front of the board. Striking each of the brown bells several times, isolate the one with the extreme lowest tone, compare it again to one or two closest in tone, and place it in the extreme left space on the board. Continue finding the lowest tone bell remaining and placing it in the extreme left vacant space on the board. Each time a brown bell is returned to the board, strike every brown bell from left to right. When all eight bells are back on the board, invite the child to strike each white and brown pair from left to right, to verify the grading.

Later, the child independently grades the eight brown bells as you have done.

(4) With the five black bells and their corresponding brown ones returned to the black stripes on the board, and now with the eight white bells and their corresponding brown ones put away, the child matches the black bells, in random order, to mixed-up brown ones, as in exercise (1).

(5) With the white bells and their corresponding brown ones put away, the child matches the five black bells, in sequence from left to right (low tone to high tone), to mixed-up brown ones, as in exercise (2).

(6) With the white bells and their corresponding brown ones put away, the child mixes up the remaining five brown bells, and grades them using only the ear as a guide, as in exercise (3).

TASTE

Tasting Cups

Aim   To help develop the child's perception of taste, and to introduce the four basic tastes (sweet, acid, bitter and salty).

Material   A tray on which rests, in a column, four pairs of small, white ceramic cups, each containing a plastic dropper (preferably with an angled tip) and a small amount of liquid as described below.
Also, a tray with paper cups and a jug of fresh drinking water.

Preparation   Fresh solutions to be tasted must be put out for each use. Just before a presentation or when the child is ready to do an exercise, fill each pair of cups halfway with a different tasting liquid, either sweet, acid, bitter or salty, fill the jug with fresh drinking water, and place out two new paper cups. Keep separate supplies of the tasting liquids, made fresh each week, in the refrigerator. The sweet liquid is sugar in water, the acid is vinegar in water, the bitter is a tiny bit of quinine in water, and the salty is a little table salt in water. The solutions should all be nearly clear, and diluted to the point where they taste distinct but not strong. The eight cups are arranged in a column of four pairs, each pair with matching liquids.

Presentation   – Prepare the material as described above.
– Name the tray of Tasting Cups and show where it is kept.

– Place on a table the tray with the eight cups (with the column of four pairs running far and near), and the tray with the water jug and paper cups.
– Move the left one of each pair of ceramic cups onto the table to the left of the tray. Fill the two paper cups with water.
– Show the child how to take one drop of liquid into the dropper from one of the ceramic cups to the left of the tray, and how to let that drop fall directly onto your tongue, without allowing the dropper to touch your tongue or any part of your mouth. Taste each of the four liquids on the table in this way, taking a sip of water from your paper cup after all four have been tasted.
– Invite the child to taste the four liquids in the same way, but make sure that the sweet one is tasted first. Remind the child to take a sip of water from the other paper cup afterwards.
– Place the four cups still on the tray in a mixed-up group on the table to the right side of the tray, saying, 'These taste the same as the others.'
– Select one ceramic cup from the left group and one cup from the right group, and place them respectively left and right in front of the tray. Taste the left one, then the right one. If they tasted different, say, 'these taste different', isolate the right cup on the table beyond the far side of the tray, and invite the child to put another cup from the right group in front of the tray. Take a sip of water. Continue comparing tastes until you find a matching

pair, say, 'these taste the same', and offer the child a taste of each to verify the match. Move the matched pair of cups to the far end of the tray. Return the rejected cups to the right side of the tray.

– Repeat until all four pairs have been matched, re-making the column of four matching pairs.
– Taste each pair in turn, from far to near, sipping water after each pair is tried, and invite the child to do the same.
– Separate the cups into two groups again, and offer the child a turn at matching them.
– When done, firmly emphasise to the child that, 'Before you can do tasting, you must ask me to fill the cups for you. Never taste anything unless I give it to you!'

(1) The child asks you to prepare the Tasting Cups and the drinking water tray, and independently separates the cups into two groups and pairs them, as in the presentation. **Exercises**
(2) Using one of each matching pair of Tasting Cups, give a Three Stage Lesson on the names of the four tastes: 'sweet', 'acid', 'bitter' and 'salty'.

SMELL

Smelling Boxes
To help awaken and refine the child's olfactory sense, and to help make the child aware of the wide variety of odours and fragrances in the environment. **Aim**

Two wooden boxes with lids, each containing six opaque, cylindrical, plastic containers with removable perforated tops and screw-on plastic caps. The contents of the cylinders in one box match those of the other box, and each set includes six different, natural, volatile substances with distinct scents (e.g. spices, herbal cosmetic oils, perfume oils, dried fruits or flowers). **Material**

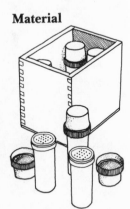

(DIY hint: For the containers, try those black plastic containers used to store 35 mm photographic film. Because they do not have a perforated top under the cap to hide the substance being smelled, put the substance beneath a ball of cotton wool, or if it is a volatile liquid, dab a ball of cotton wool in it; this way, all one sees when looking into any of the containers is the white cotton wool. Use cardboard boxes instead of wood.)

– Name the Smelling Boxes and show where they are kept. **Presentation**
– Ask the child to spread a table mat. Place one box in the far left corner of the mat and the other box in the far right corner.
– Select one cylinder from the left box, show the child how to unscrew the cap, hold the cylinder in front of your chest, and breathe through your nose deeply while moving the cylinder slightly to the left and right. Offer the child a turn at smelling the contents of the cylinder, and replace the cap.

– Select a second cylinder with a contrasting scent from the left box, smell it as above, offer the child a turn, and replace the cap.

– Repeat with each of the other four cylinders in the left box, making a group of six randomly arranged cylinders on the left side of the mat.

– Remove the cylinders from the right box, say, 'these smell the same as the others', and place them in a group on the right side of the mat.

– Select a cylinder from each group and place them on the mat in front of yourself, keeping them respectively on the left and right.

– Smell the left one, as above, and then the right one. If they smell different, say so, and isolate the right one in its box in the right corner.

– Repeat until a cylinder on the right is found to match the one selected from the left, say, 'these smell the same', and invite the child to smell the pair to confirm the match. Place the matched pair in the centre of the far end of the mat, with the boxes on either side. Return the rejected cylinders in the right box to their group on the right.

– Invite the child to select another cylinder from the left to pair, and to match this cylinder to one from the group on the right, as above.

– Repeat the pairing process until all the cylinders are matched in a column of pairs down the centre of the mat. Smell each matched pair in turn, from far to near, and invite the child to do the same.

– Separate the six pairs into left and right groups, as before, and offer the child a turn at pairing them.

Exercises (1) The child independently matches the cylinders in one Smelling Box to the cylinders in the other Smelling Box, as in the presentation.

(2) If the child is interested, give two Three Stage Lessons on the general names of the materials in each cylinder, using just the cylinders in one box.

(3) Place out the cylinders from one box on a table mat and those from the other box on a table mat a considerable distance away. At the first mat, isolate one cylinder for the child to smell, and ask the child to find the matching cylinder on the distant mat, to bring it back to verify the match, and to return it again to the distant mat. Continue as long as the child enjoys it.

(4) Make up a Smelling Box of special cylinders which coincide with actual materials in the accessible environment, especially the outdoor environment. Present these cylinders one at a time, and ask the child, 'Can you find something nearby which smells like this?'

(5) Explore and point out to one another scents in the garden or on an outdoor walk.

4 LANGUAGE ACTIVITIES

INTRODUCTION

The main purpose of language is to communicate, that is, to let others know what we are thinking. If the others are standing directly in front of us, and we want to let them know what we are thinking, our natural inclination is to speak (or if they cannot hear us, to make signs with our hands). However, if we want to save what we are thinking for our own later use, or for others at some distant time or place, or if what we are thinking may be of general interest to everyone, then speaking will not suffice. Our voices can reach only so far and they will resound only so long. The problem is how to give speech permanence.

One solution some cultures have adopted is to construct an oral tradition, such as a memorable story or song which can be taught to others, so they can repeat it often or teach it again to people they know, including their children. Many cultures have also utilised another logical solution: representing the sounds of speech in permanent visual or tactile images, so that anyone who learns to translate those images back into sounds may conveniently 'hear the speech' at any time. Written languages have always consisted of such phonetic symbols.

Just as speech is our natural response to wanting to communicate our thoughts, the child's acquisition of speech is a natural part of growing up human, as naturally human as learning to walk on two legs, or manipulating objects with the thumb opposing the other four fingers. A hearing child living around speaking adults will almost inevitably learn to speak in the first few years of life. But this is not true of writing and reading. Many people go through their entire lives, observing vast quantities of written material, and seeing other people reading newspapers, signs, books and letters, and they never pick up the ability to write or read.

Unlike speaking, writing and reading are not universal or natural human activities; they are instead cultural adaptations of the natural activity of speaking. Speech will develop naturally in the child; as cultural adaptations, writing and reading must be cultivated or taught. Montessori's Language Activities therefore presume that the child will spontaneously begin to speak with meaning, and the purpose of the Language Activities is largely to cultivate writing and reading. Also, since writing and reading are an adaptation of speech, the strategy Montessori uses to develop these cultural skills is to build on the sounds of which speech is made.

The earliest Language Activities prepare the child for writing and reading by first augmenting the toddler's existing speaking skills. These preparatory Language Activities may begin as soon as the child is talking with meaning in phrases and short sentences.

In the first two years of life, the young child sees, hears and experiences many things without thinking about them in a rational or descriptive way. All these hundreds or even thousands of impressions are stored up, waiting to be identified and understood. The very first Language Activity, the CLASSIFIED PICTURES, helps the young child define and organise this multitude of impressions by tying each impression to a clear and simple category. The child is then able to name these impressions, associate related ones, and distinguish unrelated ones. This early preparation is crucial to the learning of reading and writing, for two reasons. First, the world must appear organised before a child can express or receive written ideas about it. Second, until this point in the child's life, language has been used primarily as a means of relating personal needs and wants; the Classified Pictures show the child that things in the world can have being and meaning in themselves, and do not just exist in relation to the child. This awakens in the child ideas about the world that are of general interest to everyone, and these are the ideas that are worthwhile writing and reading.

The other preparatory Language Activities enhance the child's attention to and use of words in everyday speaking (see SPEECH) and train the child to hear the component sounds in all spoken words (see I SPY). At this point, the child is provided with the bridge between the spoken word and the written word: the component sounds in spoken words are individually associated with particular visual and tactile images, that is, letters (see SANDPAPER LETTERS).

After this early preparation, the activities that actually introduce writing and reading are conducted simultaneously. The reason for this is that it is easier to appreciate reading someone else's thoughts if the child has experienced the satisfaction of recording his or her own thoughts. Also, words the child has written will be readily recognised in reading, and words read often will naturally become part of the child's repertoire of words to write. Put simply, reading and writing are necessary complements to one another.

The key activity that introduces writing is the use of the MOVABLE ALPHABET. With the Movable Alphabet, the child applies the lessons of the Sandpaper Letters – that is, the association of specific sounds with particular images – to make words. A word is sounded out as in the I SPY activity, and plastic letters, shaped exactly like the Sandpaper Letters, are lined up on a mat to represent the sounds. The presentation of the Movable Alphabet stresses that writing is used to record a thought, and that a thought can be written instead of spoken. Introducing writing by means of pre-formed plastic letters allows the child to begin to express thoughts in written form before fully developing the manipulative skills needed to write with pencil and paper. While the child becomes familiar with the act of written expression, the manipulative skills of handwriting are gradually developed through the tactile tracing of the Sandpaper Letters and the creative use of the METAL INSETS, and other later activities facilitate the transition from the Movable Alphabet to blackboard writing and then to pencil and paper.

It is important to note that at this early stage of learning to write, words that the child writes are spelled phonetically, as best as the child can. The adult must refrain from making spelling corrections to the child's compositions in these activities. The child is allowed to misspell because correct spelling will come naturally with reading, and because the effort and anxiety connected with learning to spell may be enough to cancel the simple pleasures of self-expression. In these early stages, it is most important to cultivate confidence and enjoyment; there is plenty of time later for refining basic skills.

The key activity that introduces reading is the presentation of the OBJECT BOXES. The 'objects' these refer to are placed out on a table, and the child is invited to guess which of these objects you're thinking about. Then the child is given the object's written name as a clue. This approach clearly stresses that the purpose of reading is to find out another person's ideas. What makes this first introduction to reading easy for the child is that there are only a few things that you might be thinking of, and all of them are there on the table. So when it's time to sound out the word, the sounding need not be entirely accurate, since the child is all the while looking over the things, and thinking of their names. Starting to read is normally so difficult because the word which the child is struggling to pronounce could be virtually any word in the English language.

So reading and writing are introduced as fun and useful activities, which can help us understand and appreciate the world, and share ideas and experiences with other people.

EARLY PREPARATION

Classified Pictures

Aim   To help the child classify early impressions of the world into clear and simple categories, and to give these impressions and categories names. To lay an intellectual foundation for reading and writing by showing that things-in-themselves can have meaning, and that there is more to language than stating one's wants and needs.

Material   About fifteen sets of cards, each set bound by an elastic band, and all the sets stored in a box with a lid. Each set contains between ten and twenty cards, and each card has a picture on one side and a small symbol on the other side to show that the members of one set belong together. In any one set, the top card's picture is of an entire particular scene, situation or subject (e.g. kitchen, railway station, city street, birthday party, uniforms, vehicles) and each of the other pictures is of a particular item within that scene (e.g. in the kitchen: a kettle, a grater, a refrigerator).

How to Make the Material   You'll need: old magazines, colour advertisements, and store catalogues; scissors; non-toxic paper glue; about 300 plain index cards; a pen; thin elastic bands; a box with a lid.

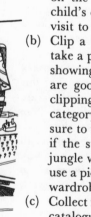

(a)   Make a list of at least fifteen scenes, situations or subjects which the child has probably seen, recording each in only one or two words. For example, most young children have had a 'bath', been at a 'birthday party', or seen a meal prepared in a 'kitchen'. If you know the child well enough, also list special situations which made a strong impression on the child, and which still sometimes come up in the child's conversation, for example, a trip to the 'airport' or a visit to the 'cinema'.

(b)   Clip a picture from an old magazine or advertisement, or take a photograph, depicting each of the scenes on your list, showing the general appearance of the entire setting. If you are good at drawing, use a colour drawing instead of a clipping or a photograph. For a subject which is more a category than a scene, picture a place where you would be sure to find lots of examples of that category. (For example: if the subject is 'wild animals', then select a picture of a jungle with animals in it; or if the subject is 'clothing', then use a picture of the inside of a clothing shop or the inside of a wardrobe.)

(c)   Collect from old magazines, printed advertisements, or store catalogues, many small clippings, each showing one common object which would be found in one of the scenes on your list. (For example, if you have 'kitchen' on your list, you can probably find a picture of a cooker, a pan, a mixer, a pinafore and a tin of soup.) If you are good at drawing, use simple colour drawings instead of clippings. Make sure that each object pictured is clearly associated with only one of your scenes. (For example, if you have both 'living room' and 'bedroom' on your list, then a picture of curtains should not be used for either, since curtains can be found in both places.) Make sure you have only one picture of each object, and collect between ten and twenty different pictures for each of the fifteen scenes on your list.

(d) Glue each picture (each picture of an entire scene and each picture of an individual object) onto a plain index card. On the back of a 'scene' card and its associated 'object' cards, lightly draw the same small symbol in the upper right corner (for example, a square, star or circle). Repeat with a different symbol for each of the other 'scene' cards and its associated 'object' cards. Put each of the sets together with an elastic band, with the picture of the entire scene on top, and store all the sets in a box with a lid.

Presentation

– Name the Classified Pictures, show where they are kept, select a set with a 'scene' that is probably very familiar to the child, and place it on a table.
– Starting with the picture of the entire scene, view each card in turn, and discuss with the child each thing pictured. Be sure to use the exact names of things (e.g. ladle, spatula, food processor). When you come to a card with a picture the child does not recognise, name and discuss it as the others, but make a mental note of it. When you are done viewing all the cards in that set, say, for example, 'all those things are found in a kitchen' or 'all those things are wild animals'.
– Show the child how to put the cards together again with the elastic band, with the 'scene' picture showing on top.
– Another day, give a Three Stage Lesson on the names of the pictures the child did not know (see Sensorial Activities for the method of a THREE STAGE LESSON).

Exercises

(1) Go through other sets of Classified Pictures with the child, as in the presentation, following the child's interests and experiences.
(2) The child looks through a set of cards independently, or with another child.
(3) The child mixes up the cards depicting individual things from two or more sets, and spreads them out picture-side-up. The 'object' cards are then sorted into piles beneath their corresponding 'scene' cards. When finished, the child turns the piles over and checks that the control marks in the upper right corners match for each pile.
(4) One day when the child has just set up to begin exercise (3), point to the spread-out pictures and say, for example, 'Can you see something found in a kitchen? Yes, what is it?' Repeat this question for the other category, saying, for example, 'Can

you see something found in an airport? Yes, what is it?'
Continue this questioning until all the pictures are sorted,
thus giving the child a chance to say the names of the objects
while sorting them.

I Spy

Aim　To make the child aware of the sounds in spoken language, and to
show how to analyse these sounds in words. (The primary sounds
in the English language: a (as pronounced in 'at'); b (as in 'sob');
c (as in 'can'); d (as in 'mud'); e (as in 'egg'); f (as in 'fun'); g (as
in 'mug'); h (as in 'hat'); i (as in 'it'); j (as in 'jump'); l (as in
'pill'); m (as in 'am'); n (as in 'an'); o (as in 'on'); p (as in 'lap'); r
(as in 'raw'); s (as in 'moss'); t (as in 'at'); u (as in 'up'); v (as in
'ever'); w (as in 'wet'); x (as in 'fox'); y (as in 'yes'); z (as in
'zoo'); ai (as in 'aim'); ee (as in 'see'); ie (as in 'pie'); oa (as in
'boat'); ue (as in 'blue'); ar (as in 'car'); er (as in 'her'); or (as in
'orbit'); oo (as in 'book'); ou (as in 'out'); oy (as in 'boy'); sh (as
in 'push'); ch (as in 'much'); th (as in 'moth'); qu (as in 'quiz').)

Preparation　Memorise the above sounds and their spellings, which are called
'phonograms'. You will probably have to train yourself not to use
the alphabetical pronunciations, and to use instead the phonetic
pronunciations. (For example, 'p' is pronounced 'puh' as in 'lap',
rather than 'pea' as in the alphabet.) Practise using the sounds by
repeatedly saying a word and then writing its component sounds
in phonograms, thereby making a phonetic spelling of the word.
(Hereafter in this book, directions on pronunciations in the
Language Activities will be written using the above
phonograms.) Practise analysing short words, and then long
words, into their component sounds.

Stages　Each child is led through the following stages over a period of
approximately one to two years. Play 'I Spy' at least once each
day. A good time to play it is when you're just waiting or relaxing
together. Play each stage for at least a few months with a child
before moving on to the next stage. When playing 'I Spy' with a
mixed age group, rotate between the various stages as necessary
to allow all ages to participate at their levels.
(1) Hold a single familiar object in your hand (e.g. a pen), so
that the child (or all the children) can see it. Look at the
object, and say, 'I spy with my little eye something that
begins with ( )', giving the first sound in the object's name
(e.g. 'p'). (Remember, 'p' is not pronounced 'pea', but 'puh',
as in 'lap'.) Prompt a guess if necessary, and when you hear
the correct answer (e.g. 'pen'), acknowledge it by
immediately repeating the word and sound (e.g. 'Pen begins
with "p"'). Repeat this process with other familiar objects in
the room.
(2) The same as Stage (1), but hold or place down two familiar

objects, the names of which do not begin with the same sound. Look at them both, but 'I Spy' just one of them by giving its first sound. When a correct answer is given, repeat the word and sound. Repeat this process with another pair of objects. Later, repeat the process with three and then more objects, only one of which has a name beginning with the given sound.

(3) The same as Stage (2), but broaden the field of possible objects to include everything in a small section of the environment, like a corner of the room. Acknowledge (by repeating the word and sound for) all answers which name an object in the field that does begin with the designated sound (since a child will probably see something you hadn't thought of). Repeat the process for the same, or another, small section of the environment. Later, repeat the process for a larger section of the environment, and then for the entire visible environment.

(4) The same as Stage (3), but indicate both the first and last sounds of the name of the object you have in mind, saying, 'I spy with my little eye something that begins with ( ) and ends with ( ).' Acknowledge correct answers by immediately repeating the word and both sounds, saying, '------- begins with ( ) and ends with ( ).'

(5) Start by playing Stage (4), selecting a small word at first, made up of only three sounds (e.g. book), and limiting the field of possible objects so that this word will be the only correct answer. After you hear the correct answer, repeat the word and the first and last sounds as before. But then draw attention to the remaining middle sound (e.g. 'oo'), and say all three sounds separately, but in sequence. Invite the child (or children) to say all three sounds in the word with you (e.g. 'book – "b", "oo", "c"'). Repeat with other small three-sound words, and gradually work up to four-sound and then five-sound words. Each time, after the object is guessed, analyse with the child (or children) all the middle sounds, and then all the sounds in sequence. Work towards the children being able to analyse words without needing to play the 'I Spy' game first.

(6) Ask, 'Can you think of a word with the sound ( ) in it?' The child here thinks of any word, without the prompt of seeing a particular object. Later, for capable children, repeat the question with two different sounds, asking, 'Can you think of a word with the sounds ( ) and ( ) in it?'

Speech

Aim To give children experience with the expression of ideas in speech, including: a sampling of their cultural heritage in language; an introduction to group discussion (including speaking to a group, listening, and combining ideas); and a technique for thinking logically about a particular theme in preparation for writing or speaking at length.

Material   Children's books and an anthology of poems or songs.

Presentations   (These activities work best with a mixed-age group of three or more children, but they may also be done with just one child.)
(1) Questioning
  – Announce to a group of children a sentence, with a subject, verb and object, concerning a recent event familiar to most of them (e.g. 'Paul washed the dishes').
  – Ask the group a number of questions about the verb, then the subject, and lastly the object, as follows: For each of these words, in turn, begin by drawing attention to the word (e.g. for the verb, 'Paul did what to the dishes?'; for the subject, 'Who washed the dishes?'; for the object, 'Paul washed what?'), and immediately afterwards ask for elaborations on the word's idea (e.g. for the verb, 'When did he wash them? Why were they washed? Where were they washed?'; for the subject, 'Who is Paul? How old is he? What was Paul wearing?'; for the object, 'What colour are the dishes? Where are the dishes now? Who made the dishes dirty?'). Ask questions which will elicit more than a 'yes' or 'no' response from the children. Acknowledge any answer, fact or fiction, which is a logical response to the question, but counter silliness with a sober 'I doubt it'. Maintain the questioning, at a rapid pace, as long as their interest holds out.
  – Repeat with other subject-verb-object sentences.

(2) The Daily News
  – Select a regular time for holding a group, with children seated in a circle.
  – Invite the children singly (but not in any set order) to offer any information, idea, experience or language expression to the group. Begin with yourself, offering a short poem or a brief personal anecdote. Be sure to invite each child, to listen attentively, and to show appreciation when the child finishes, either by thanks or applause.
  – If a topic of general interest to the group is offered, initiate an open discussion on it. In these discussions, synthesise the points brought up, and refer by name to the children who made the points you use.

(3) Storytelling
  – Select a book for reading or invent a story to tell. For children aged two, choose a story about a toddler. For ages three to four, choose repetition stories about everyday events, outings and relationships. For ages four to five, choose stories with plots, those which explain the how and why of things, simple humour, fantasies, and fairy tales with morals. Never tell any story that makes a child feel unsafe. Best are those which

stimulate the mind, clarify emotions, or answer spoken and unspoken questions.
- Seat a relatively small group of the appropriate age in a semi-circle in front of you, so that all can easily see.
- If the book is a fantasy, make clear that it didn't really happen. Read clearly, slowly and loudly, and for picture books, read a page and then stop talking and show the picture on it or facing it. Encourage all the children to say any repeated phrases along with you. Keep insecure or restless ones next to you.
- Afterwards, initiate an open discussion of the story (e.g. Was what happened fair? Could it have ended another way?).
- (If any of the children have been presented with HANDLING A BOOK (see Practical Activities), say that you will put the book in the reading corner.)

(4) Poetry and Songs
- Maintain an anthology of brief poems, songs, finger play rhymes and action songs. Memorise most of the contents.
- For a peaceful and attentive group, recite a brief poem (or a stanza from a longer poem) or sing a song. For a restless group, do finger play or action songs. Encourage the group to sing along. When teaching a song, pronounce clearly and explain all new words. When possible, relate the lyrics to reality (e.g. to personal experience or the weather or a close holiday). Portray nonsense rhymes as funny and not true.

Sandpaper Letters

Aim

To help the child associate the sounds of speech with their written symbols, as a necessary preparation for writing and reading.

Materials

Forty thin boards on each of which are glued one or two large, lower-case letters, cut from smooth sandpaper. Each board shows one of the thirty-nine English 'phonograms' (see the I SPY activity) plus 'k' (which is pronounced the same as the phonogram 'c'). The letter(s) on each board are placed a bit to the right. Boards with single-letter vowels are painted blue, those with single-letter consonants are painted red, and those with double-letter phonograms are painted green; the sandpaper cutouts glued to the boards are unpainted. The boards are stored upright in two open boxes: the single-letter boards in one box and the double-letter boards in another.

(DIY hint: Use coloured matboard instead of wood for the boards. Following a sans-serif lettering style similar to that illustrated here, make templates of the letters from index cards, cut them out with a utility knife, trace them face down on the back of fine sandpaper, and cut the shapes out of the sandpaper. Glue the letters, sandpaper side up, onto the coloured side of the matboard.)

Presentation – Name the Sandpaper Letters, show where they are kept, and select a blue, a red and a green board with contrasting shapes and sounds (e.g. 'i', 'f' and 'oy'). Place them on a table at which you can sit together.

– Sensitise yours and the child's fingers (see SENSITISING THE FINGERS in the Sensorial Activities).

– Show the child how to feel the letters, using a light, continuous touch of the index and middle fingers of the dominant hand, how to hold the board steady with the other hand, and how to sit up straight against the backrest of the chair with both feet on the floor. (To illustrate the proper lightness of touch, touch the child's arm as you would the Sandpaper Letter.)

– Play Stage (3) of the I SPY activity, using the sound on one of the three boards.

– Say 'Would you like to see what the sound ( ) looks like?'

– Place the board with that phonogram directly in front of you and the child. Pronounce the phonogram while you feel the letter(s), following the same pattern of movement that you would use if you were writing the letter(s), and invite the child to do the same. Say the phonogram while you feel the board again.

– Introduce the other two boards in the same way, and give a Three Stage Lesson, associating these sounds of speech with their symbols. In each stage, whenever the child points to or names one of the boards, the child should feel it and say the sound. After the third stage of the Lesson, play Stage (3) of I SPY again, using each of the three sounds in turn.

– Leave the boards just introduced upright on a ledge visible and accessible to the child, and say that they can be taken down and used by the child at any time.

– Privately record the letters that the child has learned.

Exercises (1) Present all the Sandpaper Letters boards, in groups of three, as in the presentation, until the child has learned them all. Occasionally include in a lesson one already introduced, to be sure earlier ones are not forgotten.

(2) Play all Stages, from (1) to (6), of I SPY, but rather than say the sound, use the Sandpaper Letters to indicate which sound you have in mind (i.e. 'I spy with my little eye something beginning with . . .' (then show one of the boards)). Ask the child who guesses the thing you 'spy' to feel the Sandpaper Letter while saying the sound.

WRITING

Metal Insets

Aim To help the child acquire proficiency in using a writing instrument, including lightness of touch, evenness of pressure, continuity of line, control of line, and familiarity with the curves and angles found in letters.

Ten flat metal squares, in each of which rests a different cut-out metal shape identical to one of the shapes in the GEOMETRIC CABINET (see Sensorial Activities). Each cut-out shape, or 'inset', is blue and has a small knob at its centre, and each border, or 'frame', is pink. The ten frames and their insets rest on two tilted wooden racks. The ten shapes are: (on one rack) curvilinear triangle, quatrefoil, circle, ellipse and oval; (and on the other rack) triangle, rectangle, square, pentagon and trapezium.

Material

    Firm, smooth, square linoleum tiles, larger than the above metal squares.

    A selection of coloured pencils.

    Pastel or white square paper, the exact same size as the outer edge of a 'frame', in an open box.

    (DIY hint: Using a utility knife, cut the frames and their insets from thick, stiff plastic or linoleum. For the knobs, use large beads, which you can attach by heavy plastic thread to the middle of each shape.)

– Name the material and show where it is kept. Take a tile, place on it a piece of paper, place on the paper a frame with its inset, and put these on a table you can sit at. (Point out how you hold the frame on the tile with your thumb when carrying the materials to the table.)

– Now get three different coloured pencils, put them next to the tile on the table, and sit at the table with the child.

– Without drawing anything yet, show the child how to hold a pencil gently but securely with the dominant hand, how to hold the inset or frame steady with the other hand, and how to sit up straight against the backrest of the chair with both feet on the floor. (To illustrate the gentle hold of the pencil, hold the child's finger as you would hold a pencil.)

– Now remove the inset from the frame and place it gently on the table. Make the outer edges of the frame coincide exactly with the edges of the paper. Select a coloured pencil. Hold the frame steady, and very carefully trace around its interior edge with the pencil, in one continuous line.

– Next, remove the frame and place it gently on the table, and put the inset on the paper so that its edges coincide exactly with the line just drawn. Select a different coloured pencil. Hold the inset steady by the knob, and very carefully trace around its exterior edge with the pencil, in one continuous line that covers the first line.

– Take the inset off the paper and place it gently in the frame on the table. Hold the paper steady, and with the third coloured pencil, starting just inside the left edge of the drawn figure, very carefully draw a continuous, tight, vertical zig-zag which reaches from the top to the bottom of the figure, and moves

Presentation

gradually to the right, so as to fill in the figure completely with nearly adjacent vertical lines.

– Observe with the child the result. Invite the child to get another piece of paper and repeat the process exactly as you performed it.

– Show the child how and where to store finished work (see STORAGE OF WORK).

Exercises   (1) The child, working independently, traces and fills in each of the Metal Insets as in the presentation.

(2) The same as exercise (1), except, after drawing around the interior edge of a frame, the child places the inset on the paper so that it does not correspond with the first drawn line, but is instead turned so that it symmetrically overlaps the line. (This is not possible with the circle.) The resulting figure will have an 'inner' section and a number of 'outer' sections. The child then fills in, with the zig-zag pattern, the 'inner' section in one colour and the 'outer' sections in another colour.

(3) The same as exercise (2), except the child combines two, and then more shapes, to create a symmetrical pattern with many sections to be filled in.

Movable Alphabet

Aim   To show the child, as an introduction to writing, that the symbols for the sounds in speech can be used to express thoughts and record experiences. Generally, to encourage self-expression.

Material   'Large Movable Alphabet': A large, shallow, two-layer box containing five of each lower-case letter of the alphabet, with each set of five resting in its own compartment. Each letter is thin plastic (blue for vowels and pink for consonants) and is identical in shape and size to its corresponding Sandpaper Letter (see SANDPAPER LETTERS).

'Small Movable Alphabet': A large, shallow box containing ten of each lower-case letter of the alphabet, with each set resting in its own compartment. These letters are identical in shape to the Large Movable Alphabet, but they are smaller and all of one colour.

'Printed Alphabet': A box containing twenty-five of each lower-case letter of the alphabet, five each of the upper-case letters of the alphabet, and fifteen each of eight punctuation symbols (? ! " " . , ; :). These letters and symbols are printed in one colour on small, white rectangular cards, are smaller and drawn with thinner lines than the Small Movable Alphabet, but are identical to them in shape.

(DIY hint: Cut the letters from coloured artboard for the Large Movable Alphabet and Small Movable Alphabet, and draw them carefully in ink on pieces of white artboard for the Printed

Alphabet. Instead of the wooden boxes with compartments, you could try using clear plastic envelopes tacked in place on a large board.)

– Name the Large Movable Alphabet, show where it is kept, and place it on a floor mat.
– Show the child how to set the box inside its upside-down lid and then place out the two layers side by side.
– Explore the alphabet with the child. First, explore the letters by sight, asking the child to point to various one-letter phonogram sounds that you name, and then asking the child to name ones you point to. Then explore the letters by touch, asking the child to place on the mat various one-letter, and then two-letter, phonograms that you name, referring back to the Sandpaper Letters when the child is uncertain. During this exploration, bring these special points to the child's attention: the separate storage of the dots for 'i' and 'j'; the fact that 'p', 'd' and 'b' are the same shape and that their identity depends upon how they are placed down; the subtle difference between 'f' and 't', and between 'i' and 'l'; and that to make the phonogram sound 'c', either 'c' or 'k' can be used. Invite the child to put the letters back in their spaces.
– Play Stage (5) of I SPY for a few minutes, until you come to an object whose name is made up of three single-letter phonograms, which the child has sounded out correctly. Then say, for example, 'j – u – g, that's right! Would you like to write the word "jug"? Let's say the sounds again: "j" – please find the letter for "j"; now "u" – please find "u" in the box; and now "g" – find "g"', and as the child hands them to you, place the letters in a row, left to right, on the mat.
– When this is done, excitedly say, for example, 'We were thinking of the word "jug" and we wrote "jug" with the letters in the box!' Ask the child to return these letters to their spaces in the box.
– Repeat this process with other words that are correctly spelled with three single-letter phonograms (e.g. cat, bus, dog), but let the child select the letters and place them in a row on the mat. (If the child had not noticed that the letters from the first word were placed in a row, show that the letters should be put in a row left to right, but not necessarily in perfect alignment. If the child selects the wrong letter for a sound in a word, do not correct it, but make a mental note so that later you can give a Three Stage Lesson on those particular sounds and letters, using the Sandpaper Letters.) After each word, emphasise the achievement by saying, 'You were thinking of the word -------- and you wrote -------- all by yourself!'

(Since the purpose of the Movable Alphabet is to introduce the child to written self-expression, and to develop an enthusiasm for it, you should not, in the following exercises, correct any spellings nor interrupt the child's writing with any suggestions. There is plenty of time for teaching spelling and composition technique when the child is older. However, because it is critical at this stage to associate sounds correctly with their phonogram letters, you should privately note errors in choosing the letters for sounds, and later correct them by Three Stage Lesson, using the Sandpaper Letters.)

(1) Play Stage (5) of I SPY and invite the child to write words with the Large Movable Alphabet, as in the presentation. First, give words with only single-letter phonograms (e.g. 'pen'), then with double-letter phonograms (e.g. 'cloth'), building up to longer and more difficult words. (If the child has difficulty selecting the letters for a double-letter phonogram, invite the child to bring the Sandpaper Letters to the floor mat, find the Sandpaper Letters board for the phonogram, and then find the Movable Alphabet letters which match the board.)

Later, play games in which the child can write things with the Large Movable Alphabet. For example: ask a simple question and invite the child to write the one-word answer with the Movable Alphabet letters (e.g. 'What is your favorite colour?'); ask the child to write all the words pertaining to something visible in the room (e.g. 'Can you name all the things on that shelf?'); or invite the child to think of words associated with a particular subject (e.g. 'What foods do you like to eat?').

(2) Name the Small Movable Alphabet, show where it is kept, place it on a floor mat, and invite the child to examine and handle the letters. Initiate a discussion on a topic of interest to the child, or ask questions on such a topic. When the child says a three- or four-word phrase of relevance to the topic (e.g. 'my dog runs fast'), say, for example, 'Let's see how we can write "my dog runs fast" with the Small Movable Alphabet.' With the child, say all the sounds in the phrase, but between each word, put two fingers up to your lips to emphasise the pause. Then say just the first word, and invite the child to write it with the letters. When the child is done writing the first word, say it again, put two fingers to your lips to show the pause that follows it, and place those two fingers down on the mat, to the right of the word the child just wrote. Your two fingers on the mat are now marking the space that must be left before the next word. Keep the two fingers there as you say the second word alone, and invite the child to write it with the letters, just to the right of your fingers. Continue in the same way to complete the phrase; each time the child adds a new word, say the phrase thus far written, including the pauses with your fingers on your lips. When the phrase is done, show much enthusiasm and say, for example, 'You were thinking "my dog runs fast" and now

you've written it!' Ask the child to put the letters back in their box. Continue the discussion and repeat the process with other phrases.

Later, invite the child to write phrases in answer to your questions, for example, to write all the things that the child did that morning (e.g. 'washed the cloths', 'drank some juice', etc.). (If the child shows some difficulty with spacing words, repeat the above process of using two fingers to indicate that the pause between two spoken words becomes the space between two written words. Also, show some books with spacings between words, to illustrate the idea.) When the child shows you the completed Movable Alphabet work on the floor mat, there will probably be some phrases you cannot understand because of their (possibly incorrect) phonetic spelling. Therefore, you must only read it silently to yourself as best you can, and discuss with interest some of the ideas, to give the child the satisfaction that you did understand. (Do not invite the child to read the Movable Alphabet work to you; the Movable Alphabet is an exercise in writing, and there will be other exercises for reading.)

(3) Remove the punctuation symbols from the Printed Alphabet and set them aside in a box. Name the Printed Alphabet, show where it is kept, place it on a floor mat, and invite the child to examine and handle the letters. Initiate a discussion on a topic of interest to the child, and build up a small set of facts which together describe an event or situation. Say, 'Let's write a story about that.' Work with the child on what to say first, and then next, but after each brief sentence is decided, leave the child alone to write it. Between each sentence, show that there is a long pause, and as with the two fingers between words, show how to leave a whole hand's space between sentences. Also help the child to align the words in fairly straight rows, and show that it is fine to start a sentence in one row and finish it on the next. After each sentence is added, say the sentences thus far written, including the short and long pauses. When all the sentences of the story are written, say, 'We thought of a story about -------, and now you've written it!' That day, read the story the child wrote, in between reading two published story books, during Storytelling time (see SPEECH). Afterwards, offer to save the story for the child (since it really was a lot of work) by copying it yourself on a piece of paper, exactly as the child wrote it (see STORAGE OF WORK). Then, ask the child to put the letters away in their box.

Repeat the process another time.

Later, invite the child to write stories independently. If necessary, suggest topics or situations to write about that come from the child's personal experiences. If this seems too difficult, invite the child to write out a song or poem that you often say together.

Writing Individual Letters

Aim   To introduce the child to the art of reproducing the shapes of letters and numbers.

Material   The forty Sandpaper Letters boards and the ten Sandpaper Numbers (see SANDPAPER NUMBERS in the Mathematics Activities), a plain blackboard, chalk in a chalk holder, blackboard eraser, a face-flannel and a towel.

Plain large paper and a pencil.

Presentation   – Name the blackboard, chalk and eraser, show where they are kept, and place them at a table. Show how to dampen a flannel, and place it at the table with a towel. Sitting at the table, show the child how to grip the chalk holder, how to erase, and how to clean and dry chalky fingers with the flannel and towel (in order to keep chalk dust off the Sandpaper Letters and Numbers).

– Invite the child to select and bring to the table one of the blue (vowel) Sandpaper Letters. Put this letter to the left of the blackboard.

– Clean and dry your fingers, feel the letter, say its sound, and then slowly draw the letter on the blackboard with the chalk. With the child, compare the drawn letter to the Sandpaper Letter. Erase the drawing.

– Repeat this process with the same letter, starting with the cleaning of your fingers.

– Invite the child to have a turn, starting with the finger cleaning.

– Ask the child to exchange the blue (vowel) Sandpaper Letter for a red (consonant) one. Invite the child to clean and dry fingers again, and then to feel, sound and draw the consonant Sandpaper Letter. Repeat with other Sandpaper Letters if the child shows interest.

– When the child is done, show how to wipe the blackboard clean with the flannel used for fingers, and request that all the materials be put away.

Exercises   (1) The child cleans fingers, and then feels, sounds and draws each of the Sandpaper Letters and Numbers boards individually, including the double-letter phonograms, on a plain blackboard with chalk, as in the presentation. Guide the child to work through the vowels first, then the single-letter consonants, then the double-letter phonograms, and lastly the numbers.

(2) The child feels, sounds, and draws every Sandpaper Letter and Number, including the double-letter phonograms, on a plain paper with a pencil. In presenting this, show how to hold a pencil, how to sharpen a pencil, how to draw several attempts of the same figure in a row on one sheet, and how and where to store finished work (see STORAGE OF WORK).

Writing Families of Letters

To give the child practice in reproducing and remembering the shapes of letters.

The forty Sandpaper Letters, a plain blackboard with chalk in a holder, an eraser, a face-flannel and a towel.
    Plain large paper and a pencil.

- Place the blackboard materials, damp flannel and towel, and the twenty-five single-letter Sandpaper Letters at a table. (There is no single-letter Sandpaper Letter for 'q'.)
- Draw on the blackboard the shape 'c', and invite the child to select from the Sandpaper Letters all the ones that 'use this shape' (a, c, e, d, g, o). Place these Sandpaper Letters in a row, then feel, sound and draw each individually (cleaning and drying your fingers each time), so that all are drawn in a row on the blackboard. Compare the drawings to the Sandpaper Letters, and erase the blackboard.
- Invite the child to make several attempts at drawing in a row on the blackboard as you did the complete family of letters based on the shape 'c'.

(1) The child independently feels, sounds, and draws in a row on the blackboard, as in the presentation: the 'c' family of letters (which are based on a curve); then the 'l' family of letters (which are based on a vertical line: b, f, i, j, k, l, p, t); then the 'r' family of letters (which are based on a line and a curve: h, m, n, r, u); and last, the '\' family of letters (which are based on slanted lines: s, v, w, x, y, z). As before, the child should clean and dry fingers between letters.

(2) The child feels, sounds, and draws the 'o' family of double-letter phonograms (oo, ou, or, oa, oy), then the 'a' family (ai, ar, aw), then the 'e' family (ue, er, ee, ie), then the 'h' family (sh, ch, th), and lastly the solitary 'qu'. Again the child should clean and dry fingers between phonograms.

(3) The child feels, sounds and draws the families of single-letter phonograms, then the families of double-letter phonograms, on plain paper with a black pencil. In presenting this, show the child how to draw several attempts of the same family in parallel rows on the one sheet, and show how and where to store finished work (see STORAGE OF WORK).

Positioning Letters on Lines

To introduce the child to the proper positioning of letters written in a row.

A board (or felt mat) on which is printed three pairs of perfectly horizontal lines, each pair just wide enough to contain an 'o' from the Small Movable Alphabet.

The Small Movable Alphabet itself.

The twenty-five single-letter Sandpaper Letters, a blackboard with three pairs of white lines the same as the board above, chalk in a chalk holder, a blackboard eraser, a flannel and a towel.

Wide-lined paper and a pencil.

Presentation
– Name the lined board (or mat), show where it is kept, and place it with the Small Movable Alphabet on a floor mat.
– Involving the child, find and place in rows on the board all the letters which generally fit within the two lines (a, c, e, i, m, n, o, r, s, u, v, w, x, z). Put these away.
– Repeat for those letters which generally extend above the two lines (b, d, f, h, k, l, t).
– Repeat for those letters which generally extend below the two lines (g, j, p, y).
– Working with the child, go through the alphabet and sort the letters into these three groups.
– Check the sorting by placing each group on the lines on the board.
– Invite the child to repeat the letter-sorting and to check it.

Exercises

(1) The child sorts the Small Movable Alphabet into the three groups (within, extending above and extending below the two lines) and checks the sorting on the lined board, as in the presentation.
(2) The child sorts the twenty-five single-letter Sandpaper Letters into the three groups, and then feels, sounds, and draws with chalk on the lined blackboard, each of the groups in turn (cleaning and drying fingers between each letter).
(3) The child sorts the twenty-five single-letter Sandpaper Letters into the three groups, and then feels, sounds, and draws with a pencil on lined paper, each of the groups in turn.
(4) The child feels, sounds, and draws with a pencil on a single piece of lined paper, the twenty-five single-letter Sandpaper Letters, in random order.

Sandpaper Capitals

Aim
To help the child associate speech sounds with the capital forms of their written symbols.

Material
Twenty-six thin boards on each of which is glued a large capital letter, cut from smooth sandpaper. Each board shows one of the twenty-six English capital letters (including 'Q'). The letter on each board is placed somewhat to the right. The boards are painted red; the sandpaper cut-outs glued to the boards are unpainted.

The twenty-five single-letter, lower-case Sandpaper Letters (all letters of the alphabet except 'q') plus the board showing 'qu'.

(DIY hint: Use coloured matboard instead of wood for the boards. Following the same sans-serif lettering style used in the Sandpaper Letters, make templates of the letters from index cards, cut them out with a utility knife, trace them face down on the back of fine sandpaper, and cut the shapes out of the sandpaper. Glue the letters, sandpaper side up, onto the coloured side of the matboard.)

Presentation

- Name the Sandpaper Capitals, show where they are kept, and place them with the twenty-five single-letter, lower-case Sandpaper Letters, plus 'qu', on a table.
- Sensitise your fingers and ask the child to do the same (see SENSITISING THE FINGERS in the Sensorial Activities).
- Say, 'There is another way to write the letters. We can write them as the "capital letters". Every letter can be written as a capital.'
- First, visually compare side-by-side the pairs of lower-case and capital letters which have nearly the same shape (c-C, f-F, i-I, j-J, k-K, m-M, o-O, p-P, s-S, t-T, u-U, v-V, w-W, x-X, y-Y, z-Z). For each pair, feel and pronounce them both (e.g. 'm, capital M'), using only the phonetic pronunciations, and feeling each letter in the exact pattern in which it is written. Invite the child to repeat, after each pair.

- Next, compare, feel, and sound the pairs of lower-case and capital letters which have different shapes (a-A, b-B, d-D, e-E, g-G, h-H, l-L, n-N, r-R), and also compare the 'q' on the 'qu' board with its capital ('Q'). Do not invite the child to repeat these.
- Select three of the capitals which have a different shape than their lower-case forms, and which contrast with each other in shape and sound (e.g. A, D and L), and give a Three Stage Lesson to associate their familiar sounds with the new symbols. In each stage, when a symbol is identified, the child should sound it and feel it. Leave the three boards upright on a ledge where the child can see and practise with them at any time. Privately record which capitals the child has learned.

(1) Teach by Three Stage Lessons the remaining seven capitals that have a different shape than their lower-case forms, to associate their familiar sounds with the new symbols.
(2) The child independently reviews all twenty-six Sandpaper Capitals, associating the symbols with their phonetic sounds.

Exercises

Storage of Work
To store only those work products which the child considers worth keeping, so that from time to time the child may review and recall the wide range and progress of the work.

Aim

Material   A Work Box, which is a large box with a lid and a wide slit in one side.

Work Folders, one for each child, divided by subject into 'Language' and other sections, stored in a place immediately accessible to the children.

A changeable date stamp, name stamps labelled with the children's photographs, and a stamp pad.

Preparation   Keep the date stamp turned to the current date.

Preliminary   – Show the child how to use a stamp and pad, practising on a
Presentation   blank piece of paper.

Method   (1) Each child independently date stamps and name stamps all finished work on paper (including Language work (from the METAL INSET activity onwards), as well as art work or later Mathematics work), and then slips it into the closed Work Box.

(2) Sort the contents of the Work Box at the end of each week, and allow the children to each pick out those few pieces that they are truly proud of and want to keep.

(3) File the selected work in the appropriate sections of each child's Work Folder.

(4) The children are free to examine their folder, or the other children's folders at any time. Parents are invited to see only their own child's folder.

READING

Object Boxes

Aim   To introduce the child to reading, by conveying the thought of an object through the written symbols learned for sounds.

Material   Object Box 1, a box with a lid, with eight small objects inside. The name of each object is a brief word spelled the same as its phonetic spelling, comprised only of single-letter phonograms (e.g. jug, bed, hen, pan, cat, bus, fan, pig). Most of the objects are not the actual item named, but a tiny toy or model version. Including the eight in the box, there is a total collection of fifty such objects to rotate weekly.

Object Box 2, a box with a lid, with fifteen small objects inside. The name of each object is a fairly brief word, spelled the same as its phonetic spelling, and containing a different double-letter phonogram (e.g. pail, boy, otter, car, ship, goat, trout). Again, most of the objects are tiny models of the item named. There is a total collection of thirty such objects to rotate weekly.

Eighty Object Box Cards, on each of which is printed, in black, the name of one of the above objects. Of these eighty cards, the eight cards which name the objects in Object Box 1 are stored in an envelope labelled '1', and the fifteen cards which name the objects in Object Box 2 are stored in an envelope labelled '2'. The remaining fifty-seven cards are bound with an elastic band and stored with the presently unused collection of objects. The cards are rotated weekly to correspond to the rotated objects.

Strips of paper, pencils, and scissors.

How to Make the Material

You'll need: two empty cigar boxes, deep blue paint, eighty index cards, a black pen, two heavy manilla paper envelopes, and an elastic band.

(a) Search in a shop that has doll-house furnishings, or any shop that sells small plastic or wooden toys, for miniatures of things whose names have the characteristics described above as necessary for each of the Object Boxes. Add to these some tiny household items whose names also have the appropriate characteristics (e.g. cap, nut, band, cork, button, cloth). Collect fifty such objects suitable for Box 1 and thirty suitable for Box 2.

(b) On the lined side of each index card, write in large lower-case letters (in the same style and size as shown on the Printed Alphabet set of the MOVABLE ALPHABET) the name of one of the objects you have collected, so that you have a name card for each object.

(c) Paint the boxes, inside and out, a deep blue. Draw a '1' on the outer lid of the eight compartment box and a '2' on the outer lid of the other box, and similarly label the envelopes '1' and '2'. Place objects in the boxes and their corresponding cards in the envelopes, as described above in the *Material* section.

Presentation

– Name Object Box 1, show where it is kept, and place it on a table with strips of paper, a black pencil and scissors.

– Take out and invite the child to name the objects one by one, helping where needed, placing them on the table in front of the child.

– Say, 'I'm thinking of one of these things. Do you know which one? I won't say which one I'm thinking of, but I'll give you a clue.'

– Write in clear lower-case letters (in the same style as shown on the Printed Alphabet) the name of one of the objects on a strip of paper. Cut the strip to isolate just the word. Place this word on the table between the child and the various objects. Say, 'Here's your clue. Now which thing am I thinking of?'

– If necessary, guide the child to say the sounds in the right order, and so that the sounds are connected. Allow the child to discover their meaning by picking out the right object.

– Say, excitedly, 'You read that word! You can read! I was thinking of ------- and I wrote the word -------. Then you read ------- and knew what I was thinking of!'

– Place the word and object aside, next to each other.
– Repeat this process for each of the other objects, placing aside each object with its associated word, and thereby gradually narrowing down the number of objects from which the child selects. (Note any constant errors in sounding out letters, so that you can correct them at another time by Three Stage Lesson. Do not correct a mistake in the child's selection of an object for a name, but stop the activity before coming to the last object in that box, since you will have already used its name; instead, repeat the presentation later, stressing the name of the previously misnamed object.)

′ Exercises

(1) Repeat the presentation, with Object Box 1, when the box has newly rotated objects.

(2) Conduct the presentation with Object Box 2. If the child mistakes the double-letter phonogram for two single-letter phonograms, underline the two letters with a single pencil stroke to suggest their connection. Repeat this presentation with newly rotated objects.

(3) Name the Object Box Cards, show where their envelopes are kept, and place the envelope for Object Box 1 with that box on the table. Show the child how to work independently, placing out the objects, selecting a card, reading it, finding the named object, and placing it on the table together with its name. The child repeats this at least once a week, matching the newly rotated objects and cards.

(4) The child works independently, as in exercise (3), with Object Box 2 and envelope 2, and repeats at least once a week, matching the newly rotated objects and cards.

Action Cards

Aim To give further introduction to reading, by conveying the thought of an action through the written symbols learned for sounds.

Material Fifty Action Cards, each printed in black with a simple intransitive verb representing an action a child can perform without materials or assistance, and all of which are spelled the same as their phonetic spellings (e.g. grin, clap, nod, run, sing, wink, spin, pout). Ten of these cards are placed in a box accessible to the child; the other forty are stored elsewhere.

Strips of paper, pencils and scissors.

Presentation – Seat at a table a child who has worked independently with the Object Boxes, and place on the table a pencil, strips of paper, and scissors.
– Say to the child, 'I'm thinking of something you can do. I won't say what, but I will write it down. Then you can read it and do it.'
– Write a word (the same as one of the Action Cards, described

above) on a strip of paper. Then cut to isolate the word, and hand it to the child.

- Invite the child to read the word aloud and perform the action; after the child starts, perform the action yourself as well.
- Repeat the process with other action words. (Note any constant errors in sounding out letters, so that you can correct them at another time by Three Stage Lesson. Do not correct a mistake in the child's acting out a correctly read action word; another day, repeat the presentation, acting out yourself the previously misperformed action.)

(1) Repeat the presentation with other action words.
(2) Name the box of Action Cards, show where it is kept, and place it on a table. Show the child how to select a card, read it, and perform the action. The child may wish to do this taking turns with another child who has also done exercise (1).

Exercises

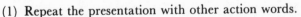

Reading Folders

To help the child learn the various spellings commonly found in English for the phonograms already learned, so as to enlarge the child's reading and writing vocabulary.

Aim

In a box, thirteen red Reading Folders in clear plastic envelopes. On the cover of each Folder is printed the phonogram, as spelled on the SANDPAPER LETTERS, of a sound that is often spelled other ways in English words. (The thirteen phonogram sounds and all their alternate spellings (in parentheses) are: e (e, ea); f (f, ph); j (j, gi, ge); oy (oy, oi); ai (ai, ei, ay, a-e); er (er, ir, ur); ee (ee, ea, e-e, ie, y); s (s, ce, ci); ou (ou, ow); ie (ie, i-e, igh, y); oa (oa, ow, o-e, oe); or (or, aw, au, ough); and ue (ue, u-e, oo, ew) (where '-' stands for an undetermined consonant between the two vowels).) Inside each Reading Folder are cards, each card bearing on one side, in large red letters, one of the alternate spellings of the sound on the Folder's cover, and on the other side, in small blue letters, the sound as it is spelled on the Folder's cover. Also in each Reading Folder are tiny books, each showing on its cover one of the spellings of the sound, and on each of its tiny pages, an example of a simple word (printed in black) which includes the sound (printed in red) as it is spelled on the book's cover.

Material

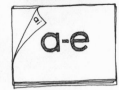

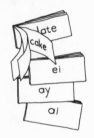

A Phonogram Dictionary, which is a small red book with twenty-seven tabulated pages. On each tab is one of the non-Sandpaper Letter spellings of the thirteen sounds in the Reading Folders (ea, ph, gi, ge, oi, ei, ay, a-e, ir, ur, e-e, ie, y, ce, ci, ow, i-e, igh, o-e, oe, aw, au, ough, u-e, oo, ew), and on the page to which the tab opens is the Sandpaper Letter spelling of its sound or possible sounds (e.g. when opening the tab 'ph', you see 'f'; when opening the tab 'y', you see 'ie' and 'ee', since 'y' could be pronounced as either). Also, on the last tab is printed 'sion/tion', and on the page to which this tab opens is the phonetic spelling of this sound: 'shun'. On the cover of the Dictionary is printed, in red, in a column, the thirteen Sandpaper Letter spellings of the sounds.

The handmade storybooks that accompany Puzzle Words Box 2 (see the PUZZLE WORDS activity).

The Printed Alphabet set of the MOVABLE ALPHABET.

Pencils and paper.

Presentation   – Name the Reading Folders, show where they are kept, and place them on a floor mat.
– Remove the folder marked 'ai', ask the child what sound it is, and say, 'Everything in this folder says "ai".'
– Show the card marked 'ai', and then show each of the other cards (ei, ay, a-e), saying for each, 'This also says "ai".' Place the cards in a straight, evenly-spaced row on the mat.
– Show the child the tiny book marked 'ai', read with the child each of the words in it, and place it on the mat exactly in front of the 'ai' card. Repeat with the 'a-e', 'ay' and 'ei' books. (When reading the 'a-e' book, point out that the 'e' on the end has no sound of its own, but affects the sound of the 'a'. Demonstrate this, using the Printed Alphabet, as follows: select the letters 't' and 'p', and put them in position on the 'a-e' card to spell 'tape'. Cover the 'e' and ask the child to read the word 'tap'. Then uncover the 'e' and ask the child to read the word 'tape'. Note with the child the change in pronunciation.)
– Put everything back in the folder and set it aside.
– Repeat the entire process with another folder.
– Invite the child to continue independently with other folders.

Exercises   (1) The child reads through the cards and books in each Reading Folder, neatly laying out a Folder's materials on the mat, as in the presentation.
(2) Name the Phonogram Dictionary, show where it is kept, and place it on a table with one of the handmade storybooks that accompanies Box 2 of the PUZZLE WORDS. Read a page or two, and show the child how, upon coming to a word which has an unfamiliar phonogram (e.g. 'ay'), it may be found on a tab of the Phonogram Dictionary, and its sound revealed on the page to which the tab opens.
(3) The child learns to associate the sound and its spellings for all thirteen Reading Folders, working with three at a time, as follows.

On a floor mat, the child mixes up in a stack the cards from three Reading Folders, and places the cardless folders in a row at the far edge of the mat. The child then picks up the cards one by one, saying the sound and placing the card in front of the folder marked with its Sandpaper Letter spelling, so as to make a column of cards in front of each folder. Lastly, the child turns the cards over, one by one down each column, to see the blue phonogram on the back, and thereby checks and corrects the sorting.

The above sorting is repeated for three Reading Folders at a time, until all thirteen have been used.

As a final variation, practised until perfect, the child mixes the cards for all thirteen Reading Folders, lays the cardless folders across the top of two floor mats, pronounces and sorts the cards, and checks and corrects as before.

(4) The child affirms the learning of the various spellings of the phonograms, as follows.

The Reading Folders and the Printed Alphabet set of the MOVABLE ALPHABET are placed on two adjacent floor mats, and the Folders are spread along the far edge of the two mats. From memory, the child places out, using the Printed Alphabet, the alternative spellings of the sounds shown on the Folders, placing them in columns as in exercise (3). The child then checks this attempt against the cards contained in each Folder, and makes corrections as needed. This exercise is repeated until done with ease.

(5) The child applies this knowledge to writing, as follows. Place a pencil and a piece of paper on a table. Ask the child to write, on the paper, the four ways of making the sound 'ie' (ie, y, igh and i-e). Then read aloud, for the child to write, various words in random order from the 'ie' Reading Folder's tiny books, each of which include the sound 'ie' spelled in one of the four ways (e.g. 'pie', 'fly', 'high', 'line', etc.). Invite the child to check his or her list of words against the tiny books.

Repeat later with the tiny books from other Reading Folders.

Puzzle Words

Aim
To help the child, in stages, become familiar with common words that cannot be sounded out, and to reinforce this learning with texts that are fully decipherable for a child at each stage.

Material
Two boxes, named Box 1 and Box 2, each holding fifteen cards, on which are printed, in black, Puzzle Words. Puzzle Words are words that cannot be correctly sounded out from the sounds and symbols the child learned from the Sandpaper Letters, nor by using the Phonogram Dictionary (see READING FOLDERS). The words are divided into two levels of difficulty, one box for each level. For example, in Box 1, Puzzle Words might include 'to, the, me, put, go, be, you, was, they, your, said, says, all, I', and in Box 2 they might include 'air, thumb, store, caught, through, knee, knot, could'.

For each box, several handmade, illustrated storybooks, the texts of which are selected from: the fifteen words on that box's Puzzle Words cards; plus, words that can be phonetically sounded out from their actual spelling; plus, for Box 2, Puzzle

Words from Box 1 as well as words that can be sounded out with the aid of the Phonogram Dictionary (see READING FOLDERS). The books contain correct capitals and punctuation.

Also, one or two specially made books, with text as described above, based on the special interests of particular children.

The Printed Alphabet set of the MOVABLE ALPHABET.

Pencils and paper.

Presentation
- Name the Puzzle Words, show where they are kept, and place Box 1 on a table.
- Select three words contrasting in sound and appearance, and give a Three Stage Lesson associating the words with their pronunciations.
- After the third stage, use the words in a discussion with the child.
- Privately record which words the child has learned.

Exercises

(1) Go through the two Puzzle Words boxes in succession, giving separate Three Stage Lessons on all fifteen words in Box 1 before moving on to Box 2. Give a Lesson about once a week, or more often if the child requests it, reviewing each time some of the words already learned.

(2) As soon as a full set of fifteen words has been introduced to the child, show the several storybooks which use those words, and invite the child to read them. For the first books, sit with the child, to share and augment enthusiasm for the story. With subsequent books, encourage the child to read independently, or after practice with a particular book, to read to a younger friend. Mentally note consistent errors in sounding letters and in identifying Puzzle Words in the story for later correction by Three Stage Lessons, but do not correct occasional errors in pronunciation.

(3) Compose and give to individual children special books which follow their personal interests and use the Puzzle Words.

(4) The child practises writing the Puzzle Words. Read aloud Puzzle Words from cards the child has learned, while the child writes them with the Printed Alphabet (or later, with pencil and paper). Invite the child to check independently the written work against the cards.

Book Corner and Library

Aim
To introduce the child to books as something natural, enjoyable and often useful.

Material
A 'Book Corner', which is an open shelving unit that displays books with the covers facing outward, placed in a quiet corner of the Montessori environment, with a table and chair nearby for reading, and a soft rug and pillow for comfortable browsing. A large collection of attractive, illustrated and interesting books

should be rotated weekly through these shelves. These books should include: picture story books; fact books focusing on a topic (e.g. boats); stories about children's common daily experiences, relationships and problems; fantasy books; word play and poetry books; and children's classics.

In another part of the room, a low shelf holding a 'Library' of fact and reference books, with their spines facing outward, near a table and chair for reading. These books are arranged on the shelf by subject matter; this arrangement is indicated by both a word and an illustration stuck to a thick divider on the shelf to the left of each subject.

Presentation

– Name the Book Corner and the Library, and show their locations.
– Include each child at some point in the group activity HANDLING A BOOK (see Practical Activities).
– Invite a child who is clearly calm and unoccupied to go with you to find a book to read in the Book Corner. Assist in picking out a simple picture story book with few or no words.
– Invite a child who voices a factual inquiry or expresses a topical interest to go with you to the library to 'research' that subject. Assist in finding a book with illustrations that address or relate to the child's idea.

Exercises

(1) The child goes spontaneously to the Book Corner for relaxation and enjoyment of the books, especially to see what new books have turned up there.
(2) The child goes spontaneously to the Library to research an inquiry or topic of interest, especially after some reading ability has developed.

5 MATHEMATICS ACTIVITIES

INTRODUCTION

Many of us feel intuitively uncomfortable about mathematics. It often seems like such a cold and inhuman pursuit, with its abstract symbols, unbending laws, and sterile logic. But for the child's sake we need to overcome this misguided impression, and learn to feel an excitement and even an affection for mathematics. We must convey to the child the belief that we have made mathematics ourselves, and that we re-make it every time we move, think, work or play. We should help the child understand that it is simply part of our being human to have a mathematical mind.

What makes us mathematically minded? Things are much too complex for us to grasp in their natural state, and so we imagine them to be, and often try to transform them into, simpler more uniform phenomena. The foundation for our mathematical mind is this inclination to simplify, or idealise, the world.

An ideal is an imaginary entity that exhibits only one particular quality. An ideal cube, for instance, would present just the form of a solid with six equal, square sides, and it would present no further aspect – no weight, no colour, no texture. Each of the branches of mathematics can be associated with the idealisation of a particular physical quality. The idealisation of form – as in cubes, triangles and spheres – leads to the study of geometry. In the same way, we can think of arithmetic as being based on the idealisation of quantity. We can also think of algebra as an idealisation of dimensions, calculus as an idealisation of motion and change, and topology as an idealisation of distance.

Once we have imagined an ideal, with its isolated quality, we cannot further our understanding of it without the use of certain basic intellectual skills. These skills include, for example, being able to judge relative amounts or degrees, being able to perceive exactness, and being able to recognise sets and series. Applying such skills to an ideal, we discover patterns inherent in it, invent symbols for those patterns, and record the patterns as laws. Then, when we again confront the world in its complex natural state, we find ourselves using these laws to predict or manipulate the behaviour of things.

So our tendency to simplify and idealise isolates qualities, and when we study these qualities in detail, we have entered mathematics. Before beginning mathematics work, the child must therefore do two things: explore and accept the notion of idealised things with isolated qualities; and gain practice in the requisite intellectual skills.

First, to introduce the idealisation of things and the isolation of qualities, the child has the early Sensorial Activities. The sensorial materials, you'll remember, are specifically designed to isolate qualities – including form, quantity, dimensions, change and distance. Think of the ideal forms in the GEOMETRIC CABINET and the GEOMETRIC SOLIDS, the ideal dimensions in the RED RODS, and the ideal gradations of the CYLINDER BLOCKS. Working with the sensorial materials gives the child a chance to deal with isolated qualities physically, and so acquire an embodied sensibility of the mathematical world of the ideal.

Second, the Montessori child is introduced to the requisite intellectual skills for mathematics by many aspects of both the Practical Activities and the Sensorial Activities. From the earliest Practical Activities, such as POURING BEANS BETWEEN TWO JUGS, to the more complex, such as SWEEPING SAWDUST, the child gradually acquires deep corporeal experience in three basic mathematical skills – exactness, calculation and repetition – evident in the child's efforts to gain dexterity in manipulating the practical materials and to organise each activity before carrying it out. The Sensorial Activities also provide the child with basic skills needed for mathematics work, including: calculation of amount or degree (e.g. PINK TOWER, RED RODS); exactness in perception and dexterity (e.g. CYLINDER BLOCKS, SORTING GRAINS); discrimination among similarities (e.g. COLOUR TABLETS, SOUND BOXES); repetition (e.g. BARIC TABLETS, SQUARE OF PYTHAGORAS); set recognition (e.g. GEOMETRIC SOLIDS and GEOMETRIC CABINET); algebraic analysis (e.g. BINOMIAL AND TRINOMIAL CUBES, CONSTRUCTIVE TRIANGLES); and recognition of progression in a series (e.g. BROWN STAIR, TACTILE TABLETS). Most of the sensorial materials provide the child with experience in more than one of these skills.

The Mathematics Activities themselves are organised into five groups, plus some FRACTIONS activities. The activities within each group are as follows. (Activities described in this book are shown in CAPITALS.)

Group 1: Introduction to Numbers
    NUMBER RODS, SANDPAPER NUMBERS, NUMBER TABLETS, SPINDLES, NUMBERS AND COUNTERS, MEMORY PLAY

Group 2: Introduction to the Decimal System
LIMITED BEAD MATERIAL, NUMBER CARDS, FUNCTION OF THE
DECIMAL SYSTEM, FORMATION OF COMPLEX NUMBERS,
Unlimited Bead Material (ADDITION, Subtraction,
Multiplication, Division), Stamps (Addition, Subtraction,
Multiplication, Division), Dots
Group 3: Introduction to Tens, Teens and Counting
INTRODUCTION TO TEENS, INTRODUCTION TO TENS, Counting
Group 4: Arithmetic Tables
Addition Snake Game, Addition Strip Board, Addition
Charts, Subtraction Snake Game, Subtraction Strip Board,
Subtraction Charts, Multiplication Tables, Multiplication
Bead Boards, Multiplication Charts, Unit Division Board,
Division Charts
Group 5: Abstraction
Short Bead Frame, Hierarchies, Long Bead Frame, Simple
Division.

Group One introduces units of quantity, and illustrates their
use in several exercises that count up to ten. Group Two is an
introduction to the decimal system (arithmetic in base ten),
giving concrete experience with units, tens, hundreds and
thousands as represented by beads, and showing how these are
combined in arithmetic operations. Group Three, which is done
concurrently with Group Two, gives experience with the decimal
system beads as applied to counting by units, by linear intervals,
and by geometric progression. Group Four uses strips, boards
and beads to give material demonstrations of addition,
subtraction, multiplication and division, and records the results
of these operations in tables to help the child remember them.
Group Five is the transition to abstraction, helping the child
internalise the functions of arithmetic and gradually disregard
the physical manipulations of materials.

The Mathematics work proceeds, as in all Montessori learning
schemes, by three stage learning (see the discussion on
'Learning by Connecting' in the first chapter): we first simply
present the components of the experience; second, we connect
those components as a circumscribed concept and bring out the
concept's characteristic attributes; and lastly, we give context to
the concept through repeated application.

Three stage learning is evident in the overall scheme of the five
groups. In Group One, the child is presented with the
fundamental components of arithmetic, as simple postulates.
Groups Two, Three and Four bring these components together in
many different ways to illustrate the workings of arithmetic. In
Group Five, arithmetic becomes an applied thought process, and
the child no longer needs the aid of the physical demonstration of
its workings. Three stage learning is the strategy within each
Group as well: for example, in Group Two, the components of the
decimal system are first experienced as a concrete given; then
they are handled and manipulated to discover their inter-

relationships; finally, the concept of the decimal system is abstracted and used by the child in symbols. Three stage learning is also the method followed for introducing each and every exercise: show the material; help the child experience the material's use and purpose; and invite the child to work with the material independently.

As you can see from the CAPITALISED activities in the above listing, this book details only the most basic Mathematics Activities. All the activities detailed in this book, if offered, are within the reach of most under-fives. But there are always a few under-fives with a special aptitude for maths, who will happily progress as far as Group 5.

In this regard, it must be remembered that the Mathematics Activities, like all other Montessori activities, are not a teaching syllabus to be followed at a set pace. They are instead to be experienced by the child as a very relaxed form of play – to be pursued or not as the child wishes. There should never be pressure, no matter how subtle, to move faster or further than the child's natural inclinations.

Similarly, when the child errs in maths, the adult has a strong urge to step in and correct the error – this seems to be a stronger impulse on our part with maths than with the other disciplines. But in the Montessori environment, you must not draw attention to error, for this may create an air of expectation, and the whole effectiveness of the Montessori approach as an aid to natural development may be tainted for the child. When an error occurs, you must decide whether it happened because the child was ·momentarily distracted or careless (in which case you simply ignore the error and continue as though it didn't happen), or if the error was fundamental to the concepts being explored (such as a confusion about terminology or organisation). In the latter case, you should gracefully and without any expression of disappointment bring the activity to a close. Later, at another unrelated time, you can give a special presentation that clears up the particular confusion in the child's mind. This may mean going back one or two activities to re-establish the necessary fundamental principles.

GROUP 1: INTRODUCTION TO NUMBERS

Number Rods

Aim　To help the child learn the names of the numbers and that each number represents a quantity separate and distinct from all others. To help the child memorise the sequence 'one' to 'ten'. To show that a number takes its significance from its place in the sequence of numbers. To show that numbers can represent either the extent of a quality or a unified set of equal parts.

Ten wooden rods, square (2.5 x 2.5 cm) on each end, varying in
length from 1 metre to 10 cm by 10 cm increments. The rods are
painted red and blue, alternating every 10 cm. The 10 cm rod is
red, and the 30, 50, 70 and 90 cm rods are red on both end
partitions.

Material

– Name the Number Rods and show where they are kept.
– Ask the child to spread a floor mat and show how to place the
rods in random order on the mat, but with all the rods parallel
and all with a red partition on the far left side.
– Invite the child to build a stair as with the Red Rods (see RED
RODS in the Sensorial Activities), making sure that the red ends
are aligned on the left.

Presentation

(1) The child builds the rod stair as in the presentation.
(2) One day when the child has built the rods, begin Three Stage
Lessons on the names of the quantities represented by the
rods (see Sensorial Activities for the method of a THREE STAGE
LESSON). Each time a rod is identified in any stage, it should
be counted and named by the child (touching each partition
from left to right, saying 'one, two, . . .').

Begin with the rods representing 1, 2, and 3, and do three
at a time until the child knows 1 through 10. If a child has
particular difficulty with a rod in a lesson, that rod should be
included in the next lesson.

Each lesson should begin by removing the relevant rods
from the constructed stair, so that it is evident where the rods
fit in the sequence.

Exercises

Sandpaper Numbers
To introduce the symbols (i.e. the written numbers) for the
quantities the child is learning to recognise, and for zero, a
quantity not previously encountered.

Aim

Ten thin boards, painted green, on each of which is glued a
number from '0' to'9', cut from smooth sandpaper. An open box
which holds the boards upright.

(DIY hint: Use green matboard instead of wood for the boards.
Following a sans-serif style similar to that illustrated here, make
templates of the numbers from index cards, cut them out with a
utility knife, trace them face down on the back of fine sandpaper,
and cut the shapes out of the sandpaper. Glue the numbers,
sandpaper side up, onto the coloured side of the matboard.)

Material

– Name the Sandpaper Numbers and show where they are kept.
– Sensitise yours and the child's fingers (see SENSITISING THE
FINGERS in the Sensorial Activities).
– Ask the child to spread a table mat and show how to remove
and replace the boards in their box without scraping them.

Presentation

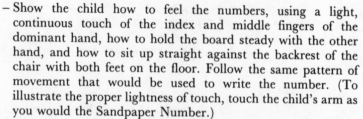

– Show the child how to feel the numbers, using a light, continuous touch of the index and middle fingers of the dominant hand, how to hold the board steady with the other hand, and how to sit up straight against the backrest of the chair with both feet on the floor. Follow the same pattern of movement that would be used to write the number. (To illustrate the proper lightness of touch, touch the child's arm as you would the Sandpaper Number.)

– Associate the symbols with their names by Three Stage Lessons. Each time a symbol is identified in any stage, it should be felt and then named by the child.

Do the first lesson with 1, 2 and 3, and then do three at a time up through 9. If the child has particular difficulty with a number in a lesson, that number should be included in the next lesson. Present a Three Stage Lesson that includes '0' only after the child has had experience with the SPINDLES activity.

Number Tablets (with the Number Rods)

Aim To associate the named quantities represented by the Number Rods with their written symbols. To give a sensorial key to the sequence 1 to 10. To develop an immediate visual recognition of the quantities 1 through 10. To provide an introductory sensorial key to addition and subtraction.

Material Ten small wooden tablets, on each of which is printed, in red, a number from 1 to 10. An open box which holds the tablets upright.

The Number Rods.

Presentation – Name the Number Tablets and show where they are kept.

– Ask the child to lay two floor mats, near to one another, and on one mat lay out the Number Rods in a random but parallel arrangement, as though they are ready to build.

– Lay out the Number Tablets, face up, in a random arrangement, on the second mat.

– Introduce the '10' tablet, name it, and ask the child to repeat the name, locate the corresponding rod and lean the tablet against it, facing you. (If necessary, do a Three Stage Lesson with '10' and two other numbers.)

– Invite the child to pick another tablet, read it, locate the corresponding rod and lean the tablet against it.

– Invite the child to do the same for another tablet, and then let the child continue, until all ten tablets are paired with their corresponding rods.

Exercises (1) The child pairs the Number Tablets with the Number Rods as in the presentation.

(2) Place the rods in random order on one mat, and the tablets in random order on another mat some distance away. At the

tablets mat, the child selects and looks at a tablet, puts it to one side on its mat, goes to the other mat to find the corresponding rod, counts the rod to ensure it is correct, brings the rod back to the tablets mat and puts it down, counts the rod again, and leans its tablet against it. This is repeated for each of the tablets on the mat, as long as the child wishes.

(3) Again place the rods in random order on one mat, and the tablets in random order on another mat some distance away. At the rods mat, the child selects a rod without counting it, puts it to one side, goes to the other mat to find the corresponding tablet, brings the tablet back to the rods mat, counts the rod to be sure the choice of tablet was correct, and leans the tablet against the rod. This is repeated for each rod.

(4) The child builds the Number Rods in a stair on one mat and then lays out the Number Tablets in random order on a nearby mat. The child slides forward the unit rod, places the '1' tablet against it, slides forward the two rod, places the '2' tablet against its right partition, and so on, until the stair is reconstructed a few inches forward, with each rod labelled by its corresponding tablet leaning against its rightmost partition. The child reads from 1 to 10, and then from 10 to 1, pointing to the tablets while reading the numbers.

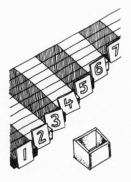

(5) Continuing one day from exercise (4), with the stair built and labelled, sit with the child at the mat, and say that you 'have something new to show'.

Isolate the ten rod and the '10' tablet leaning against it, by sliding them about a foot behind the stair. Similarly slide back the nine rod and the '9' tablet leaning against it, but leave a gap of an inch or two between the rods, and make them exactly aligned on the left. Then ask the child, indicating the space to the right of the nine rod, 'Which rod can we put here to make the two lengths the same?' When the child selects the unit rod, place it and its tablet on the right end of the nine rod. Count the nine rod, from left to right, and continue with the unit rod, calling it 'ten'. Then state the combination, saying, 'nine and one makes ten', touching the appropriate rods while speaking.

Repeat the entire process with the eight rod and two rod, then the seven rod and three rod, and then the six rod and four rod, consistently leaving a gap of an inch or two between the rods, and exactly aligning them on the left. Refer back to the ten rod as the length that is to be matched. Lastly, two fives are shown to make ten, by aligning the five rod with the others on the left, and then flipping it over so that it aligns with the others on the right. (Do not count the five rod or place its tablet against it.)

In the same way, as with the ten rod, the child combines two rods to make up the length of the nine rod, and then the eight rod, and so on down to the unit rod, which of course cannot be made from other rods. Before doing each set of sums, put away the rods and the tablets representing higher numbers than the sum being made.

To dismantle the rods and tablets for each set of sums, the child should first set aside one rod from one of the combinations and describe the subtraction, saying for example, 'ten take away three leaves seven', touching the appropriate rods while speaking. The child performs a subtraction for each of the combinations until all the rods and tablets are taken away.

As the child gains more experience making and putting away these combinations, encourage a shift in language to proper maths terms; for example, change from 'eight and two make ten' to 'eight plus two equals ten', and change from 'ten take away three leaves seven' to 'ten minus three equals seven'.

Group Play   After experience with exercise (3), work with one or more children to encourage the instant recognition, without counting, of the quantities represented by the rods. Show a child a rod, and ask the number, or conversely, show a number, and ask a child to find the rod without any counting. Immediately afterward, each time, count the partitions aloud with the group, so that if a child makes an error, it is corrected without placing blame.

Spindles

Aim   To show that numbers can represent a collection of separate objects (as opposed to the extent of a single quality). To give an experience of the quantity 'zero'. To ground the realisation that '0' to '9' are all the symbols needed for arithmetic.

Material   A tray (in two sections) with sloping partitions labelled '0' through '9'. Forty-five wooden spindles in a box. Eight pieces of ribbon increasing in length from five to twelve inches.

(DIY hint: Use new unsharpened pencils for the 'spindles', and divide two shallow cardboard boxes (wide enough for a pencil) each into five partitions, labeling them '0', '1', '2', '3' and '4' in one box, and '5', '6', '7', '8' and '9' in the other box (in the same writing style as the NUMBER TABLETS). Store the forty-five pencils in their own box.)

Presentation   – Name the Spindles and their boxes and show where they are kept.
– Ask the child to lay a floor mat. Show how to place the two sections next to each other to make a single tray of ten adjacent partitions.
– Ask the child to read the numbers on the partitions. If the child does not know one of the numbers, bring the Number Tablets over and let the child find the one that matches.

- Point to the '1' partition, say 'one', and remove one spindle from the box, counting 'one', and placing it on the mat. Then place the spindle in the '1' partition.
- Point to the '2' partition, say 'two', and remove two spindles singly from the box, counting them 'one, two', and placing them on the mat. Then place the two spindles in the partition.
- Continue in the same way to the '9' partition, after which all forty-five spindles will be divided among the partitions.
- Point to the '0' partition, say 'zero', and show that there is nothing at all in that partition.
- Replace all the spindles in their box and invite the child to have a turn.

(1) The child counts and places the spindles in the partitions as in the presentation.
(2) The same as exercise (1), except that the child uses ribbons to tie each group of two to nine counted spindles into a bundle before placing them in their partition. Show the child how to use the short ribbons first and then longer ribbons to tie the larger bundles.

Numbers and Counters

Aim To reinforce the sequence one to ten, and to give another perceptual experience of quantity as a collection of separate objects. To introduce the concept of odd and even.

Material A small box containing fifty-five small, red, round, plastic chips or 'counters'. Another box, containing solid, wooden, red-painted figures, or 'numbers', '1' to '10' (with a separate '1' and '0' for '10').

(DIY hint: Use counters as found in the children's game 'tiddly-winks', and make cardboard cut-outs for the 'numbers', following the same style lettering as the NUMBER TABLETS.)

Presentation
- Name the Numbers and Counters and show where they are kept.
- Ask the child to lay a floor mat.
- Lay out the numbers at random on the mat.
- Counting aloud ('one, two . . .'), start to place the numbers named in a row from left to right along the far edge of the mat, with a few inches between them; allow the child to finish after you've started. Specially show how to make 10.
- Lay out the appropriate amount of counters for each number 1 to 10, so as to form, for each number, a column of pairs of counters running from the number towards yourself. When placing the counters, put down the left of the first pair, counting 'one', then the right of the first pair, counting 'two', the left of the second pair, counting 'three', and so on. Leave an inch of space between the counters in each pair. For 1, 3, 5, 7 and 9,

place the last unpaired counter in the centre, rather than on the left or right.

– Visually examine the completed arrangement with interest. Put away the counters and numbers, and invite the child to re-make the arrangement independently.

Exercises

(1) The child works with the Numbers and Counters as in the presentation.

(2) The child constructs the above arrangement of Numbers and Counters. Draw the tip of your finger down the middle of each column of pairs; for each row in which your finger strikes an unpaired counter at the end of the column, move the number and all the counters a few inches towards yourself on the mat; leave the other columns in place. Teach by Three Stage Lesson that the numbers which had an unpaired counter are 'odd' numbers, and that the numbers with only pairs of counters are 'even' numbers: (Stage 1) show which are odd or even; (Stage 2) repeatedly ask the child to find one that is odd or even; (Stage 3) repeatedly ask whether a particular number is odd or even.

Memory Play

Aim

To give the child practice in recognising and counting numbers outside the context of a series. To develop the child's memory of the numbers 1 through 10.

Material

A small basket with a lid containing eleven folded cards, on each of which is written a number from '0' to '10'.

Fifty-five small, similar objects (e.g. buttons, seashells or tiny pebbles).

Presentation

– Call a group of up to eleven children (see HANDLING A BOOK in the Practical Activities for suggestions on how to call a group).

– Name the Memory Play material and show all the children where it is kept.

– Ask one of children to lay a floor mat.

– Place the basket with the cards in the centre of the mat and the box of objects on a table in another room.

– Invite each child, one at a time, to select a card from the basket, look at it once, remember the number, and put the card face down on the mat.

– Then after every child has taken a card, ask them one at a time to go to the box of objects and bring back to the mat the number of objects that was written on the card.

– Invite each child, one at a time, to count aloud the number of objects brought back, to turn over the card and see if it says the same, and then to return the card to the basket and the objects to their box. Do not comment on whether or not the child was correct. Invite each child to take another card and play again.

(The child who selects the card with '0' on it will not collect any objects. Point this out to the group, making the child feel pleased and special, rather than left out.)

(1) A child, or group of children, works independently as in the presentation. **Exercise**

GROUP 2: INTRODUCTION TO THE DECIMAL SYSTEM

Limited Bead Material

To make the child familiar with the names of the decimal categories (units, tens, hundreds and thousands) and with their relative proportions. To show that each decimal category is ten times the previous category. Perceptually, to introduce exponents as dimensions, showing units to be points, tens to be lines, hundreds to be squares, and thousands to be cubes; by having only one thousand, to suggest that the set of a point, line, square and cube completes one whole cycle of the decimal hierarchy, the cube being the 'point' in the next higher cycle of the hierarchy. **Aim**

A small wooden tray holding: nine golden-coloured, single 'unit beads' on a plank with nine indentations; nine golden ten-bead bars ('ten-bars') in a shallow open box; nine golden hundred-bead squares ('hundred-squares') in a deeper open box; and one golden thousand-bead cube ('thousand-cube') in a similar open box. **Material**

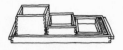

(DIY hint: You can make the bead material, but it will be time-consuming, and buying the beads individually is probably more expensive than simply buying the finished Montessori material. If you wish to make the material yourself anyway, you'll need: 1,999 identical beads with holes, each bead about 7 mm in diameter, and preferably an attractive, golden colour; stiff but pliable brass wire, slightly less in diameter than the holes in the beads; very thin brass wire; wire-cutters; and a pair of strong, narrow-pointed pliers.

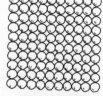

Set aside nine beads for the unit beads.

To make the ten-bead bars, string together ten beads on a straight piece of thick wire, curl one end of the wire with the pliers in a 5 mm diameter loop, cut the wire on the other side of the ten beads, and make another 5 mm loop on that end, thereby tightly locking the beads between the two loops. Make 199 of these ten-bead bars, using all the beads. Set aside nine of the bars.

To make the hundred-bead squares, lay ten ten-bead bars adjacent to one another to form a square, and weave the thin wire in and out of the ten-bead bar wires, in five straight lines across the square. As you work, ensure that all the beads on the square are in line, and tuck in all wire ends, so that they cannot poke the child's finger. Make nineteen of these hundred-bead squares. Set aside nine of the squares.

To make the thousand-bead cube, stack the remaining ten squares, with the loops all on the same two sides, and weave the thin wire in and out of the outermost layer of ten-bead bar wires, all the way around the cube, in four continuous lines (going between the weaving on the hundred-bead squares). As you work, ensure that all the beads on the cube are in line, and tuck in all wire ends.

To make the 'unit plank', take a small rectangle of hard wood and drill nine small indentations in a row, with a drill bit slightly smaller than the diameter of a bead.)

Presentation
– Name the Limited Bead Material and show where it is kept.
– Ask the child to spread a floor mat and show how to carry the tray and place it down on the mat without tipping it.
– Remove a unit bead from the tray and place it on the mat. Say, 'This is one unit.' Invite the child to hold it. Examine it with the child.
– Remove a ten-bar from the tray and place it on the mat. Say, 'This is one ten.' Invite the child to hold it. Examine it with the child. Say, 'This ten is made of units; let's see how many.' Count the beads in the ten-bar aloud with the child, holding a unit bead against each bead counted. Then say, 'There are ten units in one ten.' Invite the child to hold, compare and explore the ten-bar and the unit bead.
– Remove a hundred-square from the tray and place it on the mat. Say, 'This is one hundred.' Invite the child to hold it. Examine it with the child. Say, 'This hundred is made of tens; let's see how many.' Count the ten-bars in the hundred-square aloud with the child, holding a ten-bar against each bar counted. Then say, 'There are ten tens in one hundred.' Invite the child to hold, compare and explore the hundred-square and the ten-bar.
– Remove the thousand-cube from the tray and place it on the mat. Say, 'This is one thousand.' Invite the child to hold it. Examine it with the child. Say, 'This thousand is made of hundreds; let's see how many.' Count the hundred-squares in the thousand-cube aloud with the child, holding one edge of a hundred-square against each hundred-square counted. Then say, 'There are ten hundreds in one thousand.' Invite the child to hold, compare and explore the thousand-cube and the hundred-square.
– Examine with the child the relative sizes and weights of the unit bead, the ten-bar, the hundred-square, and the thousand-cube.
– Teach the names 'one unit', 'one ten', 'one hundred' and 'one thousand' by Three Stage Lesson.

Exercises
(1) On a floor mat, make a pile of all the units, a pile of the ten-bars, a pile of the hundred-squares, and also place out the

thousand cube, going from right to left. Remove the three boxes from the tray, but leave in the tray the unit plank with the indentations.

Sit a few feet from the mat and ask the child to bring, for example, 'four tens' in the tray. When the child brings them, touch and count aloud: 'One ten, two tens, three tens, four tens! Thank you!' Ask the child to return them to their pile. Repeat this many times, asking for any amount of the bead material, from one to nine units, tens or hundreds, or the one thousand, but ask for only one category at a time. Show the child how to place the unit beads in the indentations on the plank. If the child errs in bringing you the right number of things, then before counting them say, 'I forgot! What did I ask for?' so that by counting, the child sees the mistake.

(2) Start with the beads on the mat, and the empty tray, as in exercise (1).

Place in the tray, for example, three hundred-bead squares, and ask the child, 'What do I have?' Allow the child to touch and count aloud: 'One hundred, two hundreds, three hundreds – three hundreds!' Thank the child and return the beads to their pile. Repeat many times, placing in the tray any amount of the bead material, from one to nine units, tens or hundreds, or the one thousand, but place in the tray only one category at a time. Use the unit plank for the unit beads.

Number Cards

Aim To introduce the child to the symbols for the decimal categories, and to relate the names of the symbols to the number of zeros they have. To reinforce the notion of cycles of decimal hierarchy, in the pattern of the colours of the cards.

Material Thirty-six Number Cards printed as follows: '1' to '9' in green; '10' through '90' by tens in blue; '100' to '900' by hundreds in red; and '1000' to '9000' in green. The unit cards are only wide enough for one digit, the ten cards are the width of two digits, and so on. A box with a lid, to store the cards.

Preparation Put away the '2000' to '9000' Number Cards for later use.

Presentation
– Name the Number Cards and show where they are kept.
– Ask the child to lay a floor mat and show how to remove the cards from the box, one category at a time.
– Isolate the 1, 10, 100 and 1000 cards. Introduce the cards as 'one unit', 'one ten – with one zero', 'one hundred – with two zeros', and 'one thousand – with three zeros'. Give a Three Stage Lesson on the names of these four cards: 'one unit', 'one ten', 'one hundred' and 'one thousand'.

Exercises (1) Ask the child to lay a floor mat, and order the Number Cards in a pile, from '1' on the top, down to '1000' on the bottom.

On the mat, read through the unit cards aloud with the child, placing the cards in a pile on the right side of the mat. Rather than just reading 'one, two, three. . .', say 'one unit, two units, three units. . .' Repeat with the tens cards, saying 'one ten, two tens, three tens. . .', placing these in a pile to the left of the units. Repeat with the hundreds cards, saying 'one hundred, two hundreds, three hundreds. . .', placing these in a pile to the left of the tens. Read the last card 'one thousand' and place it to the left of the hundreds pile.

When you finish reading the Number Cards in this fashion, remind the child about the number of zeros, showing that all the units have no zeros, all the tens have one zero, all the hundreds have two zeros, and the thousand has three zeros.

Pick out a card at random from any pile and ask the child what it is. The child says, for example, 'four tens'. Repeat for other cards chosen at random. If the child errs consistently, repeat the exercise from the start another day.

Later, the child reads through the categories as above and places them in piles independently.

10	1
20	2
30	3
40	4
50	5
60	6
70	7
80	8
90	9

1000	100
2000	200
3000	300
4000	400
5000	500
6000	600
7000	700
8000	800
9000	900

(2) One day, after the child is finished placing the cards in their four piles, from right to left, ask the child to locate the card for a particular number. Say, for example, 'Please hand me the card for "three tens".' After each selection, the child replaces the card in its pile, inserting it in its correct place in the sequence.

Repeat as long as the child likes, but only ask for one card at a time.

Function of the Decimal System

Aim To show that to go beyond nine of any category, one must go to the next higher category, for both the beads and the cards. To make evident the parallel hierarchy of the quantities and their symbols. To combine the quantities and symbols in practice, and to become familiar with their correspondence.

Material The LIMITED BEAD MATERIAL and the NUMBER CARDS (excluding '2000' to '9000').

Felt lined trays, each with a cup to hold unit beads.

Presentation – Ask the child to spread a floor mat and to place on it the tray with the Limited Bead Material.

– Say, 'we must start on this side of the mat', indicating the right side.

– Place out the nine unit beads in a column running towards you on the right side of the mat, with about 10 cm between each bead, counting 'one unit, two units, three units. . .' as you place them down. When you are done, indicate that no unit beads remain, and ask, 'What comes after nine units?' Answer with the child, 'ten units'.

– Say, 'ten units are the same as one ten', and place down a ten-bar running far and near, its furthest end bead about 15 cm directly to the left of the furthest unit bead. Place out the ten-bars in a column as above, each with its furthest end bead directly to the left of the next unit bead, counting 'one ten, two tens, three tens. . .' as you place them down. When you're done, indicate that no ten-bars are left, and ask, 'What comes after nine tens?' Answer with the child, 'ten tens'.

– Say, 'ten tens are the same as one hundred', and place down a hundred-square, about 15 cm directly to the left of the furthest ten-bar. Place out the hundred-squares in a column as above, counting, 'one hundred, two hundreds, three hundreds. . .' as you place them down. When you are done, indicate that no hundred-squares are left, and ask, 'What comes after nine hundreds?' Answer with the child, 'ten hundreds'.

– Say, 'ten hundreds are the same as one thousand', and place down the thousand-cube, about 15 cm directly to the left of the furthest hundred-square. Count, 'one thousand'.

– Count through the entire layout from one unit to nine units, one ten to nine tens, one hundred to nine hundreds, to one thousand.

– Ask the child to spread a second floor mat nearby the first. Lay out the Number Cards following exactly the same procedure and language as used with the Limited Bead Material: making corresponding columns with the cards; showing that after nine of any category one must go to the next higher category; and counting through the entire layout when you are done.

– Invite the child visually to compare the arrangements on the two mats, and to discover their parallel hierarchies.

– Show the child how to follow the same hierarchical order in putting the materials back in their containers, and afterwards invite the child to construct the layouts independently.

(1) The child independently constructs the parallel arrangements on two mats, as in the presentation, and does this many times.   **Exercises**

(2) Ask two or three children who have had experience with exercise (1) to work together to lay out the bead and card arrangements on two mats, as in that exercise, but to place the mats at opposite ends of the room. Situate yourself at the mat with the Number Cards, give each child a tray with a cup, explaining that the cup is to put unit beads in. Then for each child in turn, place a single card on the tray, and ask the child to 'bring this amount of beads' from the bead mat. When the beads are brought on the tray, count them aloud. Thank the child and request that the cards and beads be put back into their respective arrangements; follow the child to be sure this is done correctly. Emphasise the need for exactness

in the replacement of the materials. Give each child many different cards to try but give only one card at a time. Repeat the entire activity a number of times over the following weeks.

(3) The same as exercise (2), but situate yourself at the mat with the beads, place a certain number of one category of beads on the tray and ask the child to 'find the card for this amount of beads'. When the child returns with a card, count the beads (for example, 'one ten, two tens, three tens, four tens – four tens'), placing them, as they're counted, in a neat column in front of the card. As before, give each child many tries, but only give beads from one category at a time. Repeat the entire activity a number of times on separate occasions.

Formation of Complex Numbers

Aim To show that in the hierarchy of the decimal system, it is the place of a digit which gives it its meaning, and that zero is a place holder for an empty category. To give the child practice in the interpretation of complex numbers and the naming of these amounts. To introduce the child to the proper wording for the teens and tens. To demonstrate that any number can be formed from the ten digits placed in their appropriate category.

Material The LIMITED BEAD MATERIAL, the NUMBER CARDS (excluding '2000' to '9000').

One felt-lined tray with a cup to hold unit beads.

Presentation – Ask a child to lay out the Limited Bead Material on one mat, and the Number Cards on another mat on the far side of the room, using the parallel column arrangements (see FUNCTION OF THE DECIMAL SYSTEM).

– Situate yourself at the mat with the Number Cards, give the child the tray with the cup, and place on it one card from the units category, and next to it, one card from the tens category, and say 'bring this amount of beads' from the bead mat. When the child returns with both unit beads and ten-bead bars on the tray, place the units cards and unit beads on the right side of the tray, and the tens cards and ten-bars on the left. Then count both sets of beads aloud, first the units and next the tens.

– Say you will now do something special with the cards. Place the units card, face up, on top of the tens card. Then with your left hand, hold the two cards together, face up, with your thumb and middle finger on the top and bottom edges. While the child is watching, gently push the right edge of the bottom card against the palm of your right hand, so that the units card slides down over the zero on the tens card.

– Pointing to the units card say for example, 'five units', and then pointing to the part of the tens card still showing, say for example, 'two tens'. Then give the correct name, saying for example, 'We call two tens and five units, "twenty-five".'

– Ask the child to replace the materials in their respective arrangements on the two mats.

– Repeat in the same way several times. Each time the child brings the beads, you should overlay the cards as above, slide the units card down into place, read and point to the two cards, and then give the number's correct name.

(1) Repeat the presentation another time.

Exercises

(2) The same as exercise (1), except place a units card, a tens card, and a hundreds card on the child's tray. When counting the beads brought back, arrange the units, tens and hundreds materials right-to-left on the tray. Overlay the cards as before, but with the hundreds card on the bottom, and slide both the tens and units cards into place, aligned on the right. Point and say, for example, 'Three units, seven tens, and four hundreds; we call this "four hundred seventy-three".'

(3) The same as exercise (2), but include the one thousand card, and place it on the bottom when overlaying the cards.

(4) The same as exercise (3), but omit either the units, tens or hundreds card. After overlaying the cards and sliding them into position, indicate that the zero shows through in the empty category. Point and say, for example, 'You brought eight units – how many tens? none! – six hundreds, and one thousand. We call this "one thousand, six hundred and eight".' Repeat this exercise many times, omitting a different category each time, and then omitting two categories.

(5) The same as exercise (3), except situate yourself at the mat with the beads (instead of the cards), place a number of beads from each category on the child's tray, asking the child to 'find the cards for these beads'. When the child returns with cards, then for each category, count the beads and read the card, while in the process arranging the categories right-to-left. Overlay the cards, slide them into position, read the categories right-to-left, and properly name the complex number, all as before.

(6) The same as exercise (5), but omit one category, and later, two categories.

(7) Repeat exercises (3) and (5) many times, but invite the child to overlay the cards, slide them into position, and read the categories right-to-left, all independently. Say and have the child repeat the proper name for the complex number.

Unlimited Bead Material

To give a sensorial impression of addition as a putting together of quantities. To reinforce the idea that ten of one category is the same as one of the next higher category; to put this idea to use in addition with 'carrying'. To build the child's sense of social

Aim

co-operation by having a number of children contribute to one goal.

Material   The Unlimited Bead Material, which includes a container with a large supply of unit beads, a box with a large supply of ten-bead bars, a box with many hundred-bead squares (or square wooden tablets representing these), and nine thousand-bead cubes (or wooden cubes representing these), all golden-coloured, and all on a large tray.

(DIY hint: See LIMITED BEAD MATERIAL on how to make the bead material; make the equivalent of three sets of the Limited Bead Material, plus six extra thousand-bead cubes.

Alternatively, provide thirty unit beads, make thirty ten-bead bars as above, and cut from wood thirty squares and nine cubes, equivalent in size to the bead material, painted with golden circles on all sides so as to look like the bead material.)

The NUMBER CARDS complete (i.e. including '2000' to '9000'). Three sets of Small Number Cards, about one third the size of the Number Cards, and otherwise the same, except that the thousands only go up to '3000'. There is a separate box for each set. Three felt-lined trays, each with a cup to hold unit beads.

Preliminary Activities

(a) Name the Unlimited Bead Material and show where it is kept. Show how to carry and place down the Unlimited Bead Material tray without spilling it. Show how to place out the beads in categories right-to-left on a floor mat, and name this 'the bank'. Show that any representational wooden materials are meant to be the same as real beads from the Limited Bead Material.

(b) Show the Number Cards, name the Small Number Cards, and show where they are kept. Show how to arrange the large Number Cards, as well as a set of Small Number Cards, in rows and columns as in the FUNCTION OF THE DECIMAL SYSTEM activity, but with the edges of the cards touching.

(c) Do a 'changing' exercise, trading at the bank ten unit beads for one ten-bar, ten ten-bars for one hundred-square, ten hundred-squares for one thousand-cube, and the converse.

Presentation

– Gather two or three ready children, and lay three floor mats: lay out the 'bank' on the middle mat, the large Number Cards on the left mat, and one set of Small Number Cards on the right mat.

– Give each child a felt-lined tray.

– Put on each tray a different four-digit number in Small Number Cards, which when added, do not involve 'carrying' between categories (e.g. 2143, 3524 and 1212). Hand each child the four cards and then tell them to stack the cards and slide them into position (as in the FORMATION OF COMPLEX NUMBERS).

– With you (or an experienced child) acting as the 'banker', each child goes to the 'bank' and gets the amount of beads shown on

his or her cards. Each child counts to verify what the 'banker' has given.
- Show the children how to place down their four-digit numbers in a neat column of three and then simply put all their beads in a big pile, on the middle mat.
- Ask each child, in turn, to sort out one category of beads from the pile, starting with the units. When a category is counted, the child gets the large Number Card for that amount of cards, and places it next to the counted category.
- When all four categories have been sorted, stack and slide the four large cards into place, read the resulting number, then place that number below the column of small cards on the mat.
- Give the proper numerical name (e.g. 'six thousand, eight hundred, seventy-nine') for the large card sum.
- Review what was done, naming the children and their actions, and call the activity an 'addition'.
- Have the children help you replace the materials in their original positions on the three mats.
- Do more additions the same way.
- Direct the children to put away the materials and mats.

Exercises

(1) Do addition another day as in the presentation.
(2) Do addition with 'changing' and 'carrying' from one category to the next. Select numbers which when added will involve 'carrying' (e.g. 2618, 1423 and 3547), though not necessarily in every category, and definitely not in the thousands category. During the counting of the categories of the big pile, starting with the units, interrupt when a child gets up to 'ten', and suggest 'changing the ten at the bank' for one piece of the next higher category. Finish as before. Sometimes try having numbers or answers with empty categories, that is, with one or more zeros.

GROUP 3: INTRODUCTION TO TEENS AND TENS

Introduction to Teens

Aim

To associate the names 'eleven' to 'nineteen' with their quantities and symbols, and to combine the quantities and symbols.

Material

Nine different bead bars, called the 'Short Bead Stair', ranging in length from one bead to nine beads, each bar a different colour (corresponding to the sequence of colours of the tiles in the Sensorial Activity SQUARE OF PYTHAGORAS). A box with a triangular compartment to hold the bars in the shape of a stair.

Nine golden ten-bead bars.

Two tall, rectangular 'Teen Boards', each divided into five sections, each section bordered above and below by a raised

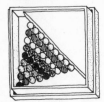

wooden slat. In each section (except the bottom section of the second board) is printed a large '10'.

Nine 'Digits' tablets, each printed with a digit '1' to '9', which can be slid between the slats on the Teen Boards to cover the '0' of each '10'.

(DIY hint: To make the Short Bead Stair, see LIMITED BEAD MATERIAL on how to string the beads, but use coloured beads as specified above. For the Teen Boards, you could simply use a long piece of matboard, divided with lines into ten sections. Holding the board lengthwise from far to near, in each of the top nine sections print a large '10'. Make matboard Digits tablets large enough to cover the '0's.)

Preliminary Activities

(a) Name the Short Bead Stair, show where it is kept, and ask the child to spread a floor mat. Show any one bar, ask the child to count it, and ask the child the name of the colour. Introduce two other bars. Give a Three Stage Lesson to associate the numbers with the bars' colours. Give more Three Stage Lessons on other occasions, until the child can readily identify all nine bars by their colours alone, without counting.

(b) Show the child how to arrange the Short Bead Stair on the mat in the shape of a triangle with the base on top.

Presentations

(1) The Beads
   - Ask the child to lay a floor mat, to arrange on it the Short Bead Stair (as a triangle with the base on top), to place on the mat the golden ten-bead bars, and to count a golden bar to make sure it is ten.
   - Place that counted ten-bead bar on the mat running left and right, and place to its right, the unit bead from the Short Bead Stair. Count, from left to right, each of the golden beads, until you get to the unit bead, at which point you say, 'eleven'.
   - In the same way – using Short Bead Stair bars added to ten-bead bars – name, place and count up to 'twelve' and 'thirteen', making these arrangements in front of the eleven on the mat, with the ten-bead bars forming an even column and the Short Bead Stair bars extending to their right.
   - Give a Three Stage Lesson on these names. (Point when saying each name; for example, point to the three-bar saying 'thir-' and then to the ten-bar saying '-teen'.)
   - On separate occasions, give Three Stage Lessons on the remaining combinations up to 'nineteen', each time first laying out the ones that the child has already learned. After the lesson, the child counts through the whole sequence learned so far.
   - On separate occasions, ask the child several times to make a particular number, 'eleven' to 'nineteen', with the beads.
   - Later, you repeatedly make a different number with the beads, and ask the child what it is.

(2) The Boards
  - Name the Teen Boards and Digits and show where they are kept. Place the two boards on a floor mat to make one long column of '10's, with the five '10's on top. Place the Digits on the mat in an ordered stack with the '1' on top.
  - Slide the '1' digit over the '0' of the top '10', and call the resulting figure 'eleven'. Using more Digits from the stack, make and name 'twelve' and 'thirteen' in the same way, just below the '11'.
  - Give a Three Stage Lesson on these names.
  - On separate occasions, give Three Stage Lessons on the remaining combinations up to '19', each time first laying out the ones the child already knows, working from the top of the board downwards. After the lesson, the child reads through the whole sequence learned so far.
  - On separate occasions, ask the child several times to make a particular number, 'eleven' to 'nineteen', with the Teen Boards and Digits. (The child may use any '10' on either board.)
  - Later, you repeatedly make a different number with the Teen Boards and Digits, and ask the child to name it.

(3) Combining the Boards and Beads
  - Ask the child to lay a floor mat, to build on it the Short Bead Stair (as a triangle with the base on top), and to place out the golden ten-bead bars, the Teen Boards and the Digits (in an ordered stack with the '1' on top).
  - Place a ten-bead bar running left and right, to the right of each '10' on the boards.
  - At the top '10' on the board, place the unit bead from the Short Bead Stair to the right of the ten-bead bar, and slide the '1' Digit over the zero of that '10'. Say 'eleven'. Do '12' and '13' below, in the same way, and continue down through '19'.
  - Count through the sequence, pointing to each bead combination and its symbols.
  - Disassemble the arrangement and invite the child to construct it again and count through the sequence.

(1) The child independently arranges the beads and boards as in presentation (3).   **Exercise**

Introduction to Tens

To associate the names 'ten, twenty, thirty, forty, fifty, sixty, seventy, eighty, ninety' with their quantities and symbols, and to introduce counting from 1 to 99.   **Aim**

Two tall, rectangular 'Ten Boards', each divided into five sections, each section bordered above and below by a raised wooden slat. On one board, the five sections are marked '10', '20',   **Material**

'30', '40' and '50', and on the other board, the top four sections are marked '60', '70', '80' and '90'.

Nine 'Digits' tablets, each printed with a digit '1' to '9', which can be slid between the slats on the Ten Boards to cover the '0' of each number.

Nine golden ten-bead bars and ten loose golden unit beads in a container with a lid.

(DIY hint: For the Ten Boards, you could simply use a long piece of matboard, divided with lines into ten sections. Holding the board lengthwise from far to near, print in the sections from top to bottom: '10', '20', '30', '40', '50', '60', '70', '80' and '90'. Make matboard Digits tablets large enough to cover the '0's.)

Presentations

(1) Ten Boards with Beads
  – Name the Ten Boards and show where they are kept.
  – Ask the child to lay a floor mat, and to place on it the Ten Boards, the Digits tablets, and the golden ten-bead bars. Arrange the two boards to make one long column of numbers in their correct order. Arrange the Digits on the mat in an ordered stack with the '1' on top.
  – Place a ten-bead bar to the right of the '10' section on the top board, and say 'ten'; add another ten-bead bar and slide both down next to the '20' section, and say 'twenty'; add another ten-bead bar and slide all three bars down next to the '30' section, and say 'thirty'; and so on, all the way down to the '90' section.
  – Place the nine ten-bead bars to the left of the boards and invite the child to repeat the making and naming of 'ten' to 'ninety'. If the child has difficulty with any of the names (since 'twenty', 'thirty' and 'fifty' alter the pronunciation of the corresponding digits 'two', 'three' and 'five'), then give a Three Stage Lesson on those names only.

(2) Counting One to Ninety-nine
  – Ask the child to lay a floor mat and to place on it the Ten Boards, the Digits tablets, the golden ten-bead bars, and the loose unit beads. Arrange the Ten Boards in one column, and about six inches to the left of that column, place the Digits tablets in their own long column, in ascending order from far to near.
  – Place a unit bead to the right of the '1' tablet, and say 'one'; add another unit bead and place both to the right of the '2' tablet, and say 'two'; add another unit bead and place all three next to the '3' tablet, and say 'three'; and so on, up to 'nine'.
  – Add another bead, but say 'ten units are the same as one ten', and exchange the ten unit beads for one ten-bead bar, then place the bar to the right of the top '10' section on the top board, and say 'ten'.
  – Add a unit bead to the ten-bar, slide the '1' tablet over the zero, and say 'eleven'.

– Add another unit bead to the unit bead and ten-bar, replace the '1' tablet with the '2' tablet, and say 'twelve'.
– Continue to add one bead at a time, use the appropriate tablet to make the number on the board, and then say the number's name. Whenever you add the tenth unit bead, change the ten beads for another ten-bead bar, and slide all the bars down to the right of the next section on the board.
– Invite the child to finish the process (in your presence), counting all the way up to ninety-nine.

(1) The child works with ten-bead bars and the Ten Boards as in presentation (1).
(2) The child uses the unit beads and the ten-bead bars, together with the Ten Boards, to count from 1 to 99, as in presentation (2).
(3) One day, after the child places on a floor mat the materials used in exercise (2), name any number from 'one' to 'ninety-nine', and ask the child to place out the bead quantity for it, and then to make the symbol for it using the Ten Boards and Digit tablets. Repeat this as long as the child likes.

FRACTIONS

Fractions

To introduce the child to the idea of fractions as the division of a whole into equal parts.

The Fraction Insets, which are ten green, square metal plates, into each of which is cut a red, circular inset, divided by radii into between one and ten equal sections, each section having a small knob. The ten plates are arranged in two long wooden trays, increasing in the number of their sections from left to right.

(DIY hint: Using a utility knife, cut the frames and their insets from thick, stiff plastic or linoleum. For the knobs, use large beads, which you can attach by heavy plastic thread to the middle of each shape.)

– Name the Fraction Insets, show where the two trays are kept, and place them on a floor mat.
– Invite the child to handle the material freely for a long while, taking out the sections, comparing them, putting them back, mixing and sorting them, counting them, and so on.
– Explain to the child that each circle represents a fraction, which is 'a breaking into parts that are all exactly the same'. Show how the full circle has one part, the next circle has two parts the same, the next circle has three parts the same, and so on.
– The child explores the insets independently.

6 CULTURE ACTIVITIES

INTRODUCTION

In the mid-nineteenth century, biologists developed the theory of 'evolution by natural selection'. This theory was intended to explain how life on earth came to assume such a wide variety of forms and functions.

According to the theory, organisms possess 'genes', which are heritable determinants of outward characteristics. Genes vary slightly among the individuals of a 'species' – any closely related family of organisms that can produce viable offspring. Over innumerable generations, the natural variation in characteristics produced by the combination of slightly differing sets of genes, or produced by occasional errors in the transfer of genes from adult to offspring, can cause new heritable characteristics to occur. The majority of these new characteristics are either innocuous or detrimental to the survival or reproduction of the offspring who bear them. Occasionally however, one of these heritable characteristics makes an organism's survival, or its reproduction, more likely, for the particular environment in which it lives. As a result, the genes causing these characteristics are more likely to be conveyed to the organism's own offspring. If this 'selection' of a helpful characteristic is repeated over many generations, it may result in the characteristic becoming a new norm of the species. The theory proposed that the reason this natural selection process has led to widely differing life forms is that the environment which forces the selection keeps changing. The environment changes primarily in two ways: first, by gradual changes in physical conditions, such as climate, terrain and soil composition; second, by the coming and going of other evolving organisms which pose competition for limited sources of food, water, light and shelter. Each evolving species must continually cope with both these types of changes.

Nineteenth-century biologists deduced from this theory that the natural tendency of 'evolution by natural selection' is the gradual perfection of each species' adaptation to its environment (i.e. survival of the fittest), and the gradual perfection of harmony among all the various life forms sharing a particular environment (i.e. ecological stability).

If one accepts this theory, it has all kinds of implications for us, the human species. Predictably, some late nineteenth-century thinkers drew the conclusion that humans are simply advanced apes. But it is obvious even to non-academicians that there are profound differences between people and other animals, even the higher apes. What makes us somehow different from other animals in the evolutionary chain?

You can probably think of a lot of things that make us humans a very special sort of animal. For instance, we have art, religion, laws, scientific pursuits, and recorded language. But all our uniquely human attributes can be neatly summed up in one word: 'culture'.

We are different from other animals because rather than 'inherit' adaptations to the environment through genes, we humans appear to 'learn' adaptation through our culture – our society's unique interpretation of the world – and we transform the world, with our hands, in accordance with our understanding. If we accept the notion that humans evolved from a long line of ape-like animals, then we should also believe that at some point in that evolution, the human species largely ceased adapting to the environment through biological evolution, and instead began to depend upon adaptations afforded by social and cultural activities. In the last few thousand years, at least up until recently, cultural adaptation has proved to be a more rapid and direct means of adjusting to changing environmental conditions, and it seems to give far greater potential for winning out over competing species.

The human race's biological evolution must have specifically prepared it for, and made possible, its subsequent cultural evolution. Conversely, cultural evolution must be a direct product of, and augmentation of, biological evolution. It would seem to follow, then, that the two types of adaptation must operate on similar principles.

Indeed, in cultural development, as in evolution by natural selection, beneficial traits are transmitted from one generation to the next, and there is a pool of variables to draw on. In the natural environment you have the genes to do the transmitting, and you have natural genetic variations and mixings to provide the pool of variables. Similarly, in culture, you have adults teaching children rules of behaviour, values, traditions and useful facts, and you have individual dissent, innovation and cross-cultural mixing. Also, just as biological evolution produces a wide variety of species with unique adaptations to the environment, so does cultural evolution yield a wide variety of societies. And just as biological evolution tends towards the perfection of each species' adaptation, and gradually towards the harmonious cohabitation of all species in the environment, so does cultural evolution tend towards an improvement of the quality of life for individual citizens, and gradually towards the harmonious co-existence of all societies on earth.

Montessori had some very specific ideas about the way in which our early biological evolution prepared us for a later evolution of adaptation through culture. Montessori believed that mankind's early biological evolution resulted in a unique combination of certain predominant behaviour patterns, universal among humans, which she called the 'tendencies of man'. This inherited combination of 'tendencies' towards certain types of behaviour has enabled our species, and our species alone, to transcend biology and live instead by culture. That is, these 'tendencies', operating together, constitute the endpoint of mankind's formative biological evolution, and have made possible our continued evolution on the cultural level. Evolving now in this higher plane, we depend upon these particular innate behavioural 'tendencies' for our survival and continuity.

During her many years of observing children in a great variety of cultural environments, Montessori was able to identify fourteen specific behavioural traits which she considered to comprise these 'tendencies of man'. The fourteen universal tendencies are: exploration; order; gregariousness; communication; abstraction; curiosity; calculation; work, aided by repetition, concentration and self-control; perfection; creativity; and independence. Some of these tendencies appear individually in other species of animals, but this special combination of fourteen is found only in us.

All these 'tendencies of man', according to Montessori, operate upon our behaviour like a single force, and all are apparent to some degree in each of our cultural, or adaptive, activities. Nevertheless, each of the various tendencies seems to complement precisely the effects of certain others, and we can identify specific aspects of culture which derive primarily from certain tendencies acting in concert. These clusters of tendencies also appear to compound their effects in a particular sequence, building up – in two phases – the process of cultural adaptation.

Our initial contact with the environment arises largely from our tendency to 'explore' and perceive 'order' in the world. Exploration entails seeking unfamiliar stimuli, and searching for new and unknown perspectives. Order is used to orient ourselves to the world, to understand our position in relation to all of the world's parts. The aspect of culture most clearly associated with these two tendencies is natural history. Practitioners of natural history explore and classify the world around them.

It is often said that we are social animals, and our tendency to 'gregariousness' leads us to share with others our experiences of the environment. In addition to being in one another's presence, the tendency to 'communicate' helps to bind participants through shared experiences, and increases the degree to which common experiences are mutual. Shared discoveries through exploration further bind us spiritually and emotionally, and our communal classifications of these discoveries allow us to agree upon signs to represent them, grounding the formation of language. So the aspect of culture which is supported by gregariousness and communication is of course language, consisting of speech, messages, records and literature.

The use of language helps to bring out our tendency to 'abstract' our experiences of the environment, and by perceiving relationships among these abstractions, we construct an understanding of the world and how it works. Its driving force is our tendency to 'curiosity', an intellectual desire to know the how and why of things and events. Together, abstraction and curiosity are the basis of that aspect of culture called pure science. Indeed, the ultimate goal of pure science is to establish a mathematical system of inter-related abstractions which accurately model or explain our physical world. This understanding of the environment completes the first phase in cultural adaptation.

Applied (as opposed to pure) science comes in when this mathematical system is directed to the modification of the environment for some immediate human benefit. This begins the second phase in cultural adaptation: the modification of the environment, in accordance with our understanding of it, for survival and continuity. This second phase is based on our tendencies to 'calculation' and 'work'. Driven by material needs, we design environmental modifications by measurement and calculation, and then effect these modifications through work.

The tendency to 'work' is in itself just a drive to exert personal effort, but our work is made competent by means of three subordinate tendencies: 'repetition', which provides the necessary feedback to achieve exactness; 'concentration', which helps us focus on one step at a time in our work; and 'self-control', which allows us to direct our efforts towards a specific goal.

Again, the primary object of our 'calculations' and 'work' is the assurance of our survival and continuity. The by-products of these two tendencies is a collection of artefacts and tools generally termed technology. Technology is often the most evident aspect of culture, since it is the initial physical product of cultural adaptation.

You will recall that successful biological adaptation consists in something more than mere survival. For the individual species it also means the perfection of its adaptations for the environment in which it lives. Similarly, in cultural evolution, we act upon our human tendency to 'perfection', and each society naturally extends its efforts beyond the level required for survival and continuity. We not only aim to modify the environment in accordance with our understanding of it, but we also aim to perfect the form of those modifications. In other words, we seek perfection, or beauty, in the visual form, sounds and movements of our technology. Often, because the roots of cultural adaptation lie in biological evolution, our concepts of beauty are based on adaptive forms found in nature. These natural concepts of beauty are then combined in a unique way with the ideal forms inherent in each culture's abstract understanding of the world. So each culture ends up with its own special technological style, as in architecture or clothing. To help develop this style and give it fluidity, we use our natural tendency to 'creativity' – an ability to envision a world which does not exist. The aspect of culture which arises from our tendencies to perfection and creativity is, of course, art. Through art, our cultural adaptations are brought closer to perfection. Art is often the aspect of a culture which is most valuable to its people, since it embodies the strivings of cultural evolution, like biological evolution, towards perfection.

Finally, because cultural evolution, like biological evolution, is progressive in its strivings towards individual perfection and systemic harmony, we have a natural desire to trace the progress of culture over time. Every culture has an account of its own history, often mixed up with myths and legends. In tracing our culture's history, we look for signs of ever-increasing perfection in our environmental modifications, and ever-increasing co-operation and organisation among our fellow citizens: in sum, an ever more successful adaptation to the environment. So history is the aspect of culture which satisfies our tendency to realise an ever greater degree of adaptive success, that is, 'mastery over our destiny' – or in a word, 'independence'. Our tendency towards independence suitably stands alone as the endpoint in the process of cultural adaptation.

Table 1 summarises the two phases and the six steps leading to cultural adaptation, the fourteen 'tendencies of man' that make these steps possible, and the aspects of culture which are the manifestations of each step.

The activities described in this Culture Activities chapter cover several of these 'tendencies of man' and their related cultural aspects. First there are three geography activities, based on the tendency to 'explore', and introducing the idea that there are many kinds of environments in the world and that as a result, the cultures in each place are different. These are followed by natural history activities, which introduce some simple ways to 'order' the many kinds of plants and animals we would find in our explorations, and which emphasise the diversity of life and the rigours of survival. Next there are a few examples of pure science presentations, which demonstrate some simple 'abstractions' of Nature, such as magnetism and optics, and which pique the child's 'curiosity'. Finally, there are three activities to introduce the idea of history. One of these activities, the Time Line, traces the child's own progress towards 'independence'.

Table 1

Steps to Cultural Adaptation	Tendencies of Man	Related Aspect of Culture
Phase 1		
Exploring and classifying the environment	Exploration Order	Natural history
Sharing experiences of the environment	Gregariousness Communication	Language
Understanding the environment	Abstraction Curiosity	Pure science
Phase 2		
Modifying the environment in accordance with our understanding of it to ensure survival and continuity	Calculation Work Repetition Concentration Self-control	Technology
Perfecting our environmental modifications	Perfection Creativity	Art
Assessing the progress of our adaptations	Independence	History

GEOGRAPHY

Land and Water

Aim To launch the child's exploration of the world's physical environment in the context of a simple distinction: land versus water. To help the child use this distinction to differentiate, and then identify, several types of geographical landmarks. To help the child find examples of these landmarks near home and then throughout the world.

Material A Land and Water Globe, resting on a tilted metal pin sticking out of a round wooden base. The surface of the globe, which represents the surface of the earth, only shows two features: land (represented by a sandpaper surface) and water (shown as a smooth, blue surface).

(DIY hint: For the Land and Water Globe, take a small, ordinary non-relief globe of the earth, paint the water areas with light blue matt paint and let it dry, and then paint glue onto the land areas and roll the globe around in a tray of fine sand until all the land areas are covered with sand.)

Four pairs of Land and Water Forms Trays, which are waterproof relief models set in deep, metal trays. Each pair of trays represents a particular land formation and its converse water formation: an island and a lake; a peninsula and a gulf; a cape and a bay; and an isthmus and a strait.

(DIY hint: For each of the eight trays, start with a two-inch-deep, square, metal cake pan or tin. In each, make a roughly finished Plaster of Paris formation in the desired shape. Coat the formation and the pan entirely with pale-blue high-gloss paint, and let it dry. Then paint all the higher-elevation land portions with brown high-gloss paint. In the trays, each land formation is brown and raised where its converse water formation is blue and sunken, and each land formation is blue and sunken where its converse water formation is brown and raised.)

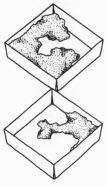

There are five required accessories to the Land and Water Forms Trays: a pale-blue plastic jug; a pale-blue plastic bucket; a small toy boat, one inch or less long, that floats; a similar toy car, one inch or less long, that does not float; and a drying cloth.

Land and Water Forms Pictures: in a labelled envelope, ten square cards, eight illustrating the patterns of the Land and Water Forms Trays as seen from above (showing pale blue for water and brown for land), plus two more water formation cards, one illustrating the generalised idea of an ocean and the other of a sea.

(a) Pouring water from a jug to a particular depth.
(b) Pouring water from the corner of a square tray into a bucket.
(c) Drying wet objects with a drying cloth.

Preliminary Practical Activities

– Name the Land and Water Globe, show where it is kept, and bring it to a table. Show the child how to carry it with one hand around the base and the other hand on top of the globe.
– Say, 'We live on the earth. This globe is much smaller than the earth, but it shows you what the earth looks like.'
– Introduce 'land', where 'there is dry ground to stand on', as the rough, brown parts of the globe. Invite the child to feel the land portions of the globe.
– Then introduce 'water', where 'fish swim and boats sail', as the smooth, blue parts of the globe. Invite the child to feel the water portions of the globe.
– Explore the globe with the child, for example finding the 'largest area of land' or 'largest area of water'. Note that there is more water than land on the earth.

Presentation

(1) The child explores the Land and Water Globe independently.
(2) Introduce the Land and Water Forms Trays in four separate presentations, using a different corresponding pair each time.

Exercises

In each presentation, slowly pour water from the jug into each of the two trays until the level of the water just reaches, but does not touch, the brown 'land' level on the formation. Then feel, with two fingers, along the dry side of the border between the 'land' portion and the 'water' portion on each tray, calling it the 'shoreline', and noting that the shape traced by your fingers is the same for both trays in the pair. Repeat the exploration of the shorelines with the toy car and toy boat, guiding each along on the very edge of its appropriate medium. When you're done, show the child how to empty the water from the trays into the bucket (pouring from the corner), and show how to dry the trays and their formations with the drying cloth. Invite the child to repeat these activities independently, eventually using all eight trays together in a row of four pairs.

Later on, teach the names of all eight Land and Water Forms in several Three Stage Lessons, using two pairs of trays in each lesson.

On another day, pour water into a tray and then tell stories about an imaginary traveller who perhaps gets lost or has an adventure, moving the car and boat around on the forms to illustrate the story's action. In these stories, refer to the forms by their proper names.

(3) One day, when the child is using all eight Land and Water Forms Trays independently, name the Land and Water Forms Pictures, show where they are kept, and place them on a separate table near the trays. Show the child how to match the pictures to the trays, naming them and placing them on the nearby table in the same order and arrangement as the trays. Name and discuss the cards for 'ocean' and 'sea', and place them as an additional pair in the row.

(4) Working with the child, create models of other, different land and water forms, following the same process used to make the eight Land and Water Forms Trays. Allow the child to fashion freely the shapes of the forms. When they are made, invite the child to use and study them as in exercise (2).

Maps

Aim   To show the child that the world's land areas have been divided by name and government, and to help the child become acquainted on a 'sensorial' level with these divisions and the governments' locations.

Material   A Continents Globe, resting at an angle on a metal pin in a wooden base. The surface of the globe, which represents the surface of the earth, shows water as a smooth, blue surface, and each continent as a raised but smooth surface, coloured as follows: green for Africa, red for Europe, yellow for Asia, brown for Australasia, orange for North America, pink for South America, and white for Antarctica.

Eight large, rectangular wooden Puzzle Maps. Each Puzzle Map is fashioned from two layers: the bottom layer is a thin, solid piece of Masonite board; the top layer is a piece of wooden board into which is cut a number of puzzle-like pieces that can be removed, revealing the bottom layer; the outer edge of the top layer, which surrounds the removable pieces, is fixed to the bottom layer. The removable pieces represent the political or geographic divisions of land that together are the subject of the map. Each removable piece is painted a bright colour different from all adjacent areas on the map, and each removable piece has a small white knob protruding from its coloured surface. The fixed outer edge of each map's upper layer represents surrounding water, painted blue, and surrounding land which is not part of the subject of the map, painted pale yellow.

The Puzzle Map material includes:

A 'Continents of the World' Puzzle Map, showing two separate blue circles in a background of pale yellow, each circle representing a hemispheric view of the earth, in which each removable puzzle piece represents a continent. (Antarctica, visible from both hemispheric views, is represented by one white puzzle piece in each circle.) Each continent piece is painted the same colour as on the Continents Globe, and each has a small knob in its centre.

Six more Puzzle Maps, one for each of the world's continents (except Antarctica), in which each removable puzzle piece represents a different country. The location of the knob on each of these puzzle pieces corresponds to the location of the country's capital city.

One Puzzle Map for the child's own country, in which the removable puzzle pieces represent the largest political divisions thereof (e.g. Counties).

A wooden rack which stores all eight Puzzle Maps so that they are readily accessible to a young child.

A clear, plastic circle, the same size as the hemisphere circles on the Continents of the World Puzzle Map.

(DIY hint: For each Puzzle Map, find a coloured, wall-hanging map representing the desired area and divisions, and glue it, thoroughly and evenly, to a thick piece of corrugated cardboard, the same size. To make the puzzle pieces, take a utility knife, and cut out each pertinent land division. Glue the surrounding, unremoved part of the mounted map to another thick piece of corrugated board, the same size. For the knob on each puzzle piece, poke a small hole through the centre (if it's a continent) or through the capital city (if it's a country or smaller), and glue in a 1.5 cm piece of wooden dowel, about the same diameter as a pencil.)

A black pencil, sheets of art paper in many colours, child's scissors, large sheets of white paper, and non-toxic glue.

Presentation – Name the Continents Globe, show where it is kept, and bring it to a table, showing the child how to carry it with one hand around the base and the other hand on top of the globe.
– Ask the child to get the Land and Water Globe and bring it to the table as well.
– Invite the child to examine and compare both globes, leading to the discovery that the land masses on the Land and Water Globe have been divided into coloured areas on the Continents Globe.
– Say 'We call the big pieces of the earth's land the "continents". How many continents are there?' Point and count them aloud with the child.
– Explore the Continents Globe with the child. For example, locate the largest continent, or a spot where two continents meet. In these explorations, only name the continents by their colours (e.g. 'the red continent').

Exercises (1) The child explores the Continents Globe independently.
(2) Name the Puzzle Maps, show the child where they are kept, how to remove and replace a Puzzle Map in the map stand, how to carry a Puzzle Map (level, held by the middle of the two shorter sides), and how to place a Puzzle Map on a floor mat (leaving room on the front portion of the mat for removed puzzle pieces).

Name the Continents of the World Puzzle Map, and ask the child to remove it from the stand and place it on a floor mat, along with the Continents Globe. Show how the globe has been translated onto the map: first, demonstrate how each circle on the map is 'a picture of one side of the globe'; second, point to particular continents on the globe, one at a time, and ask the child to find them on the map.

Put the globe away. Demonstrate the use of the Puzzle Map, taking out three pieces and then putting them back, emphasising how to hold the knob between the thumb, forefinger and middle finger of one hand, how to keep the piece level horizontally, how to place the pieces in a random arrangement on the floor mat, how to select randomly a piece for replacement, how to examine visually where the piece goes before trying it, and how to put it in its place gently and silently, without forcing it. Invite the child to repeat the removal and replacement of three pieces, and then to do the whole puzzle, removing all the pieces and then replacing them.

A week later, introduce the child's home continent Puzzle Map by name (e.g. 'Europe') and invite the child to work with it in the same way as the first. Repeat these introductions with each of the other Puzzle Maps over a number of weeks, starting with the child's home-country Puzzle Map (e.g. 'Britain'), and moving on to the other continent maps. (When introducing the continent Puzzle

Maps, select the appropriate piece from the Continents of the World Puzzle Map, call it by its continent name, and ask the child to look through the stand to 'find the Puzzle Map that shows this shape'. Similarly, when introducing the child's home-country Puzzle Map, select the appropriate country piece from its continent map, call it by its country name, and ask the child to 'find the Puzzle Map that shows this shape'.)

The child works independently with any of the Puzzle Maps, one at a time, until they are each mastered as puzzles.

After the child has mastered a particular Puzzle Map as a puzzle, show how to re-assemble the removed pieces on a separate floor mat, without using the Puzzle Map base to contain them.

After the child is able to do this for each of the individual continent maps, show how to lay six floor mats to form a huge rectangle, and then how to construct on it a complete map of the world by country, reproducing the configuration of continents shown on the Continents of the World Puzzle Map.

Later, show the child how to trace the puzzle pieces onto matching-colour paper (using the tracing technique learned with the Metal Insets) (see METAL INSETS in the Language Activities), how to cut out the outlined shapes, and how to glue them onto a large sheet of white paper to form replicas of the Puzzle Maps that the child can take home. Again, the child does this first for the Continents of the World Puzzle Map, then for the child's home-continent Puzzle Map, then for the child's home-country Puzzle Map, and last for the other continents Puzzle Maps. The clear plastic circle is used to help reproduce the blue hemispheres shown on the Continents of the World Puzzle Map.

(3) Teach the names of all the removable Puzzle Maps pieces by Three Stage Lessons, starting with the Continents of the World Puzzle Map, next doing the countries in the child's own continent, then the divisions in the child's own country, and lastly, the countries in the other continents. Complete all the pieces in one Puzzle Map before going on to the next one. Emphasise the names of the child's own continent, country and local division, and discuss the child's experience with these names – for example, their appearance on pieces of mail or their mention on television or radio news programmes.

Places

To connect the child's map knowledge with a few impressions of the places that the shapes and names represent. To introduce the idea that life is different in places away from home, and that such differences are natural.

Aim

At least six sets of Classified Place Pictures, stored in a box with a

Material

lid, each set containing between ten and thirty cards. (See CLASSIFIED PICTURES in the Language Activities.) In each set, the top card bears a black silhouette of a country's Puzzle Map piece, labelled in its centre with the country's flag and printed name. Each of the other cards in the set illustrates a characteristic aspect of that country, such as a well-known feature of landscape, a kind of dwelling, or a species of indigenous wildlife, and each of these cards is labelled on the back with the country's flag. There is a set of Classified Place Pictures for at least one country in every continent (except Antarctica), including the child's own country.

Picture Folders, each containing photographs of a particular country's landscape, wildlife, land and water formations, and/or human culture, cut from magazines (such as *National Geographic*). Each folder is clearly labelled with the name, flag and Puzzle Map piece silhouette of the subject country. Several countries from every continent (except Antarctica) are represented.

A group of tangible artefacts, from a single foreign country, including samples of plants (e.g. foods), animals (e.g. shells, fossils), culture (e.g. clothing, musical instruments), or terrain (e.g. stones, minerals). The display of artefacts is changed monthly, representing a different country each month. The display is labelled, as on the Picture Folders, with the name, flag and Puzzle Map piece silhouette of the country.

Geography books, magazines, films, slide presentations and storybooks about life in foreign lands, and especially about life for the children there.

Preliminary Practical Activities

(a) Handling photographs stored in a folder (i.e. holding them gently by the edges, placing them in an orderly pile, and ensuring they are not creased by closing the folder).

(b) Handling delicate objects (practising with, for example, a hollow eggshell, a facial tissue and uncooked spaghetti noodles).

Presentation

– Name the boxes of Classified Place Pictures, show where they are kept, select a set, and place it on a table mat.

– Point out the label that shows which country the selected set concerns, name the continent it is in, and ask the child to bring to the table the Puzzle Map of that continent. Show and name the puzzle piece for the selected country, compare the puzzle piece to its silhouette on the top card, and say, 'All the pictures in this box show what you might see if you visited -------' (giving the country's name).

– View each card in turn, and discuss with the child the thing or scene pictured, using precise terminology (e.g. pizza, gondola, Colosseum), allowing the child to share previous knowledge and to ask questions.

– Give Three Stage Lessons on the names of things pictured which the child did not know.

(1) Go through the other boxes of Classified Place Pictures with the child, as in the presentation.

(2) The child looks through the boxes of Classified Place Pictures independently, or with another child, first finding the Puzzle Map piece that matches the silhouette.

(3) The child mixes up the cards from two or more sets of Classified Place Pictures, spreading out the cards face up on a table, and then sorts them into piles next to their country silhouette cards. Afterwards, the child turns over each pile to check that the flags all match.

(4) As the child begins exercise (3) one day, for example with the cards for Japan and Brazil, and has spread out all the cards on the table, sit down and say, 'Can you see something found in Japan? Yes, what is it?' and then, 'Can you see something found in Brazil? Yes, what is it?' Repeat, alternating between the countries, giving the child an opportunity to combine vocabulary use with the sorting.

(5) The child looks through the Picture Folders independently, or with another child, first finding the Puzzle Map piece that matches the silhouette on the folder's cover.

(6) The child carefully handles and examines the artefacts, independently or with another child, first finding the Puzzle Map piece that matches the silhouette labelling the display.

(7) Read fact books and stories, and present films and slides, about life in faraway places, always first showing the appropriate continent Puzzle Map and country piece.

Exercises

NATURE STUDIES

Animals

Classifying Animals

To help the child classify impressions of animals into clear and simple categories, and to give these impressions and categories names. To help foster the child's respect for the world's diverse animal life by showing that every type of animal has a natural environment which is its home, and a way of life that is special.

Aim

Twelve sets of Classified Animal Pictures, stored in a box with a lid, each set containing between ten and thirty cards. (See CLASSIFIED PICTURES in the Language Activities.) Six of the sets of cards are pale yellow, and the other six sets of cards are pale blue. In each of the six yellow sets of Classified Animal Pictures, the top card bears the black silhouette of a generalised form of one of the following animal types: insect, fish, amphibian, reptile, bird and mammal (e.g. for the 'amphibian' set – a generalised silhouette of a frog or toad); each of the other cards shows a full-colour picture of one particular species of that animal type (e.g. in the 'fish' set – a flounder, a tuna, a trout, etc.); and every card is labelled on the back with a small version of the animal

Material

type silhouette on the top card. In each of the six blue sets of Classified Animal Pictures: the top card bears a colour silhouette of Australasia, Asia, Africa, Europe, South America or North America, exactly as shown on the Continents of the World Puzzle Map (see MAPS); each of the other cards shows a full-colour picture of one particular species indigenous to that continent (e.g. for the 'North America' set – a black bear, a copperhead snake, etc.); and every card is labelled on the back with a small version of the continent silhouette on the top card. Taken all together, the yellow cards in the six 'animal type' sets have exactly the same animal pictures as the blue cards in the six 'continent' sets. In other words, the same animals are classified by 'animal type' in the six yellow sets and by native 'continent' in the six blue sets.

Binoculars, a magnifying glass and a battery-operated cassette tape recorder.

Story and fact books about animals, emphasising their natural environment and respecting their right to live there.

Films and slide presentations about animals.

Preliminary Practical Activities

(a) Using binoculars to focus on specific, distant objects.
(b) Using a magnifying glass to examine specific small objects or surfaces.
(c) Using a tape recorder to record particular sounds.
(d) Observing at a zoo, a public aquarium, a 'safari' park, a bird sanctuary, a wildlife preserve, or a farm with livestock.

Presentation

– Name the yellow Classified Animal Pictures, show where they are kept, select the 'mammals' box of cards, and bring it to a table. Show the mammals silhouette card, and say, 'This kind of animal is called a mammal; all the animals shown in this box are mammals.'
– View each card in turn, and discuss with the child each animal pictured, using their common but precise names (e.g. chimpanzee, California sea lion). Consistently invite the child to share personal knowledge and experiences.
– Give Three Stage Lessons on the names of pictured animals which the child did not know.

Exercises

(1) Work through the other five boxes of yellow Classified Animal Pictures, as in the presentation. The child then looks through the boxes of yellow cards independently or with another child. Later, the child combines the cards from two or more yellow sets, sorts them into piles next to their animal type silhouette cards, and checks the sorting against the animal type silhouettes on the backs of the cards. One day, sit with the child during this sorting, and occasionally ask, for example, 'Can you find one of the mammals? Yes, what is it?', to give the child experience saying the newly learned names of animals.
(2) Name the blue Classified Animal Pictures and show where

they are kept, saying that they 'show the same animals as in the yellow Classified Animal Pictures'. Place the set of cards for South America on a table. Ask the child to get the Continents of the World Puzzle Map, and to find the puzzle piece which corresponds to the South America silhouette on the top card. Say, 'All the animals shown in this box are ones you might see if you visited South America.' View and discuss the cards. Say any animal names that the child does not remember from exercise (1).

(3) Work through the other five boxes of blue Classified Animals Pictures, as in exercise (2). The child looks through the boxes of blue cards independently or with another child. Later, the child combines the cards from two or more blue sets, sorts them into piles next to their continent silhouette cards, and checks the sorting against the continent silhouettes on the backs of the cards.

(4) The child lays out two floor mats, touching side-by-side, and places all six boxes of yellow cards on one mat, and all six boxes of blue cards on the other mat. The child next places out the six animal type silhouettes and the six continent silhouettes, evenly spaced, across the tops of their respective mats, and combines all the yellow cards into one pile (leaving all the remaining blue cards in their boxes). The child then sorts all the yellow cards among the continent silhouettes on one mat, collects them again into a pile, and re-sorts them among the animal type silhouettes on the other mat. If the child is inclined, the process is repeated.

(5) The child reads and listens to books about animals, watches animal films, television nature shows and slide presentations about animal life.

(6) The child uses the binoculars to watch birds and keep records of the types seen, to spot small animals in a field, or to observe deer or other wildlife from a distance. The child uses the magnifying glass outdoors to watch insects' behaviour in their natural habitats, and indoors to examine animal fossils, bones and feathers. The child uses the tape recorder to record forest sounds (especially in the evening), noises around a pond, and bird songs. All observations by the child can be written down in a 'Natural History Records Book', with the date, time and location of each observation. These records can then be built into a study over time – for example, a study of 'Birds in the Park at Different Times of the Year', or they can be extended into a research project, such as making a map showing 'Geese Migrations in Western Europe'.

Parts of Animals

To help the child recognise and name the body parts of various animal types. **Aim**

Material   Six sets of Classified Animal Parts Pictures, stored in a box with a lid, each set containing between seven and ten cards. (See CLASSIFIED PICTURES in the Language Activities.) In each of the six sets, the top card bears a black line drawing of a generalised form of one of the following animal types: insect, fish, amphibian, reptile, bird and mammal. Each of the other cards in the set show that same black drawing with one particular body part (which is peculiar to that animal type) coloured-in (black for insects, blue for fish, green for amphibians, grey for reptiles, orange for birds, and brown for mammals.)

Presentation   – Name the Classified Animal Parts Pictures, show where they are kept, select a box, and bring it to a table.
          – View each card in turn and discuss with the child the coloured-in body part, using exact terminology (e.g. mandible, beak). Consistently encourage the child to share personal knowledge and experiences, and to ask questions.
          – Give Three Stage Lessons on the names of pictured body parts which the child did not know.

Exercise   Work through the other five boxes of Classified Animal Parts Pictures, as in the presentation. The child then looks through the boxes independently or with another child. One day during one of these sessions, sit down next to the child and occasionally ask, for example, 'What is this part of a bird called?', to give the child experience saying the newly learned names of animal parts.

Plants

Classification by Leaf

Aim   To help the child classify impressions of plants into clear and simple categories (in this instance, classifying them by the shapes and arrangement of their leaves), and to give these impressions and categories names. To help foster the child's respect for the wide diversity of plant forms in the world.

Material   A wooden Leaf Cabinet, similar in most respects to the Geometric Cabinet (see GEOMETRIC CABINET in the Sensorial Activities), except that there are only three drawers, the removable insets are painted green, and the fourteen insets found in the drawers are generalised leaf shapes (positioned with the stem pointing down), as follows:

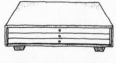

Drawer 1: reniform (kidney shape with the stem attached to the middle of the inner curve), triangular (with the stem attached to the centre of the triangle's base), elliptical (like an ellipse, with the stem attached to one narrow end) and orbiculate (round).
Drawer 2: spatulate (like a spoon), aciculate (two needles joined at one end), hastate (shaped like a fish, with the stem attached between the tail fins), sagittate (like the head

of an arrow, with the stem attached where the rod of the arrow would be), linear (long, thin and straight) and lanceolate (like the tip of a lance, with the stem attached at the rounded end).

Drawer 3: ovate (egg shape with the stem attached to the wide end), obovate (egg shape with the stem attached to the narrow end), cordate (heart shape with the stem attached between the curves) and obcordate (heart shape with the stem attached to the pointed end).

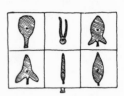

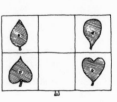

A blunt toothpick with a large round bead glued on one end.

A small, wooden shelf unit with three shelves, on which are stored three sets of thin, white, square Leaf Cards, similar in most respects to the Geometric Cabinet Cards. Each set of fourteen cards contains one card for each figure in the Leaf Cabinet. The cards on the upper shelf bear solid green representations of the Leaf Cabinet shapes. The cards on the middle shelf show thick green outlines of the shapes. The cards on the lower shelf bear thin green outlines. All the representations on the cards are exactly the same size as the insets in the Leaf Cabinet, and the cards themselves are the same size as the flat, wooden squares that form frames for the insets.

A handmade Leaves Book: a binder containing firm cardboard pages, on each of which are pressed one or two actual leaf samples (collected locally by you and the children), each page then covered and sealed with a clear, stick-on plastic sheet. Each leaf sample displayed in the Leaves Book is chosen to represent one of the following characteristics: *simple* (being a continuous, undivided blade); *compound* (consisting of a single blade divided into smaller, leaf-like parts); *palmate* (a compound leaf divided around a centre point); *pinnate* (a compound leaf divided along a linear axis); *paripinnate* (a pinnate compound leaf with its smaller, leaf-like parts in directly opposing pairs); *imparipinnate* (a pinnate compound leaf with its smaller, leaf-like parts attached singly, on alternating sides, along the centre axis, and with one part attached at the far end of the axis); *reticulated* (with branching veins); *parallel* (with columns of parallel veins); *entire margin* (with an edge consisting of one smooth line); *crenate margin* (with outward-curving bumps in the edge); *dentate margin* (with inward-curving dents in the edge); *serrate margin* (with dents all curving in at the same angle, i.e. a serrated edge); *lobed* (a simple leaf with several large indentations reaching less than half-way in towards the leaf's middle); *fid* (a simple leaf with several large indentations reaching about half-way in); *partite* (a simple leaf with several large indentations reaching more than half-way in); *sect* (a simple leaf with several large indentations reaching almost all the way to the middle – almost, but not quite, a compound leaf); *opposite* (an arrangement of leaves on the stem in opposing pairs); *alternate* (an arrangement of leaves on the stem singly, on alternating sides, with one at the end); *whorled* (an arrangement of leaves on the stem in a climbing, spiral pattern); *reniform*; *triangular*; *elliptical*; *orbiculate*; *spatulate*; *aciculate*; *hastate*; *sagittate*; *linear*; *lanceolate*; *ovate*; *obovate*; *cordate*; *obcordate*; *oblanceolate* (like the tip of a lance, with the stem attached at the lance's point); *ensiform* (curved and sword-like); *peltate* (circular, with the stem attached to the centre); *lyrate* (shaped like a lyre); or *runcinate* (partite, with the lobes all curved towards the stem).

Preliminary Practical Activities

(a) Collecting fallen leaves, pressing them, and sealing them onto cardboard pages in a book.
(b) Using a magnifying glass to examine small objects.
(c) Handling a toothpick safely.

Presentation

– Name the Leaf Cabinet, show where it is kept, and gently place Drawer 1 on the far portion of a table mat, leaving about six inches of the mat in front.
– Present the Leaf Cabinet drawer the same way as you did the Geometric Cabinet's Presentation Tray. However, because some of the leaf shapes have more finely detailed edges than the Geometric Cabinet shapes, show the child how to feel the inserts and their frames with the side of the toothpick (instead of with your fingers), holding the toothpick by its bead.

Exercises

(1) The child works independently with Drawer 1 of the Leaf Cabinet, as in the presentation, and later does Drawer 2, and then Drawer 3.
(2) The child works with any one drawer in the cabinet, but performing only the second half of exercise (1), that is, putting all the shapes on the mat and replacing them one-by-one.
(3) The child works with two, and then all three drawers at one time.
(4) Teach by Three Stage Lessons, the full name (as given in this activity's *Material* section) for the shape of each inset in the Leaf Cabinet.
(5) Name the Leaf Cards, show the shelf unit in which they are kept, and show the child how to use them in the same way as the Geometric Cards are used with the Geometric Cabinet (see exercises (5) through (8) of the GEOMETRIC CABINET activity in the Sensorial Activities).
(6) Name the Leaves Book and look through it with the child, discussing the different leaf characteristics represented. When you come to one of the leaf shapes represented in the Leaf Cabinet, see if the child spontaneously recognises the shape. Invite the child to bring the inset from the Leaf Cabinet that best corresponds to the shape of the sample leaf.
(7) Invite the child to start a personal leaf collection, encouraging the habit of noticing, on walks and outings, fallen leaves with interesting shapes, saving them, pressing

them between sheets of newsprint under a flat, heavy weight, and then classifying them (by comparing them to the samples in the Leaf Book) as: being *simple* or *compound* (and if compound, then *palmate, paripinnate* or *imparipinnate*); having *reticulated* or *parallel* veins; having an *entire, crenate, dentate* or *serrate* margin (and if dentate, then *lobed, fid, partite* or *sect*); being attached to the stem in an *opposite, alternate* or *whorled* pattern; and finally, being similar to one of the nineteen common leaf shapes represented in the Leaf Book. Once classified, each collected leaf can be placed on cardboard, sealed under plastic, and put in a looseleaf notebook marked with the child's name.

Parts of Plants

To help the child recognise and name the parts of various types of plants.   **Aim**

Six sets of Classified Plant Parts Pictures, stored in a box with a lid. (See CLASSIFIED PICTURES in the Language Activities.) The subjects of the sets, and what each of the cards in those sets shows, are as follows: **Material**

Parts of a Plant: root, stem, leaf, flower, fruit. (The top card shows a black line drawing of a generalised fruit tree. The other cards each show the same black tree, but with one part coloured-in green.)

Types of Roots: tuberous (e.g. dahlia), fusiform (e.g. radish), conical (e.g. carrot), napiform (e.g. turnip), fasciculated (a cluster of roots).

(The top card shows the same black line drawing of a generalised fruit tree, with the roots coloured-in green. The other cards each show a green, generalised drawing of one type of root.)

Types of Stems: climbing (e.g. ivy), procumbent (e.g. strawberries), woody (i.e. tree trunk and branches), shrubby (shrub trunk), herbaceous (like the stem of most annual flowers), corm (e.g. gladiola bulb), rhizome (extending just under the surface of the ground), bulb (e.g. onion, tulip), tuber (e.g. potato).

(The top card shows the same black line drawing of a generalised fruit tree, with the trunk and branches coloured-in green. The other cards each show a green, generalised drawing of one type of stem.)

Parts of Stems: node (the part where the leaf's stem joins the main stem), internode (the part of the main stem between the leaves), axil (the curve of the leaf's stem at the node), axil bud (a bud at the axil which grows into a new leaf or flower), terminal bud (a bud on the internode which grows into a new leaf or flower).

(The top card shows the same black line drawing of a generalised fruit tree, with the trunk and branches coloured-in green. The other cards each show one green branch enlarged, with one part of it highlighted in yellow.)

Parts of Flowers: calyx (the part which supports the flower from beneath), corolla (the petals), stamen (the part which produces the pollen) and pistil (the part which produces the egg and catches pollen).

(The top card shows the same black line drawing of a generalised fruit tree, but now it is flowering, with the flowers coloured-in green. The other cards each show one green flower enlarged, with one part of it highlighted in pink.)

Types of Fruit: capsule (e.g. foxtail), legume (a pod which opens completely, e.g. beans), follicle (a pod which splits along one side only, e.g. peas), silique (a pod with seeds sticking to a membrane in the middle, e.g. wallflower), pome (a fruit with a hard centre, e.g. apple), berry (soft throughout, e.g. orange), pepo (e.g. cucumber, melon, pumpkin), drupe (a fruit with a stone in the middle, e.g, cherry).

(The top card shows the same black line drawing of a generalised fruit tree, but now bearing fruit, with the fruit coloured-in green. The other cards each show a green generalised drawing of one type of fruit.)

Presentation
– Name the Classified Plant Parts Pictures, show where they are kept, and place the 'Parts of a Plant' set on a table.
– View each card in turn and discuss with the child the plant part coloured-in, using exact terminology. Encourage the child to share personal knowledge and experiences, and to ask questions.
– Give Three Stage Lessons on the names of pictured plant parts which the child did not know.

Exercise
(1) Work through the other five boxes of Classified Plant Parts Pictures, as in the presentation. The child then looks through the boxes independently or with another child. One day during one of these sessions, sit down next to the child and occasionally ask, 'What is this called?', to give the child experience saying the newly learned names of plant parts.

Plant Life Cycles

To familiarise the child with the life cycle of plants, including **Aim**
their growth from seeds, their method of reproduction, their
needs for water, nutrients and sunlight, and the changes they go
through each year and throughout their lives.

Indoor plants (including ferns, cacti, mosses and flowering **Material**
plants) in pots with draining dishes, and a watering can.
  A soft cloth.
  Small clear pots with draining dishes, grass or flower seeds,
and potting soil.
  Gardening scissors and vases.
  A rake.
  An outdoor garden area divided as follows: a wild,
uncultivated area; cultivated flowers; vegetable rows; cultivated
lawn; compost heap. Gardening tools, seedling boxes, cloths for
cleaning the tools, plastic pots for transplanting, gloves (both
adult and child-size), seedling boxes and a seed catalogue.
Materials for food preparation.

(1) The child waters indoor plants, first feeling the soil to see if it **Activities**
    is dry, then filling the watering can, and pouring in a little at
    a time until some appears in the draining dish.

(2) The child dusts the leaves of indoor plants with a damp, soft
    cloth.

(3) All year long, the child plants seeds in small, clear pots
    indoors, waters them regularly, and observes their sprouting.

(4) In winter, the child helps you pick out and order seeds from
    the seed catalogue, and in late winter, the child hoes and
    smooths the soil in the garden to get it ready for planting. At
    about this same time, the child plants the seeds into seedling
    boxes, and waters and cares for them. When warm weather
    arrives, the child transplants the seedlings from the boxes
    into the garden, and cares for them there.

(5) Throughout the spring and summer, the child waters and
    weeds the garden, pulling all of one kind of weed before
    starting on another. The child practises weeding first in the
    lawn area, then in the vegetable rows, and lastly in the flower
    area.

(6) Also in the spring and summer, the child cuts flowers from
    the flower garden, selecting only a few fresh stems with
    unopened petals, and arranges them in vases indoors. Later,
    the child cares for the flower arrangement, changing the
    water daily, and re-cutting the stems while holding them
    underwater (to prevent airlocks in the stems).

(7) In the summer and autumn, the child examines and picks
    ripe fruits and vegetables from the garden, washes them, and
    helps prepare them for use in meals and snacks for the
    children.

(8) Also in autumn, the child rakes leaves, saving the more

interesting or colourful ones (for use in the activity CLASSIFICATION BY LEAF).

(9) Through the autumn and winter, the child adds food scraps, weeds, and organic waste to the compost heap, and helps to blend it into the soil in the gardens in the spring.

Matter and Energy

Air

Aim   To make the child aware that air is an important part of the physical environment, and to demonstrate some of air's properties.

Preliminary Practical Activities
(a) Pouring water from a jug to a particular depth.
(b) Drying wet containers with a cloth.
(c) Respect for matches; understanding fire dangers.

Activities
(1) Empty Bottle
Materials: A plastic mat; a very large, deep bowl; a small, empty, transparent plastic bottle; a bucket; a drying cloth; a jug; a source of water.
Method: Gather the materials. Pour water from the jug into the bowl to a depth of about six inches. Ask the child if the bottle is empty; the child examines the bottle and answers 'yes'. Holding the bottle upside down, place the mouth of the bottle in the water, slowly move the bottle into a horizontal position, and attentively observe and listen to the bubbles coming out. Say, 'The bottle was not empty; it had air in it!' Show how to pour the water out of the bottle into the bowl, and begin again. Invite the child to try the activity and to repeat it several times. When the child is done, show how to dry the bottle, pour the water from the bowl into the bucket, dry the bowl, empty the bucket where used water goes, and finally dry the bucket.
The child later repeats the activity independently.

(2) Blowing Bubbles
Materials: The same as in activity (1), except in place of the plastic bottle, a supply of plastic straws.
Method: Gather the materials. Pour water from the jug into the bowl to a depth of about six inches. Take one straw and give another to the child. Show the child how to blow through a straw, while feeling the blowing air with one hand. When the child has perfected blowing air 'out' without drawing any air 'in', show the child how to put the end of the straw in the water, and then blow, thereby making bubbles. Say, 'We have air in our lungs. When we blow through the straw, we blow air.' Invite the child to try the activity and to repeat it several times, and then to dry the materials. Instruct the child to dispose of used straws and get new ones next time.
The child later repeats the activity independently.

(3) Sails
Materials: The same as in exercise (2), plus three tiny boats:

one, a folded paper boat (with a canopy if you know how to fold it that way); another, a half of a walnut shell filled with wax and equipped with a toothpick mast and paper sail; and last, a proper toy sailboat, with cloth sail and weighted keel.
Method: Gather the materials. Pour water from the jug into the bowl to a depth of about six inches. Place the folded paper boat on the water, and show the child how to blow through the straw onto the boat to make it move along the water's surface. Invite the child to repeat this with the walnut shell boat, and then with the proper toy sailboat. Prompt the child to experiment with different directions and intensities of blowing on different parts of each boat.

The child later repeats the comparisons independently.

(4) Pump
Materials: A small, light bicycle-tyre pump; several light and fluffy feathers; a table-tennis ball; fine sawdust in a plastic container.
Method: Name the pump, show where it is kept, and bring it with a feather to an area of open floor space. Show the child how to work the pump and direct the air flow, and then how to use the pump to blow the feather along the floor. Invite the child to try it.

The child later repeats this use of the pump independently, first using several feathers, then the table-tennis ball, and lastly the sawdust.

(5) Windmill
Materials: A square piece of thin card; scissors; a pin; two small beads; a short wooden dowel.
Method: Tell the child you are going to make a 'windmill'. Gather the materials. Fold the card diagonally in both directions, and then cut along each crease to within 1/4-inch of the centre. Push the pin through one bead, then through all the corners of the card bent in towards the centre, through the centre of the card, through the other bead, and firmly into the side of the dowel, near one end.

Show the child that any movement of air (e.g. blowing, a moving fan or outdoor wind) makes the windmill spin.

On a day with gusty weather, fix the windmill upright just outside a window, so the child can watch the wind stopping and starting with varying velocity.

Another day, take the windmill along when you go with the child to the top of a hill. Show how to hold the windmill in front of your chest, pointing away, and then slowly turn your body to face different directions. Tell the child that the direction you are facing when the windmill is spinning fastest is 'where the wind is blowing from'. This direction can be recorded with the help of a compass (see MAGNETISM) and a daily or weekly record of wind direction can thereby be maintained by the child.

(6) Hot Air Spiral
Materials: A round piece of thin card; a pencil; scissors; the

receiving part of a metal snap used on clothing; glue; a knitting needle; a thick nail; a hammer; a metal lid from a jar. *Method*: Using the hammer and nail, punch a hole in the centre of the lid, and push the knitting needle through the hole so that it can stand upright with its pointed end up. With the hammer, pound smooth any sharp edges on the lid.

Say you will make a 'hot air spiral'. Glue the snap, open side facing upwards, to the very centre of the card, and with the pencil draw a spiral from the snap to the outer edge, making at least five full revolutions. With the scissors, cut along that line from the outer edge all the way in to the snap. Balance the snap on the pointed edge of the standing knitting needle, so that the spiral hangs down around the needle.

Show the child that when the spiral is placed over any source of heat, the hot air moves up and makes the spiral spin. Try placing it above a radiator or an oven, making sure that it doesn't come near a live electrical element or open flame.

(7) Candle in Limited Air

Materials: A candle attached by wax drippings to the inside centre of a deep, metal cake tin; a box of matches; a metal can filled with fine sand; a narrow glass jar several inches taller than the candle; a jug; a bucket; a drying cloth; a water source.

Method: Gather all the materials and sit with the child at a table. Pour water from the jug into the cake tin to a depth of one inch. Strike a match with the match box closed, light the candle, blow out the match, and place it head down in the can of sand. Gently but swiftly, in one movement, place the jar over the candle, so that the jar's lip is submerged in the water. Watch the flame subside and go out, and point out the rising water in the jar. Say, 'Fire needs air to burn. The fire quickly used up the air in the jar, and then it couldn't burn any more. As the air was used up, water came into the jar to take its place.'

The child does NOT attempt this activity independently. Explain that matches are very dangerous, even for grownups.

(8) Water Upside-down

Materials: A thin-lipped glass jar; a square of firm, smooth cardboard; a drying cloth; a large bucket; a jug larger than the jar; a water source.

Method: From the jug, fill the jar just to overflowing, so that the water's surface bulges slightly above the jar's lip. Place the bucket on the table. Say, 'The air all around us pushes on everything; it pushes so hard, that it will hold this piece of cardboard on the jar, even when I turn it over.' In one movement, slide the cardboard square onto the jar so that it seals the lip all the way around, and then holding the card against the jar with one hand, lift and invert the jar over the bucket, and when it is completely inverted, remove the hand supporting the card, allowing air pressure to hold it up. Say, 'Air must push very hard to hold all this water in the jar.' Put your hand against the card again, turn the jar right side up, and remove the card. Repeat the demonstration if the child wishes, using the dry side of the card.

Water

To demonstrate two ideas about water: that things either float or sink in water; and that falling water is a ▓▓▓ ▓▓ ▓▓▓ ▓▓ ▓▓▓▓▓▓. **Aim**

(a) Pouring water from a jug into a small-mouthed jar. **Preliminary**
(b) Pouring water into a funnel. **Practical**
(c) Drying wet objects with a cloth. **Activities**

(1) Sink and Float   **Activities**
   Materials: A plastic mat; a large, deep bowl; a jug; a bucket; a drying cloth; a source of water; at least ten small objects, changed monthly, half of which float (e.g. cork, table-tennis ball, plastic straw, wooden ice lolly stick) and half of which sink (e.g. stone, coin, golf ball), all stored in a box; thick golden syrup; cooking oil.
   Method: Gather the materials, and pour water from the jug into the bowl to a depth of about six inches. Say, 'Some things will float on top of water, and other things will sink down into water.' Place one of the buoyant objects on the surface of the water, and say, for example, 'A cork floats.' Remove the object, dry it with the cloth, and set it to one side on the mat. Repeat with other objects in the box, separating the ones that float from the ones that sink. Invite the child to finish sorting the remaining objects in the box.
   Show the golden syrup and the oil, and pour a little of each into the bowl of water. Note that 'oil floats because it is lighter than water' and that 'golden syrup sinks because it is heavier than water.' Help the child clean out the bowl, using soap, at a sink.
   Later, the child independently conducts the sink and float activity with the objects (but not with the liquids).
(2) Modelling Clay Boat
   Materials: A plastic mat; a large, deep bowl; a jug; a bucket; a drying cloth; a source of water; Plasticine modelling clay.
   Method: Gather the materials, and pour water from the jug into the bowl to a depth of about six inches. Put a round lump of modelling clay onto the surface of the water and note that it sinks. Roll the lump of modelling clay into a stick shape, put it on the water, and note that it too sinks. Pat the stick of modelling clay into a flat, pancake shape, put it on the water, and again note that it sinks. Finally, mould the pancake of

modelling clay into a boat shape, gently place it on the surface of the water, and show excitement when it floats. Say, 'When it holds air, it is lighter than water, so it floats.'

The child later repeats this activity independently.

(3) Fountain

Materials: A jug; a large basin; a funnel connected to a long, flexible, clear plastic tube; a drying cloth; a water source.

Method: Gather the materials. Place the basin on the floor beneath the front edge of the table. Ask the child to hold the open end of the tube pointing upwards, just above the basin. Hold the funnel at table-top level, and pour water from the jug into the funnel. Note the little stream squirting up from the tube's open end. Say, 'Falling water can be made to go up again in a fountain.'

Switch places with the child: you hold the end of the tube upwards over the basin, while the child pours water into the funnel.

(4) Waterwheel

Materials: A jug; a basin; a toy waterwheel on a stand; a drying cloth; a water source.

Method: Gather the materials. Put the waterwheel in the basin and place the basin on the floor. Kneel on the floor over the basin, and show the child how to pour water in a steady stream from the jug onto the horizontal paddles of the waterwheel, making the wheel spin. Say, 'Falling water can be used to turn a wheel.' Try pouring from a higher or lower position of the jug, and try pouring onto the vertical paddles, instead of the horizontal ones, noting the effects of these changes.

The child tries it, and later repeats this activity independently.

Magnetism

Aim To illustrate the phenomenon of magnetism and some of its general uses.

Preliminary Practical Activities
(a) Keeping a horseshoe magnet strong by remembering to store it with its 'keeper' – a metal bar placed across the two open ends of the horseshoe.
(b) Handling a needle without injury.
(c) Pouring water from a jug; drying with a cloth.

Activities
(1) Sorting Magnetic Objects
Materials: A horseshoe magnet with a 'keeper' in a small box with a lid; at least ten small objects, changed monthly, half of which are magnetic (i.e. can conduct electricity, e.g. a piece of uninsulated copper wire, a brass screw, a steel nail) and half of which are non-magnetic (i.e. are not good conductors, e.g. a quartz stone, a wooden ice lolly stick, a piece of string), stored in a box.

Method: Name the magnet, show where it is kept, and place the magnet box and the box of objects on a table. Show the child how to ease the 'keeper' off the magnet and place the 'keeper' back in the box. Open the box of objects and select an object which you know to be magnetic (e.g. the steel nail). Hold this object close to the open ends of the magnet, show that you feel a pull, and invite the child to feel it and to let the object stick to the magnet. Remove the object and place it to one side, saying, 'this is magnetic'. Next select an object you know to be non-magnetic (e.g. the wooden ice lolly stick), show that no pull occurs, invite the child to feel it, and place the object distinctly apart from the first, saying, 'This is not magnetic.' Repeat this test with several other objects, continuing to sort them into two groups: magnetic and non-magnetic. Invite the child to sort the remaining objects. When the materials are being put away, remind the child about replacing the 'keeper' on the magnet.

The child later repeats this activity independently.

(2) Searching for Magnetic Things

Materials: The horseshoe magnet in its box.

Method: Show the child how to test objects in the room to see if they are magnetic. Go up to something, place the magnet gently against all parts of its surface, and feel whether there is any pull. When there is a pull, say, 'This is magnetic.' Invite the child to test other things in the room. (Ensure that any watches, recording tapes and computer diskettes are out of the child's reach, as the magnet can damage them.)

Later, the child continues to explore the environment, and takes the magnet along on walks, to try testing outdoor objects.

(3) Magnetising a Chain of Objects

Materials: The horseshoe magnet in its box; a box of steel paper clips.

Method: Place the magnet, without its 'keeper', on its side, on a table. Place a paper clip against it, so that it bridges the magnet's two open ends, like the 'keeper'. Lift the magnet, noting that the paper clip lifts too, and then put it back down on the table. Place another paper clip on the table, its end just touching the first paper clip. Lift the magnet, noting that the second paper clip is lifted too, and say, 'While a magnetic thing is touching a magnet, it also acts like a magnet.' Place more paper clips on the table, each just touching the end of the last one. Lift the magnet with each addition to see how far the original magnetic force will extend. Invite the child to continue experimenting with the magnet and paper clips.

The child later repeats this activity independently.

(4) Magnetic Pull through a Card

Materials: The horseshoe magnet in its box; in a thin, wooden frame, a piece of card, eight inches square, on which is pictured a tiny roadway, one inch wide, winding through pictures of trees and houses; a piece of thin card, 1 x 1½ inches, folded and glued to form a triangular prism, with the top two surfaces picturing a car seen from the side, and a steel paper clip glued to the inside of the bottom surface.

Method: Show the child the little car, pointing out the paper clip inside, and show how to hold the large square of card level, by its frame, with one hand. Place the little cardboard car, paper clip down, on the card, on the pictured 'road'. Show the child the magnet, and place it against the underside of the card, beneath where the cardboard car is resting. Move the magnet about slightly until you see its magnetic force 'grab' the car and hold it. Now slowly move the magnet along the underside of the card, which will pull the car along on the top. Follow the pictured 'road', and remark on the 'scenery' that the car passes on its route. At some point say, 'The magnet pulls on the paper clip, even through the picture.' Invite the child to play with the car, framed scene and magnet, showing how one edge of the frame can be placed on the edge of a table, to help hold it up.

The child later repeats this activity independently.

(5) Sand and Iron

Materials: The horseshoe magnet in its box; a wide, plastic bowl containing fine sand; a plastic container with a lid containing smooth 'iron' filings; a fine, white handkerchief.

Method: Name the Sand and Iron materials, show where they are kept, and bring them to a table with the magnet. Place the magnet inside the handkerchief, and in one hand, grip the loose ends of the handkerchief and the magnet inside. Rub the wrapped magnet around inside the iron filings container, and lift it out, noting that 'Iron filings are magnetic.' Holding the filings-covered portion of the handkerchief inside the container, carefully remove the magnet from it, allowing the filings to fall off the handkerchief, back into the container. Invite the child to repeat this part of the activity.

Again place the magnet in the handkerchief, and now rub it around inside the sand container. Note that 'Sand is not magnetic.' Invite the child to repeat this, too.

Now say, 'Let's hide the iron filings in the sand, and see if the magnet can find them.' Empty the iron filings container into the sand container, and stir the mixture with your finger. Place the magnet in the handkerchief as before, and rub it around a number of times in the iron filings and sand mixture. Lift it out, and show the child that all the iron filings have stuck to the covered magnet, while only sand is left in the container. Remark with a tone of astonishment, 'Even when the magnet was covered and the iron filings were hidden, the magnet could still find them all.' Invite the child to repeat this last part of the activity.

The child later repeats the entire activity independently.

(6) Compass

Materials: The horseshoe magnet in its box; a sewing needle; a round piece of paper, with a diameter the same as the length of the needle; a round piece of plastic with a lip (e.g. the cap from a small container), which is the same size as the paper, and which floats; a plastic bowl; a jug; a drying cloth; a water source; the Continents Globe (see MAPS); a pencil; a simple, commercially-made compass.

Method: Say to the child, 'We will make a compass.' Gather all the materials except the ready-made compass. Fill the bowl with water from the jug. Say, 'Now we'll magnetise the needle.' Rub the needle about thirty times against one open end of the magnet, pinch the centre of the paper circle and slip the needle in and out of it so that both its ends are showing. Place the paper on the plastic circle, and then gently float them on the water in the bowl. Allow the needle to align itself, and say, 'A magnetised needle will always point to the same place on the earth, because the earth is like a big magnet.'

Show the child the North and South Poles on the Continents Globe, and explain, 'One end of the earth's magnetic pull is called the "North", and the other end is called the "South".' Point out that the needle in the bowl is being pulled North and South.

Using your knowledge of the geography of your area, note which end of the needle is pointing North. Gently lift the paper disk off the plastic disk, and use the pencil to write 'North' and 'South' on the paper at the appropriate ends of the needle. Replace the paper on the plastic disk and say, 'Now we have a compass!' Allow the compass to align itself with the earth again. Review where North and South can be found on the Continents Globe, and use your compass-in-a-bowl to show the child which directions in your environment are North and South.

Introduce the commercially-made compass, saying, 'This needle is just like the one in the bowl; it always points North and South.' Show the 'N' for North and 'S' for South. Also name 'East' and 'West', showing the 'E' and 'W' on the compass, and indicating it on the globe. Explain that because, wherever you are, a compass will always point North and South, it can help you if you are lost.

The child independently observes the compass-in-a-bowl, or the ready-made compass, and later takes the ready-made compass on outdoor walks and trips, eventually using it to help identify a location or navigate a route.

To illustrate the phenomenon of ▓▓▓▓ and how things react to it. **Aim**

(a) Clapping hands to a musical beat. **Preliminary**
(b) Handling and drawing with chalk. **Practical**
(c) Building with wooden blocks in an orderly fashion. **Activities**

Exercises   (1) Bouncing Ball

Materials: A high-density rubber ball; pieces of chalk; an outdoor area with a concrete floor next to a concrete or brick wall that you have permission to mark with chalk.

Method: Name the Bouncing Ball, show where it is kept, secure a piece of chalk, and take the child to an outdoor spot as described above. Mark with the chalk the highest spot you can reach on the wall. Hold the ball at that height and drop it. Each time the ball hits the ground, clap your hands, and count the bounce: 'One, two, three. . .' Next to the mark on the wall, write the number of bounces you counted. Repeat this process several times, marking the wall at various heights, inviting the child to drop the ball when the height is within the child's reach, and in any case inviting the child to clap and count along with you. After a number of trials, read the numbers on the wall from the lowest mark to the highest.

The child later repeats this activity independently, or with another child.

(2) Pendulum

Materials: A solid rubber ball with about three feet of kite string attached to it by a large, U-shaped tack.

Method: Name the Pendulum and show where it is kept. Say, 'The earth pulls down on everything – this pull is called "gravity". Let's watch how gravity pulls down on this ball.' Hold the loose end of the string at arm's length, and high enough so that the ball does not touch the ground. With your other hand, lift the ball towards one side, and with the string taut, release it. Keep the end of the string in the same position in the air, allowing the ball to swing back and forth, less and less, until it stops.

With you still holding the end of the string, invite the child to pull the ball to one side and release it.

(3) Roman Arch

Materials: The Roman Arch (a special Montessori material), which includes: a rectangular, wooden platform with two, upright planks, side-by-side, separated by a few inches, and each having a step-like pattern cut into its top, inside corner; thirty-five specially-made wooden blocks, of particular shapes, which can be built into an archway connecting the two planks; a three-piece wooden arch support, which raises and lowers by moving the middle piece, to hold up the arch while it is being built or disassembled; a large box to keep the Roman Arch material in.

Method: Name the Roman Arch, show where it is kept, and bring the box to a table. Open the box and place the stand on a table mat. Say, 'Remember that the earth pulls down on everything, and that this pull is called "gravity". Let's see how gravity helps to hold up an archway.'

First show the child how to assemble the pieces of the arch support, how to adjust the support up and down, and where

to place it between the upright planks. Next, lay out all the blocks on the table mat. Build the trapezium-shaped blocks around the curve of the support, adjust the height of the support to make these blocks lean on one another, and then place the small rectangular blocks (some with one slanted side) around the arch-shape so far built, filling in the stair-like pattern on the planks, and putting the rectangular 'keystone' over the middle trapezium-shaped block. Lastly, build the large rectangular blocks on top of this construction, row-by-row in a triangular design. Gently lower the arch support, and slide it out from under the constructed archway. Show delight and amazement that the arch stays up without the support.

Reverse the building process to dismantle the arch.

Invite the child to repeat the building of the arch. Sit with the child and when asked to help, help only in the selection of the correct blocks, but allow the child to place the blocks on the construction. After admiring the completed, free-standing arch for a moment, the child dismantles it by reversing the building procedure.

The child later repeats the arch construction independently.

Later, when building the arch, the child tries leaving out one or more blocks to see the effect on the stability of the structure. One day when the child is doing this, name and identify the 'keystone' (the small rectangular block placed above the middle trapezium-shaped block), and suggest leaving it out to see what happens.

Sound

To demonstrate the transmission of sound through things other than the open atmosphere.

Aim

– Listening (see BEING SILENT in the Practical Activities).

Preliminary Practical Activity

(1) Table Amplifier
Materials: A solid wood table; a ticking watch.
Method: Bring the watch to the table. Say to the child, 'When I talk, the sound I make goes through the air', pointing from your mouth to the child's ear. 'But sound can also go through solid things – like this table.' Tap on the table loudly and ask if the child can hear it. Show the child how to put one ear down against the surface of the table, and then tap on the table again, repeatedly, gradually getting softer. Say, 'You could hear even the softest tap because the sound goes right through the table to your ear.'

With the child sitting upright again, hold the ticking watch next to the child's ear, and ask if the tick can be heard. When

Activities

the child answers 'yes', gradually move the watch away, carrying it over the table top, to a distance where the child says it can't be heard at all. At just that distance from the child, place the watch directly down onto the table, and invite the child to put an ear down against the table surface again. Ask, 'Can you hear the watch now at that distance?' When the child answers 'yes', note that 'the sound couldn't be heard through the air, but could be heard through the table'.

(2) Speaking Tube

Materials: A 10 to 15 foot length of plastic hose-pipe. (Ensure that the ends have no sharp edges.)

Method: Name the Speaking Tube, show where it is kept, and say, 'Sound can be kept in a closed space, like this tube.' Show the child how to speak and listen through the tube, speaking very quietly, directly into the tube, and listening with the open end right against your ear. Try it with the tube stretched out in a straight line, and then make it go around a corner, being careful not to knock into things or trip someone with it.

The child later uses the Speaking Tube together with another child.

(3) Tin Can Telephone

Materials: Two empty tin cans (tins of soup are the right size), minus their lids, each taped around the open rim with thick, cloth tape (to cover any sharp edges), and each with a small hole punched inward in the centre of its base (with any resulting sharp edges pounded smooth); 10 to 15 feet of kite string, threaded through the holes in the cans, and knotted at each end to keep it from slipping through the holes.

Method: Name the Tin Can Telephone, show where it is kept, and say, 'Sound can go through a string.' Show the child how to wind and unwind the string around one can, for storage purposes. Then show how you can each hold a can, and keeping the string very taut, speak and listen through the cans. When speaking, completely cover your mouth with the can, and when listening, completely cover your ear with it. Point out that care must be taken to avoid knocking into something or tripping someone with the string.

The child later uses the Tin Can Telephone with another child.

Optics

Aim   To demonstrate how light can be bent or re-directed by what it passes through.

Preliminary   – Polishing a magnifying glass or glass prism with a soft cloth.
Practical
Activity

Activities

(1) Magnifying Glass

Materials: A magnifying glass with a handle comfortable for a child; a box containing at least ten small objects, changed monthly, all of which have interesting details or textures (e.g. a leaf, a strand of wool, the mechanism of an old watch, a colour photograph clipped from a magazine).

Method: Name the Magnifying Glass, show where it is kept, and bring it with the box of objects to a table. Say, 'Light bouncing off things lets us see them', pointing from the table to your eyes. 'But a magnifying glass bends the light and makes things look bigger.' Show the child how to hold and look through the magnifying glass, slowly moving it closer or further away from the object you're observing, to bring it into focus. Invite the child to continue examining the contents of the box.

The child later examines the things in the box independently. Invite the child to use the Magnifying Glass to examine things around the room and outdoors.

(2) Pinhole Camera

Materials: A Pinhole Camera, fashioned as follows. Take a shoebox, completely cut away one narrow end, paint the box's interior black (including the inside of its lid), tape the lid shut on the box, and poke a pinhole in the centre of the other narrow end. Fix a piece of thin, white tracing paper in a stiff cardboard frame, slightly smaller than the open end of the box, and attach one edge of the frame perpendicularly to the end of a long, cardboard triangular prism. The latter construction (effectively a 'screen' on a 'rod') is then slid into the open end of the box, with the paper 'screen' inside and the triangular 'rod' sticking out.

Method: Name the Pinhole Camera, show where it is kept, and bring it to a brightly lit place in the room where there are large and colourful things. Say, 'Remember that light bouncing off things lets us see them', pointing from the things to your eyes. 'When light from something goes through a little hole, like this', indicating the pinhole in the camera, 'it comes in upside down.' Show the child how to hold the box with one hand, point the box's pinhole at a brightly lit object, peer into the opening, and then gently pull or push the triangular 'rod' until the image is brought into focus on the 'screen'. Say, 'Light coming in the little hole in our eyes also comes in upside down, but our minds turn it "right side up" again!' Invite the child to continue looking at things through the Pinhole Camera.

Later, the child freely uses the Pinhole Camera indoors and outdoors.

(3) Glass Prism

Materials: A glass triangular prism, with dull edges, in a soft protective case.

Method: Name the Glass Prism, show where it is kept, and

bring it to a table in a brightly lit area. Say, 'Remember that light bouncing off things lets us see them', pointing from things to your eyes. 'But when light goes through a triangular glass prism, it is broken into lots of colours.' Show the child how to look at the objects in the room through the Glass Prism, holding it by its ends and putting one of its flat rectangular edges across your eyes.

One bright, sunny day, show the child how to position the Glass Prism, standing it on one end, on a window sill in the room, where it will catch a beam of direct sunlight. Invite the child to 'find the rainbow' that the prism makes somewhere on the walls or ceiling of the room. Observe the rainbow for a few moments, and note that it moves and shifts as the sun moves through the sky.

HISTORY

Past and Present

Aim   To help the child understand the distinction between past and present, how the present becomes the past, and how past events have led to the present situation.

Material   An Events Board, made from a large, rectangular noticeboard, its top half painted grey, its bottom half white, and its entire front surface covered with a thick coat of rubber cement.

A subscription to a newspaper that prints many photographs of current events.

Scissors.

Preparation   Choose a recent and cheerful news story which is: currently being reported in the newspaper; likely to be of interest to young children; illustrated with clear and interesting photographs; and likely to develop for several months into the future (e.g. an engagement between two famous people, or the events leading up to the visit of a foreign dignitary).

Clip two or three recent pictures from the newspaper that can serve to introduce the story.

Presentation   – With the above photograph clippings in hand, name the Events Board and show where it is hanging in the room.

– Discuss the subject of the pictures, emphasise that the event illustrated is happening now, and stick the pictures on the white area, explaining that because it is happening 'now, or in the present', it belongs in the white area of the Events Board.

– If, in the next few days, more photos of essentially the same event are published, discuss them with the child and stick them, alongside the first photos, in the white area of the Events Board.

– When a new event that represents a further development in the same news story has been pictured in the paper, cut out the pictures, and discuss this new event with the child. Emphasise that the new event is happening now, and that the pictures of it belong in the white area. Stick the new pictures to the white area of the Events Board.

Note with the child that the other, older pictures in the white area 'are not happening now; they happened before, in the past', and say, 'because they are in the past, they belong in the grey area'. Remove these older pictures from the white area and stick them on the grey area of the Events Board.

Review the situation. Pointing to the white area, say, 'these events are happening now, in the present', and pointing to the grey area, say, 'these events happened before, in the past'.

– Repeat this last step whenever photographs appear which describe a new event in the developing story, inviting the child to stick the new photos on the white area, and re-stick the old photos on the grey area. Allow the grey area to become quite cluttered with photos, even overlapping when necessary.

– When the story ends or has gone on for several months, study the Events Board with the child, reviewing all the events 'in the past' that now result in the situation pictured 'in the present'. Do not emphasise the order in which the past events occurred, but only that they are 'in the past'.

(1) Select another news story, and invite the child to look through the newspaper each time it arrives, to cut out any relevant photographs, to decide whether they represent the same event or a new development, and to stick pictures of new developments on the white area of the Events Board, moving older pictures to the grey area. Allow the child to work independently; only correct the error of using white for 'past' and grey for 'present'; do not correct the child's judgements about whether a new photograph depicts a new development. **Exercise**

Stories about the Past

To enhance the child's appreciation of the 'present', by opening up the 'past' as a field for learning, enjoyment and caring. **Aim**

Kept on a special shelf in the Montessori environment: fact, picture, and story books about people, places and events in the past; antique objects and old photographs. **Material**

Brief dramatic films depicting historical events.

Children's plays based on history.

– Set up and introduce the child to a special shelf in the room for **Presentation** books and objects that concern the past, calling it 'the history shelf'. Invite the child to explore the things on it independently.

Exercises (1) The child goes often to the history shelf, finding new things on it every week.

(2) Show films that 'tell a story about events in the past'.

(3) Put on a history play, with costumes, props and scenery, about an event in the past. Emphasise to the children that by being in the play, they can 'see what it was like to live in that period of history'.

(4) Occasionally introduce to a group of children a particularly interesting antique object or old photograph from the history shelf, and invent a simple, pleasant and thoroughly feasible story about it. When you tell the story, stress that it did not really happen, but that you think something like it could have happened.

(5) Tell the child to ask a parent, grandparent or other senior friend or relative to tell a particular story about his or her past (e.g. to ask grandmother how she and grandfather first met).

Time Line

Aim To help the child understand that events can be recorded in relation to a fixed measurement of time (in this case, years), and therefore that past events have occurred in a particular order. To allow the child to contemplate the progress of his or her life so far, as an example of history writing.

Material A sample Time Line, constructed as follows. Take a large, long sheet of paper and print three centred headings at the top: 'Time Line', your full name and the statement, 'I was born on (day, month, year)', giving your actual birth date. Beneath these headings make a vertical Time Line, as follows, representing your first seven years: glue thin paper strips, of the same length but different colours, vertically end-to-end down the left side of the sheet. To the left of each point where two strips join, write from top to bottom: '1 year', '2 years', etc. Then, to the right of each strip, glue one or more photographs (or photocopies of photographs) of yourself at the indicated age, preferably doing something characteristic of your age (e.g. holding a teddy bear in your favourite chair).

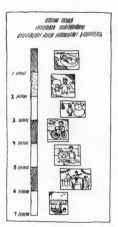

Materials to make a Time Line for the child: a large sheet, a black marker, coloured art paper, scissors, glue and many photographs (or photocopies of photographs) of the child from birth to the present.

Presentation – Show the child the Time Line you made for your own first seven years, and discuss it, connecting each year strip (e.g. 'this part is when I was three; I'd lived three years by then') to the photos

(e.g. 'here I am riding my tricycle; I learned to ride it when I was three').
- Ask if the child would like to make a Time Line.
- If the child says 'yes', arrange to obtain photographs from the child's family, photocopy and return them, and then make the Time Line, as above, with the child.
- Put the Time Line up in the room where the child, the child's friends, and visitors can easily see it.

(1) The child occasionally looks at the Time Line, and shows it to friends and visitors. **Exercises**
(2) Each year, up to seven years, the child adds pictures to the Time Line.

FURTHER READING

Montessori, Maria. *The Absorbent Mind*. Second revised edition. (Translated from the Italian by Claude A. Claremont) India: Kalakshetra Publications (1973). ISBN 0 7229 0170 4

Montessori, Maria. *Advanced Montessori Method*, Vol. 1. New edition. (Translated from the Italian by F. Simmonds and L. Hutchinson) India: Kalakshetra Publications (1965). ISBN 0 7229 9085 5

Montessori, Maria. *Advanced Montessori Method*, Vol. 2. New edition. (Translated from the Italian by A. Livingston) India: Kalakshetra Publications (1965). ISBN 0 7229 9086 3

Montessori, Maria. *Discovery of the Child*. India: Kalakshetra Publications (1966). ISBN 0 7229 0160 7

Montessori, Maria. *Education for a New World*. India: Kalakshetra Publications (1963). ISBN 0 7229 7341 1

Montessori, Maria. *The Formation of Man*. Fifth edition. (Translated by A. M. Joosten) India: Kalakshetra Publications (1978). ISBN 0 7229 7077 3

Montessori, Maria. *From Childhood to Adolescence*. Second edition. (Including 'Erdkinder' and The Functions of the University) New York: Schocken Books (1976).

Montessori, Maria. *The Secret of Childhood*. (Translated by Barbara Barclay Carter) India: Orient Longman (1978).

Montessori, Maria. *Spontaneous Activity in Education*. New edition. (Translated from the Italian by F. Simmonds) New York: Schocken Books (1972). ISBN 0 8052 0097 5

Montessori, Maria. *To Educate the Human Potential*. New issue. India: Kalakshetra Publications (1973). ISBN 0 7229 7207 5

Montessori, Maria. *What You Should Know about Your Child*. India: Kalakshetra Publications (1966). ISBN 0 7229 7448 5

INDEX